The
American
Woman
1990-91

Edited by Sara E. Rix for the Women's Research & Education Institute

W·W·NORTON & COMPANY

NEW YORK · LONDON

The American Woman 1990-91

A Status Report

Printed in the United States of America.

The text of this book is composed in Goudy Old Style, with display type set in
Bodoni Bold Condensed. Composition and manufacturing by the Haddon
Craftsmen, Inc.

First Edition

Library of Congress Cataloging in Publication Number 88-648742

ISBN 0-393-02840-2
ISBN 0-393-30686-0 (pbk)

W. W. Norton & Company, Inc., 500 Fifth Avenue, New York, N. Y. 10110
W. W. Norton & Company Ltd., 37 Great Russell Street, London WC1B 3NU

1 2 3 4 5 6 7 8 9 0

Contents

Women in Brief

Appendices

Tables and Figures

Appendix · American Women Today: A Statistical Portrait

Editor's Notes

LIKE ITS PREDECESSORS, this third edition of *The American Woman* attempts to provide an overview of how America's women and their families are faring. Its contents include a wealth of statistics as well as probing articles by researchers and other experts on women's issues.

As did earlier editions, this volume documents continued progress for and by women. Since the second edition of *The American Woman* was prepared, women's labor force participation has continued to rise. More women are working full time. The wage gap has narrowed somewhat. Women have made advances, admittedly sometimes modest ones, in business, the military, science, and engineering, on corporate boards, and in Congress, where there are now 29 women— four more than there were in the 100th Congress and the largest number to date.

American women have become increasingly active in the peace movement and in the field of international development, and here at home the women's movement flourishes at the national and grassroots levels. This book notes some impressive "firsts" by individual American women: the first female bishop in the history of the Episcopal Church; the Navy's first female "sailor of the year"; the first American woman to scale Mt. Everest; the first black female to become staff director of a Senate full committee.

Yet the months since the last edition was published have by no means been a period of consistently good news for women. If there is a single recurrent message in the various segments of this book, it is that progress has bypassed millions of American women, particularly minority women and women who head families on their own.

Commenting on the second edition of *The American Woman*, Charles Whited of the *Miami Herald* observed that despite "giant strides," women's status as documented in that volume is "far from equal," which "does not bode well for the nation" (Whited, 1989). Indeed, this country's failure to reduce significantly the poverty rates of the millions of American families headed by women virtually guarantees that the children in these families face a future as bleak as their present.

As the statistical appendix in this volume shows, the median income for families headed by women is about half that of two-parent families in which the wife does not have a paid job, and just over one-third that of the families in which both spouses are in the paid labor force. Female-headed families are three times as likely as other families to have incomes below the poverty level, and over half of all children in female-headed families are poor. The problem is especially acute for minority children: one of the most startling statistics in the statistical appendix is that nearly four out of five—79 percent—poor black children are in female-headed families. This represents a 50 *percentage point* increase over the comparable figure for 1960.

The American Woman paints a graphic picture of who America's families are and how they are struggling to cope. It reminds us that the two-parent family is still the dominant American family type, even though both the number and proportion of families headed by single parents, predominantly women, continue to rise. It shows that the majority of women today—including wives and single mothers—are working for pay. Yet, like earlier generations of women, contemporary women usually retain primary—and often sole—responsibility for the care of family members. And, while women today typically have fewer children to rear than their forebears, they are more likely to have frail elderly relatives to care for.

According to the 1989 Mother's Day report prepared by the Older Women's League (OWL), the typical woman can expect to spend 17 years caring for children and 18 years caring for older family members. OWL estimates that nine out of 10 women "will be caregivers either of children or parents, or both" at some time in their lives (Older Women's League, 1989: 1). Since most of these women are also employed, they cannot devote full time to family caregiving—unless they quit their jobs or cut back on their hours of paid work.

But it is doubtful that our economy could survive if a substantial number of the 55 million women in the American labor force decided to stay at home, even if one ignores the billions of dollars that women workers contribute to their families' incomes and to the gross national product. Given acute labor shortages in some parts of the country, severe skills shortages in other parts, a decline in the number of young people entering the labor force, and a projected increase of about 20 million jobs between now and the turn of the century, even the eight million-plus working women with children under age six would be missed if they opted for full-time homemaking.

Yet it is surely not easy for working women with families to manage. Working parents in the United States lack guaranteed job-protected leave to care for new babies or sick children or parents. Many cannot find adequate, affordable care for their children while they are at work. Relatively few are offered the flexible work options that make juggling family and work responsibilities easier. A theme that surfaces again and again in this book is that public and private policies have been very slow to adapt to the changes in the lives of workers and their families.

Articles in all three editions of *The American Woman* highlight the extent to which public policy has played a major role in enhancing women's educational and employment opportunities. Barriers to women's advancement have been reduced by Title VII of the Civil Rights, the Equal Pay Act, Title IX of the Education Act Amendments, and the Pregnancy Discrimination Act, to give but a few examples. While this is not to suggest that women have yet achieved full equality and equity in the workplace, their employment experiences and occupational profiles are vastly different from what they were a generation ago because legislative changes have made it easier for women to compete in the workforce.

But as the barriers that denied women access to job opportunities just because they were female have fallen, other barriers have been revealed. Many people argue, for example, that women cannot hope to achieve true equality in the workplace until they are assured of a more equitable division of labor at home, but data in this book suggest that a 50-50 sharing of home and family responsibilities between husbands and wives is a long way off.

Many employers—especially small firms—don't provide maternity leave. Their employees, who are often low-wage workers, have to patch together days of sick leave, vacation time, and unpaid days off to care for a new baby or for a sick child or other relative. As of mid-1989, U.S. parents remain in the unenviable position of living in one of the two countries in the industrialized world that do not have laws requiring job-protected leave for care of the newborn.

Defenders of the status quo, i.e., those who oppose government mandated fringe benefits, argue that intense competition for qualified labor will force employers to provide the types of employee benefits that working parents need, but economist Barbara Bergmann counters that "only the government can threaten penalties that will motivate more employers to allow women to compete fairly for the most interesting and best-paid work" (Bergmann, 1986: 300).

In their collective and individual reports in this book, members of the executive committee of the Congressional Caucus for Women's Issues discuss what they think the federal government must do to help women compete. What comes through especially loud and clear is the need for child care and family leave policies. These congresswomen and their allies may meet with some success this year or next. Nevertheless, it should be noted that if the 101st Congress approves a family leave bill, it will be limited to *unpaid* leave, probably of no more than 10 weeks, and will not reach the millions of workers who are employed by smaller firms.

Moreover, it may be true that "child care has moved into the national spotlight," as the authors of this book's chapter on child care contend; it may even be the case that some additional federal funds for child care will be committed within the next two years. There is little evidence, however, of a willingness to commit funds sufficient to ensure safe, affordable child care, preferably with an educational component, for the millions of children who need it.

And, unfortunately, it appears that the women's movement and others who support women's rights will have to devote precious time and resources to fighting other battles that had been considered won. Several recent Supreme Court decisions seem likely to unravel employment programs and policies that have helped women and minorities get a foot in

the door and a chance to compete effectively. These disturbing decisions (e.g., *Wards Cove Packing Co. v. Antonio* and
Martin v. Wilkes) are briefly described in "In Review" (formerly "Year in Review"), *The American Woman's* summary of
legislative, judicial, social, and economic developments affecting women. Preserving affirmative action and equal opportunity measures will mean getting Congress to reaffirm its
support for them as, after several years of intense struggle by
women's advocates, it finally reaffirmed Title IX in 1988.

And employment discrimination battles are not the only
ones that women's advocates must fight in the coming
months and years. One of the most significant Supreme
Court rulings, in *Webster v. Reproductive Health Services*, was
handed down on July 3, 1989, when the Court upheld a Missouri state law declaring that life begins at conception and
requiring that physicians ascertain the viability of a fetus
before performing an abortion. Missouri's ban on the use of
public funds or facilities for abortions was also upheld.

While the Supreme Court did not explicitly overturn the
1973 *Roe v. Wade* decision that legalized abortion, women's
right to choose is clearly now in jeopardy, and additional
restrictions may be in the offing, since the Court has agreed to
hear three new abortion cases next term.

Moreover, because the *Webster* decision returned to the
states a right to regulate abortion that is unprecedented since
the *Roe v. Wade* decision, both pro-choice and anti-abortion
activists are gearing up for what promise to be years of lobbying and litigation at the state level. (Several states have already moved to tighten restrictions on abortion.) The next
edition's "In Review" can be expected to include updates on
abortion rights developments across the country.

Indeed, "update" is probably the key to what *The Ameri-*

can *Woman* is all about. The overall purpose of "In Review," the chapters long and short, the congresswomen's reports, and the statistical appendix is to keep readers informed about the current status of women in this country, and to provide women's advocates, activists, and others with the facts and figures—the information tools—that will assist them in their work on behalf of women and families.

The longer chapters explore, in some depth, a number of important issues; in this edition, scholars consider the problems of the black family, the crisis in affordable housing, the day care crisis, and employment policy. The shorter chapters simply highlight the status of women in a variety of fields or activities—in art, in television, and in international development, for example. Similarly, "In Review" and the statistical appendix help the reader sum up where American women have been going and what has been happening to them since the last edition of *The American Woman* was compiled.

In designing *The American Woman*, the Women's Research and Education Institute has sought to be responsive to suggestions about content and to requests for particular information. (This edition, for example, presents considerably more separate material on minority women—black women and their families, Asian Americans, Hispanics, and American Indians—than did earlier editions.) We have tried to offer readers a little bit of everything, with the inevitable result that some do not get all of what they want and others get more than they want. We have yet to examine every issue of importance to women, and some of those we have covered in earlier editions need to be revisited. Future editions will provide that opportunity.

SARA E. RIX

Acknowledgments

THE THIRD EDITION of *The American Woman*, like the first two volumes, has enjoyed a broad base of support from several foundations and many individuals who have made generous financial or in-kind contributions to WREI and its work.

We are extremely grateful to the Ford Foundation for underwriting a large portion of all three editions of the book. June Zeitlin and Alison Bernstein deserve special thanks for their advice on and encouragement of our efforts to produce *The American Woman*.

We are also grateful for the generosity of AT&T, Chevron U.S.A. Inc., the George Gund Foundation, the Prudential Foundation, RJR Nabisco, Sears, Roebuck and Company, and the Warner Lambert Foundation, without whose assistance there would be no book.

Sincere gratitude goes to Jean Stapleton, president of the Board of WREI, who has been an enthusiastic and untiring spokeswoman for all three editions of *The American Woman*, and to Mary Emrick of Chevron U.S.A. Inc., whose extensive and effective promotion of the book and enthusiastic support of all our efforts have been deeply appreciated.

We are in debt to Anne Bryant of the American Association of University Women and Jill Miller of the Displaced Homemakers Network for providing practical assistance in promoting the first two editions.

Our editor at Norton, Mary Cunnane, and her assistant,

Rebecca Castillo, never tired in providing constructive advice and precious encouragement.

An excellent and supportive advisory board continues to share time and expertise on matters that will make *The American Woman* an ever more valuable resource. That board consists of Jessie Bernard, Mariam Chamberlain, Jane Chapman, Beverly Ellerman, Beverly Guy-Sheftall, Harriette McAdoo, Irene Natividad, Brenda Pillors, Sarah Pritchard, Ida Ruben, Ann Schmidt, Margaret Simms, Elizabeth Waldman, and Franklin Wallick.

Wholehearted thanks are extended to Debbie Blake, Nancy Duff Campbell, Pam Holcomb, Joseph Piccione, Allison Porter, Marc Rosenblum, Ronnie Steinberg, and Wayne Welch—writers, editors, reviewers, or just plain boosters of the book. Judy Dollenmeyer's ability to share her expertise at the last moment was an enormous help. Kathryn Reith of the Women's Sports Foundation provided her time and expertise, as did many individuals at the Bureau of the Census and the Bureau of Labor Statistics, especially Howard Hayghe.

As always, I want to express my appreciation to the staff at WREI. Sara Rix, the editor, and Anne Stone, the associate editor, dedicated countless hours of research, writing, and editing to *The American Woman*. Thanks are due to interns Amy Coursen, Cynthia Doran, Kitty Gretch, and Mary Anne Jorgensen, who gathered information for many sections of the book, as did research assistant Barbara Andrew, who also prepared the statistical portrait of American women today. The tireless promotion and dissemination efforts of WREI's Alison Dineen and Terry Walker have contributed greatly to the success of *The American Woman*.

Finally, I want to stress that neither the funders nor any of the advisors, reviewers, or editors are responsible for any errors or misstatements that may appear in the book. In addition, the opinions expressed herein do not necessarily represent the opinions of anyone other than the authors of the chapters.

BETTY PARSONS DOOLEY
Executive Director
Women's Research and Education Institute

Introduction

JEAN STAPLETON

WOMEN HAVE MUCH to celebrate, much to safeguard, and much to achieve. Their prospects for exercising unique leadership stretch to the horizon of the post-Cold War world now in the making. Here at home, painful barriers remain; some are higher than they were a year ago. But women are also more aware of how to surmount obstacles and are more canny about tactics and resources. We women are better prepared for the long haul—less divided among ourselves and more experienced in working with each other.

The international scene calls for conciliation, world rule of law, and new perspectives, not prolonged confrontation. Borders are becoming more transparent, while outworn definitions of national interest are shifting. Women have fewer vested interests in things as they are; less connected to the international old-boy networks that have guided foreign and defense policies since World War II, women may be able to hasten the advent of a workable post-nuclear world order. Internationally, women's comprehension of the web of interconnected life is needed more than ever. We can help overcome all sorts of man-made boundaries in order to protect the planet we have jeopardized.

Broader social justice is demanded to match and hasten economic development. Changes in work and the workplace must come, not only for women's benefit, but also to strengthen our economy for the future. This is true not only in less developed nations, but also in Europe, Asia, and the United States. In today's European Community, a social charter with strong provisions for women moves forward in tandem with the economic integration directives that culminate in 1992. Ironically, says the head of a European national bureau of women's affairs, the women's movements inspired by American counterparts in the late 1960s and early 1970s have produced strong new European initiatives that U.S. women may soon envy.

In this country, many women are double- or triple-working in families, jobs, and public roles, and they are often stretched to the limit. Much has been achieved. But, as the writers of the essays in this edition of *The American Woman* show, dark places remain. Many women are alone—with children, but without jobs or adequate support. Many are ill-housed, undereducated, and underemployed. There are not only glass ceilings atop women who have risen part way in corporate life; plenty of steel caps still hold the lid on initial opportunities. The presence of left-out and left-behind women in our society prevents self-congratulation about how far we've come.

Several chapters in this collection draw a general picture of the international and intellectual support system women have built. Sarah Harder opens her essay with an overview of the effectiveness of U.S. women's organizations in public policy and legislative advocacy. She definitely finds the glass half full. Women were dismayed by the 1982 failure to ratify the ERA and by stalled federal action for women during the Reagan years. Despite—or perhaps because of—these events, the 1980s generated new alliances among women's groups.

Agreeing to disagree in some cases, specialized and single-issue women's groups as well as the larger federations forged "alliances . . . to address issue priorities on the basis of opportunity and need." Permanent state and local alliances numbered more than 30 in 1988, with 10 more in formation. Since 1985, a Council of Presidents of national women's organizations has been regularly meeting. In 1988, it launched a nonpartisan issues strategy under the banner of the Women's Agenda, in collaboration with more than 40 organizations representing millions of women around the country.

These organizations have agreed to push this agenda, and Harder believes their "chorus on a shared song sheet" will prevent women's issues from being marginalized, as often happens with partisan solutions. To regain lost momentum, Harder suggests that the time may have come for a new federal council for women, perhaps based on the Canadian model.

Arvonne Fraser widens our field of vision in her essay on women and international development, where poverty and inequality go hand in hand. "Women in development" as a perspective made its debut only 20 years ago, when Ester Boserup of Denmark challenged the standard development doctrine that ignored women's key role in economic life.

Fraser sees no coincidence in the fact that International Women's Year, the 1976-85 U.N. Decade for Women, and women-in-development programs all began after a new U.S. feminism flowered. She writes that American women have been major contributors to development because they have exercised "four basic freedoms" many other women lack: freedom of speech, of association, of publication, and of travel. U.S. women's contributions to a newly revived international women's movement include helping to define new ideas, publicizing them, creating new international organizations or networks around specific issues such as domestic violence, conducting research, and organizing conferences. Although Fraser cautions that American women often lack the awareness and international experience of their overseas colleagues, "they have often been the model builders because they have the freedom, energy, and means" to get involved.

A whole new generation of women leaders in the so-called developing world is now taking the stage. They resent condescending attitudes. Far from defining equality as parity with men, these new leaders assert that, to achieve true equality, men must become more responsible for families. American men and women have surely fallen short of this goal, so for women "the whole world is [still] developing."

Kate McGuinness's interesting history of women in the peace movement notes that the most active times of women's participation in international peace activity coincide with periods when women vocally claim greater roles in society at large. Concern for social issues has always partnered women's activism for peace. Social work pioneer Jane Addams led the Women's Peace Party at the outbreak of World War I, and women today clearly comprehend the tradeoffs between defense and day care, helicopters and housing.

Mariam Chamberlain discusses the emergence and growth of the women's studies programs and research centers that have given a solid grounding to women's advocacy. (In fact, centers for women's research outside government are only at the brink of adequate support in other nations; even in societies more legislatively advanced than the United States, women would like to match our research capacity.)

Even though current women's studies programs emerged first on the East and West Coasts, it jars our "bicoastal" arrogance to learn that the earliest known American course on women was offered by the department of sociology at the

Jean Stapleton, actress and president of the board of the Women's Research and Education Institute. *Peter Kredenser, photographer*

University of Kansas in 1892. At the University of Washington in 1912, Professor Theresa McMahon gave a course on "Women and Economic Evolution, or the Effects of Industrial Change on the Status of Women." Chamberlain suggests that challenges to traditional assumptions, raised by a new look at conventional topics from a woman's perspective, have mostly occurred where there are women faculty members.

In a lively way, Chamberlain follows the stages of integration and institutionalization of women's studies since 1969. What has been the overall effect? The original aspiration was less for separatism than for honest integration of women into the whole apparatus of traditional scholarship. Indeed, women's studies have not only challenged assumptions, but even the so-called established facts and rules. For example, "the Dark Ages" were a period of relative ascendance for women. "The Renaissance," a period of economic rebirth for princes, was rather dimly lit for women.

A second cluster of essays in this collection paints group portraits of American women from American Indian, Hispanic, and Asian Pacific backgrounds. C. Matthew Snipp's discussion of American Indian women's labor force participation finds that poverty among Indians hits women most keenly. The poor in Indian communities tend to marry the poor, and often both are unable to get work. Educational horizons are narrow and social isolation is great. Snipp shares our dismay that these very first Americans are the last to share in their country's wealth.

Gloria Bonilla-Santiago's portrait of Hispanic women locates them in one of the fastest growing segments of the U.S. population. Concentrated in nine states which contain nearly 90 percent of American Hispanics, their communities are largest in California and Texas. Poverty is a serious problem, especially for families headed by women: more than half such families in 1987 were poor. Although considerable differences exist among the poverty rates of Hispanic subgroups, the overall proportion of Hispanic families who live in poverty is 2.5 times that of non-Hispanic families.

Hispanic women are at best marginal in the U.S. labor market today. They are a bit less likely than non-Hispanics to be in the labor force at all. Yet they will enter the future U.S. workforce in unprecedented numbers. One key reason is that Hispanic women are a youthful population compared to the U.S. female population in general, and their fertility rate is high. Improving the educational and job status of Hispanic women, Bonilla-Santiago says, will thus help ensure not only their own futures, but the future of a qualified U.S. labor force.

Juanita Tamayo Lott celebrates Asian and Pacific American women, who have been comparatively successful in the U.S. economy. For the first time in 1980, the census showed that a majority—52 percent—of the 3.7 million Asian and Pacific Americans were women, and women now dominate immigration from those regions. Lott says it is important to grasp that Asian Pacific women "do not define themselves in relation to white men, white women, or other women of color. Their identities are rooted in civilizations that are thousands of years old." For the time being, it seems, they will surely be affected by the rough-and-tumble of the American experience.

The median income of Pan Asian women is slightly higher than that of the overall U.S. female population, yet remains less than that of any group of U.S. males. Lott believes that the talents and contributions of these women are finally beginning to be acknowledged and that their linguistic and cultural skills "are beneficial to a global economy and pluralistic society."

Another group of essays considers women who work in

fields dominated by men. For example, Janet Bickel's chapter highlights the growing proportion of women gaining entry to medical schools. In 1988, the number of female physicians exceeded 100,000, more than double their number a decade ago. This is a staggering increase. What's behind it? The total number of applications to medical school has dropped more than 30 percent in the past 15 years; half the number of males apply today as did so in the mid-1970s. As for medical faculties, more women than men enter academic medicine. Yet by 1987, women were still only 19 percent of medical school faculty members, and few advance to full professorships. Is this a repeat of the cliché that professions have become devalued when women enter them in great numbers? Bickel has no definitive answers, but her questions are pointed.

Faith Ando looks at women in business through women who are sole proprietors. "Women have been starting businesses in such record numbers in recent years," she says, that "the proportion of businesses owned by women—25 percent of the 12 million U.S. firms in 1982—may reach 50 percent by the year 2000." Ando assumes that some of the same factors that encourage men to strike out on their own also apply to women.

She sees differences, too: women's other employment options may be less attractive than those available to men of comparable background; entrepreneurship is one way out. Though extremely demanding, it may also allow more flexibility for child care. Finally, women reentering the labor force after a hiatus may find that establishing their own businesses is the only way to capitalize on the skills they have acquired in nonformal work. Ando doesn't avoid the bad news that black and Hispanic (but not Asian) women are underrepresented among women business owners. Business women identify access to commercial credit as a key ingredient for success—another reason antidiscrimination enforcement is so important for American women.

Women in the art world is Elsa Honig Fine's theme. She gives an engaging tour, starting with the genteel tradition of women dabblers and angels, who are in the wings of art but not the limelight. Only in the 1980s have women been appointed museum directors or chairs of art departments. As with women in academic medicine, "critical mass" in administrative power is often as important to equality as attracting more women practitioners. There remains a lot of work to do in behalf of those who make and sell art. As late as 1988, relatively few gallery or museum exhibitions were of women artists' work.

A new generation of women art historians and critics appeared in the 1970s, and their work of "archaeology and extrication" goes on. They are unearthing lost or neglected work by women, giving crafts their due, and extricating art by women from the assumptions of a largely male critical and curatorial establishment. Fine is dubious about attempts to identify or dictate certain artistic forms or styles as "women's," but she implies that artistic equality partly depends on making certain that women have seats at the table where decisions are being made.

Some women opposed the National Museum of Women in the Arts a few years ago in Washington; they saw it as letting major art institutions "off the hook" about buying and exhibiting women's work. That didn't happen—in fact the reverse occurred, says Fine, and separatist operations probably need to exist "because there is still so much catching up to do."

Several other essays look at American women today

through the longer lens of social, economic, and demographic trends. These chapters consider problems especially serious for women over the next decade: contingent work, employment policies, the effects of persistent poverty on black families, and affordable housing.

Elizabeth Conway writes that temporary, part-time, and contract work, collectively known as "contingent work," has a long history among American women. Such jobs have grown more commonplace in the past decade, now occupying a quarter to a third of the U.S. labor force. Most contingent workers are women. Lower wages, few or no benefits, and little protection in bad times are among the problems. Conway thinks the public sector needs to help the private sector remedy these problems. Changing business needs and vocal advocacy by part-time professionals may soon raise the issue's profile and result in some changes. Women need to strive toward ensuring that contingent work is innovative rather than merely exploitive, as it has often been.

Surveying the occupational landscape, Deborah Rhode says one view sees women and work as a *Pilgrim's Progress* saga of rising opportunity. Another view spies occupational segregation and stratification "and concludes that we're still pushing the same rocks up the same hills." Rhode's overview leaves the story somewhat more open-ended. Her eloquent legal analysis suggests that "equal opportunity is inadequate as a means and an end; what is needed are fundamental changes in workplace practices, premises, and priorities." Obstacles for women are more entrenched in culture, economics, and social expectations than a strict equal opportunity remedy acknowledges.

Employment issues must become part of a larger political agenda touching education, housing, social services, and the tax structure. Too many policies reflect old assumptions about women's secondary status as workers, while "too few address the structural problems that still confine many women to that role."

Harriette Pipes McAdoo discusses the history and growing diversity of African American families. She dismisses the current rage for explanations hinging on a black "underclass." Poverty is nothing new, she says, but rather, a widening of poverty has hit middle-class, working-class, and already impoverished people. The major difference "is that traditional avenues for upward mobility are now blocked, as the economy has slowed and the job skills demanded by the labor market have changed." Discrimination and economic isolation, shared by all people of color in McAdoo's belief, haunt our attempts to improve the situation.

For African American women, too, a shortage of adult males "has obvious implications for marriage prospects." More single women and families headed by women alone mean more female poverty. Looking ahead to a situation where American "minorities" may become "majorities" in the new century, McAdoo warns that we must not lock racial differences into permanent status differences.

Cushing Dolbeare's and Anne Stone's penetrating analysis of federal housing policies and American women identifies affordable housing as an acute and rapidly worsening problem. Women are most likely to live in bad housing, or to pay an inordinately large slice of their incomes for housing, or both, primarily because most poor Americans are women. Not only do women-maintained households form 58 percent of all households with incomes below $10,000, but almost half of all women householders fall into that income range.

Federal policies are out of balance for women. Dolbeare

and Stone write that the cost of housing assistance for low- and moderate-income people is dwarfed by the cost to the federal Treasury of "housing assistance" given through the tax code to middle- and upper-class Americans through deductions, credits, and the like. The current supply of subsidized housing should be protected. To obtain a rapid increase in affordable housing, policies should center on providing it through nonprofit sources. Housing assistance should become an entitlement. Solving America's housing crisis—for the poor in general or the homeless, battered, or displaced women in particular—will demand persistent advocacy.

Now that we have been rolling out the red carpet for women over nearly 20 years, we may often feel as if someone is rolling it up right behind us. But 1989 differs from 1969 partly because women now have public voices, visibility, and partial access to centers of political and economic power that were closed two decades ago. Even if momentary pessimism rules our thoughts, optimism must carry our actions.

No difficulty comes to us without a gift in its hands, like Shakespeare's toad with a jewel in its forehead. I do believe that women's unity, determination, and resourcefulness will be quickened by the challenges that are so clearly before us today. I share the belief of a Zimbabwean artist that "a woman's place is in the struggle." Today, women across the world will no longer take "no" for an answer. Nor will we make do with *no* answers to our need for equality, sufficiency, dignity, and participation in decisions touching our lives and livelihoods.

In Review:
January 1, 1988 – July 3, 1989

ANNE J. STONE

1988

January 1 / Wives are still doing the bulk of the housework even if they are employed outside the home, according to a study reported in this month's issue of *Psychology Today*. Researchers at the University of Florida found that wives average about 30 hours a week on household tasks, their husbands about six hours. Wives employed full time do about 70 percent of the housework, full-time housewives about 83 percent.

January 12 / The U.S. Department of Education releases a survey showing that women and people of color are rare among public school administrators, especially superintendents (96 percent male, 97 percent white). Among principals, 76 percent are male and 90 percent are white.

January 19 / The U.S. Information Agency (USIA) is ordered to notify some 4,400 women who applied unsuccessfully for USIA jobs between 1974 and 1984 that they may be entitled to back pay and preferential hiring status. Today's order by U.S. District Judge Charles Richey follows his 1987 ruling that the USIA had discriminated against female job applicants.

January 19 / Sponsors of the upcoming bipartisan Women's Agenda Conference in Des Moines, Iowa, express dismay that none of the Republican presidential hopefuls has agreed to address the conference, where more than 40 national women's organizations—including the American Association of University Women and the Business and Professional Women/USA—will be represented. Five of the seven Democratic candidates have accepted invitations to appear at the conference.

January 21 / The Census Bureau reports that almost one-fourth (24 percent) of American children lived with only one parent in 1986 and projects that more than half of all American children alive today will live in single-parent households at some time before they grow up.

January 21 / Couples with sons are less likely to divorce or separate than are couples who have only daughters, according to study results announced in today's *New York Times*. The three researchers at the University of Pennsylvania who conducted the study report that sons promote marital stability more than daughters because fathers are more involved in rearing sons, and that "beliefs about the importance of male role models for sons act as a deterrent to divorce" for the mothers as well as the fathers of sons.

January 28 / By a vote of 75-14, the U.S. Senate passes the Civil Rights Restoration Act (S. 557), after amending the bill to permit universities and hospitals to refuse to pay for or perform abortions—a development that dismays many of the bill's supporters. The bill was designed to restore the broad coverage of federal antidiscrimination statutes (such as Title IX) that prevailed before the Supreme Court greatly limited their reach in its 1984 *Grove City College v. Bell* decision.

February 2 / The *Federal Register* publishes the Reagan administration's new regulations barring family planning clinics that receive federal funds from informing a woman with an unintended pregnancy that her options include abortion. Clinics would also be forbidden to refer a woman directly to an abortion facility, even if she asks for such a referral. (Federally funded clinics have for some time been prohibited from performing abortions.) The Planned Parenthood Federation of America, the National Family Planning and Reproductive Health Association, and several state governments immediately file lawsuits to keep the new regulations from going into effect.

February 2 / At a Senate Judiciary Committee hearing, Senator Edward Kennedy (D-MA) notes that President Reagan's 367 judicial nominations to date have included only 6 blacks and 31 women.

February 2 / The Department of Defense orders the military services to enforce rules against sexual harassment more vigorously and to open more positions to women.

February 3 / Ruling in the "Baby M case," the New Jersey Supreme Court declares the $10,000 surrogacy contract between William Stern and Mary Beth Whitehead-Gould invalid. In a unanimous opinion reversing a lower court finding that the surrogacy contract was legal, the state's highest court says the contract amounted to "baby selling" and violated three specific New Jersey adoption statutes. While awarding custody of Baby M to Stern and his wife, the Supreme Court restores Whitehead-Gould's right to visit the child.

February 5 / President Reagan signs S. 825, the Housing and Community Development authorization bill, into law. Included in the omnibus legislation is a provision authorizing $5 million annually (for two years) for child care services in public housing facilities.

February 11 / The national executive board of the Boy Scouts of America votes to end the Scouts' requirement that troop leaders be male.

February 14 / Regular, intensive exercise impairs

women's fertility, at least temporarily, although such exercise does appear to help protect women against a number of serious diseases, according to findings presented today at the annual meeting of the American Association for the Advancement of Science. Harvard University researchers who studied more than 5,000 women believe that intense physical activity interferes with the production of estrogen.

March 2 / By a vote of 315-98, the House of Representatives approves the Civil Rights Restoration Act (S. 557), as amended and passed by the Senate on January 28. President Reagan has said he will veto the bill.

March 3 / The federal government announces that it will suspend application of the new anti-abortion regulations which were issued on February 2 and were to have taken effect on March 2. Legal challenges have resulted in injunctions against the regulations by federal courts in Denver, New York, and Boston, whose rulings cover the majority of federally funded family planning clinics.

March 8 / Catalyst, a not-for-profit group that works with corporations to foster career development for women, honors the Gannett Company, the DuPont Company, Corning Glass Works, and Avon Products for their exemplary efforts to recruit, retain, and promote women.

March 16 / President Reagan vetoes the Civil Rights Restoration Act.

March 18 / The Air Force announces that it has formally adopted a policy directing that commanding officers neither "impede . . . or otherwise interfere with" the decision by a service member's spouse to work outside the home, nor allow that decision to be a "factor . . . [affecting] the evaluation, promotion, or assignment of the military member." Some Air Force wives have complained that they were pressed by higher-ups to quit their jobs or risk harm to their husbands' careers.

March 22 / By substantial bipartisan majorities, the House and Senate vote to override President Reagan's veto of the Civil Rights Restoration Act, thereby reinstating the broad federal protections against sex, race, age, or disability discrimination in federally funded institutions that prevailed before the Supreme Court's *Grove City College v. Bell* decision.

March 23 / The Subcommittee on Civil and Constitutional Rights of the House Judiciary Committee begins two days of oversight hearings on sex harassment and other obstacles to women's employment in skilled, blue-collar jobs.

March 28 / The Justice Department announces that the city of Chicago has agreed to pay more than $9 million in back pay and to adjust seniority dates for victims of discrimination on the basis of race, national origin, and sex in the Chicago police department. The agreement resolves a suit filed in 1973.

March 28 / The National Committee on Pay Equity makes public a survey finding that more than 1,500 local governments, school districts, and community colleges in 24 states and the District of Columbia "have taken steps to identify or eliminate race or sex bias in the wages of civil service employees."

March 28 / President Reagan signs an executive order removing references to gender in the official code of conduct that guides military personnel if they become prisoners of war.

April 8 / The University of Connecticut's trustees approve a resolution asking the state's legislature to appropriate sufficient funds to eliminate male-female disparities in faculty salaries. A study of the university's salaries found that no explanation other than sex discrimination could account for $1,700 of the average difference between male and female faculty members' salaries. If the Connecticut legislature approves the funds, women faculty members will receive raises averaging $1,700 over the next two years.

April 8 / U.S. Secretary of Agriculture Richard E. Lyng signs a five-year plan to improve his department's performance in hiring and promoting women and minorities. Conceding past shortcomings, Lyng promises that the Agriculture Department will speed up the promotion of women to more responsible positions and bring the percentage of women up to the average for the government as a whole.

April 14 / The Oxford University Press publishes 30 volumes of *The Schomberg Library of Nineteenth-Century Black Women Writers*, which includes fiction, poetry, essays, and biographies by or about black women writers of the 1800s. Ten more volumes are planned in the set, which is edited by Henry Louis Gates, Jr.

April 25 / Burnita Matthews, the first woman ever to serve as a federal district judge, dies at the age of 93. President Harry S. Truman appointed Matthews to the District Court for the District of Columbia in 1949. She was active on the bench until late 1983.

April 26 / The House Committee on Small Business begins hearings on difficulties faced by women-owned enterprises. Equal access to commercial credit is a particular problem, according to many witnesses. Business and commercial loans are currently exempt from the antidiscrimination requirements of the federal Equal Credit Opportunity Act, which prohibits discrimination in lending on the basis of sex or marital status.

April 27 / Deciding a key child support enforcement matter, the Supreme Court rules unanimously in *Hicks v. Feiock* that in civil proceedings for contempt of court against parents who fail to pay court-ordered child support, a delinquent parent who claims inability to pay may be required to prove that inability. However, the Court's opinion makes clear that in a criminal contempt proceeding where inability to pay is an element of the crime, placing the burden of proof on the defendant might violate his/her constitutional rights.

May 3 / The General Conference of the United Methodist Church votes overwhelmingly to approve a revised hymnal that is gender neutral.

May 5 / The Congressional Caucus for Women's Issues announces the results of the Child Care Challenge it issued in 1987, calling on members of Congress to nominate model employer-sponsored child programs in their congressional districts and states. Of the 160 employers nominated, 43 were selected by a blue ribbon panel of child care experts to receive recognition for their achievements in providing child care benefits to their workers.

May 9 / In San Francisco, a federal judge raps the U.S. Forest Service and its parent, the Department of Agriculture, for failing to comply with a 1981 court-ordered plan to end discrimination against women Forest Service employees in California. The judge orders the Forest Service to establish a $1.5 million fund to assure compliance with the affirmative action plan. In addition, the Forest Service must pay the fees of Equal Rights Advocates, who represented the women plaintiffs in the case.

May 11 / Two congresswomen introduce bills to give job protection to congressional employees. H.R. 4576, introduced by Rep. Lynn Martin (R-IL), would entitle congressional and federal court employees to the civil rights protections that are afforded to other American workers by Title VII of the Civil Rights Act of 1964. H. Res. 445, introduced by Rep. Patricia Schroeder (D-CO), would set up a board to hear discrimination complaints from House of Representatives employees and would allow appeals to the House Committee on Ethics. Under present law, congressional employees are not covered by major federal antidiscrimination statutes.

May 14 / The Coalition of Labor Union Women (CLUW) sponsors the American Family Celebration in Washington, D.C. Attended by almost 50,000 people from around the country, the event seeks to highlight the importance of policies to help families balance work and family life.

May 23 / The Food and Drug Administration approves the cervical cap for use in the United States. This contraceptive device has long been used in Europe.

May 25 / The House approves a foreign aid appropriations bill that includes a provision requiring the Agency for International Development (AID) to allocate at least $5 million per year—more than twice what it currently spends—to the Women in Development program. The measure seeks to ensure that women are participating in AID-assisted activities/programs overseas in approximate proportion to women's traditional participation in those activities.

May 26 / The U.S. Navy names Petty Officer 1st Class Beth Blevins its "sailor of the year." She is the first woman to win that honor, which brings Blevins a promotion to Chief Petty Officer, an assignment to work in Washington with the Master Chief Petty Officer, and the Navy Commendation Medal.

June 1 / "Symbolom" by Pulitzer Prize-winning American composer Ellen Taafe Zwilich is given its world premiere

performance in Leningrad by the touring New York Philhar-
monic Orchestra. Commissioned especially for the orchestra's tour, Zwilich's score is believed to be the first American
work to have its world premiere in the Soviet Union.

June 7 / The great majority (87 percent) of parents think
that participating in sports is just as important for girls as for
boys, according to a survey released today by the Women's
Sports Foundation. Less encouraging is the finding that
girls'—especially black girls'—participation in sports drops
off in their mid- to late teens.

June 8 / The Senate gives final approval to H.R. 2470,
the Catastrophic Health Care Insurance Act (the House approved it on June 2). President Reagan is expected to sign the
bill, which includes two provisions of particular relevance to
women: one to ensure that the noninstitutionalized spouses
of institutionalized persons will not be left impoverished by
Medicaid eligibility requirements and one to provide Medicare coverage for breast cancer screenings.

June 13 / Female athletes at Temple University will be
treated comparably to male athletes under a "ground-breaking agreement" reached today in *Haffer v. Temple University*.
According to the National Women's Law Center, which represented the plaintiffs in the eight-year-old sex bias case, the
agreement lays out specific improvements and safeguards for
women student-athletes in such areas as participation opportunities, athletic scholarships, and overall resources.

June 20 / The U.S. Supreme Court rules unanimously
(in *New York State Club Association, Inc. v. City of New York*)
that the First Amendment does not prohibit a city from barring sex and race discrimination in large clubs where members make important business and professional contacts. The
case involved a New York City ordinance prohibiting dis-

crimination in public accommodations which had been extended to include private clubs that have more than 400 members, provide regular meals, and receive payments for dues, meals, or other services from members' employers.

June 22 / The Supreme Court rules 5-4 in *Florida v. Long* to limit the retroactive relief available to employees under a 1983 Supreme Court decision which invalidated the use of sex-based actuarial tables in calculating pension benefits under employer-operated pension plans. Today's ruling means that only those employees who retired after the effective date of the 1983 decision are entitled to compensation for a disparity in benefits that arises from the use of gender-based criteria.

June 26 / The *Washington Post* reports that a *Washington Post*/ABC News voter survey conducted earlier in the month (June 15-19) found that while men split evenly between Democratic front-runner Dukakis and Republican front-runner Bush, women preferred Dukakis to Bush by 57 percent to 33 percent.

June 27 / A study on the status of women in 99 countries finds the United States ranking third, behind Sweden and Finland. Published today by the Population Crisis Council, the report evaluates women's status in five major areas: health, control over childbearing, education, employment, and legal protection.

June 29 / The U.S. Supreme Court today hands down two decisions with particular relevance to women. In *Bowen v. Kendrick*, the Court rules 5-4 that the Adolescent Family Life Act, a federal law that grants federal funds to religiously affiliated organizations for the purpose of promoting chastity among teenagers, does not, on its face, violate the constitutionally mandated separation of church and state.

In *Watson v. Fort Worth [Texas] Bank & Trust*, the Court rules unanimously that in employment discrimination cases involving challenges to employers' subjective criteria for hiring or promotions, employees may use statistical evidence showing disparate impact (such as underrepresentation of women or minorities in the workplace) and need not prove an intent to discriminate. The ruling in *Watson* does not determine the burden of proof (i.e., on employees and employers, respectively) applicable in disparate impact challenges to subjective employment criteria, but four members of the Court indicate that they would increase the burden on employees to prove discrimination.

June 29 / By a vote of 376-23, the House of Representatives votes to add families with children and the handicapped to the groups protected against housing discrimination by federal fair housing law. The bill also strengthens the government's powers to enforce prohibitions against all forms of illegal housing discrimination.

June 29 / Forty-two percent of the federal government's female employees and 14 percent of its male employees experienced some form of sexual harassment between May 1985 and May 1987, according to a survey released today by the U.S. Merit Systems Protection Board. Harassment against women was most pervasive in the State Department and related agencies, where more than half of the female employees surveyed said that they had been sexually harassed at work.

June 30 / At the steps of the U.S. Capitol, National Organization for Women (NOW) president Molly Yard delivers to Rep. Don Edwards petitions that contain 100,000 signatures calling for passage of the Equal Rights Amendment. Edwards (D-CA) has promised to reintroduce the ERA, which is the top priority on NOW's agenda.

July 1 / The Marine Corps' Security Guard School in Quantico, Virginia graduates its first women. Graduates of the school are assigned to security forces guarding naval bases and other installations; heretofore, female Marines have been barred from these assignments.

July 6 / The Coalition for Women's Appointments is officially launched, spearheaded by the National Women's Political Caucus and involving 45 organizations with more than five million members. The goal of the bipartisan coalition is to get more women appointed to top-level federal jobs. The group will develop a list of Democratic and Republican women who would be qualified to serve in whatever administration is elected this fall.

July 7 / Only three of the 13 key maternal and child health goals that the government set in 1979 for achievement by 1990 are likely to be met on time, according to the Centers for Disease Control. Expected to be achieved or surpassed are a reduction of neonatal death rates, having most babies leave the hospital in car safety seats, and the widespread institution of programs for screening newborns for metabolic disorders. Those targets not likely to be met include an infant mortality rate of no more than nine deaths per 1,000 live births and a maternal death rate that does not exceed five per 100,000 live births in any county, or among mothers of any race or ethnic group.

July 8 / Hubert I. Teitelbaum, a federal judge in Pittsburgh, tells lawyer Barbara Wolvovitz that he won't allow anyone in his courtroom to use the honorific "Ms." and orders her to use her married name or go to jail.

July 14 / Judge Teitelbaum apologizes to Ms. Wolvovitz and "recognize[s] [her] right to be addressed in any manner in which [she] see[s] fit."

July 28 / Sterilization and "the pill" are by far the two most common contraceptive methods relied on by fertile, sexually active American women, and the condom is a distant third for the unmarried as well as the married, according to a survey report released today by the Alan Guttmacher Institute. Despite rising concern about AIDS and other sexually transmitted diseases, the survey found that between 1982 and 1987 condom use rose only slightly (from 12 percent to 16 percent) among sexually active unmarried American women age 15 to 44 who wished to avoid pregnancy. The survey also found that more than three-quarters (76 percent) of never-married women in this age group were sexually active in 1987—up from 68 percent in 1982.

August 1 / Phyllis Holmes begins her term as president of the National Association of Intercollegiate Athletics (NAIA). Holmes is the first woman to serve as president of any national coed sports organization.

August 3 / The 1988 Summer Olympic Games in Seoul, Korea, come to a close. Two hundred twenty-eight U.S. women competed in 22 sports, and U.S. women won gold medals in 12 events, including basketball. Sisters-in-law Jackie Joyner-Kersee and Florence Griffith Joyner between them won five gold medals in track and field events, and each set one world and one Olympic record.

August 10 / The American Bar Association's (ABA) House of Delegates adopts a resolution committing the ABA and its members to "refuse to participate in, acquiesce in, or condone barriers to the full integration and equal participation of women in the legal profession."

September 2 / The *Washington Post* reports that the Securities and Exchange Commission (SEC) last month agreed to pay Veronica Awkard $145,000 in a "confidential settlement" arising from Awkard's claim that she was a victim of pervasive sex harassment when she was employed as a branch

Jackie Joyner-Kersee sets an Olympic record of 7.40 meters in the long jump at the 1988 Olympics. *AP/Wide World Photos*

chief in the Office of Applications and Reports Services at SEC headquarters in 1983.

September 29 / Stacy Allison of Portland, Oregon, reaches the summit of Mt. Everest. She is the first American woman (and the seventh woman) to make it to the top.

September 29 / The Federal Equitable Pay Practices Act of 1987 (H.R. 387) passes the House of Representatives by a vote of 302-98. The bill would require a pay equity study of the federal government's wage and job classification system.

October 4 / The U.S. House of Representatives votes 408-12 for H. Res. 558, to prohibit discrimination against House employees on the basis of race, color, national origin, religion, sex (including marital and parental status), handicap, or age. The measure applies only to the House and must be reapproved in the 101st Congress.

October 4 / The Equal Employment Opportunity Commission (EEOC) issues a directive advising employers that they may not single out females for exclusion from jobs because of a potential hazard to either reproductive health or the fetus unless these three conditions are met: (1) the weight of scientific evidence shows that the hazard is substantial, (2) the hazard has been shown to affect women only, and (3) no feasible, less discriminatory alternative is available.

October 6 / The Manpower Demonstration Research Corporation (MDRC) releases a study showing that pregnant teenagers and young welfare mothers who participated in programs offering special educational, medical, and counseling services between 1980 and 1982 earned significantly more money five years later than did nonparticipating women in similar circumstances.

October 7 / Hopes that the 100th Congress will adopt a federal pay equity study die in the Senate. Senate sponsors, who offered the pay equity measure in the form of an amendment to another bill (S. 2388) under consideration, withdraw the amendment when approval seems unlikely.

October 7 / S. 2488, the Parental and Temporary Medical Leave Act of 1988, which would require the federal government as well as private sector employers with 20 or more employees to grant up to 10 weeks of parental leave and up to 13 weeks of medical leave, dies in the Senate after failing to gain the 60 votes necessary to cut off debate. The full House has not yet acted on parental leave.

October 13 / President Reagan signs the welfare reform bill into law. The measure's central purpose is to reduce welfare dependency by helping AFDC recipients become gainfully employed, and to that end it provides both "carrots and sticks."

For example, the new law requires states to establish Job Opportunity and Basic Skills programs (JOBS) to educate, train, and employ adult welfare recipients. It requires that most AFDC recipients participate in JOBS, and that child care be made available to those who need it in order to participate. It provides transitional child care and medical benefits for one year to welfare recipients who leave the JOBS program for a full-time job.

The law also seeks to strengthen child support enforcement. It requires automatic withholding from an absent parent's paycheck for all new or modified child support orders involving families whose cases are handled by the Office of Child Support Enforcement (OCSE); beginning in 1994, automatic withholding will be required on all child support orders regardless of whether a parent has applied for OCSE assistance.

October 17 / IBM announces a package of employee benefit options including up to three years of unpaid leave for such purposes as caring for a new baby, sick child, or elderly relative. IBM will continue to provide such fringe benefits as health insurance. Employees taking leaves of a year or less would be guaranteed their old, or an equivalent, job at the same location. Those taking longer leaves would be assured of reemployment with IBM, but not necessarily in the same job or location.

October 17 / Gertrude Elion gets word that she and her long-time colleague George Hitchings have been awarded a Nobel Prize in Medicine for their pioneering pharmaceutical research. Although her title is scientist emeritus, Elion still works at Wellcome Research Laboratories in North Carolina.

October 21 / The 100th Congress adjourns without action by the full House of Representatives on H.R. 925, the Family and Medical Leave Act of 1987.

October 25 / President Reagan signs H.R. 5050, the Women's Business Ownership Act, into law. A key provision applies the same antidiscrimination rules to commercial credit transactions that presently apply to consumer credit transactions. Among the measure's other provisions is one to create a guaranteed "mini-loan" program in the Small Business Administration. These loans would be particularly helpful for businesses in the service sector of the economy, where women owners are concentrated.

November 4 / Bill and Camille Cosby give $20 million to Spelman College, a historically black women's college in Atlanta, Georgia. The Cosbys' gift is the largest single contribution ever made to a historically black college.

November 5 / The Baseball Hall of Fame in Cooperstown, New York, unveils a new permanent exhibition, Women in Baseball. Helping to celebrate are veterans of the long-defunct All-American Girls Professional League (1943-1954).

November 9 / The U.S. Army announces that more than 3,000 active-duty positions that were previously open only to men will now be open to women, as will 6,000-plus National Guard positions and some 1,700 Reserve positions. Federal law still bars women from combat positions.

November 11 / Detailed analyses of the *New York Times*/CBS election day exit polls published today show that 52 percent of all Americans who voted on November 8 were women and that half (50 percent) of the women voted for George Bush. However, a gender gap is evident: Bush got 57 percent of the men's vote. The polls also found gender-related differences by such other variables as marital status (Bush did best among married men [60 percent] and least well among unmarried women [42 percent]); race (nine percent of black women, and 15 percent of black men, voted for Bush, compared with 56 percent of white women and 63 percent of white men); and age (among voters age 60 and over, for example, 53 percent of the men but only 48 percent of the women voted for Bush).

November 15 / Speaking at the annual meeting of the American Public Health Association, a researcher who studied 198 large chemical and electronics companies in Massachusetts reports that nearly 20 percent of them had policies restricting women's employment options on the grounds of possible risk to their reproductive health from exposure to one or more of four substances (lead, radiation, glycol ethers, and mercury). None of the companies restricted male employees' exposure to these substances, although all but one (mercury) are known to be hazardous to males as well as to females.

November 15 / S. 2042, authorizing a memorial to the women who served in the Vietnam war, becomes law. As finally approved by Congress, the bill calls for a statue to be placed on federal land in the Washington, D.C., area, but does not specify the site. The memorial will be funded from private contributions raised by the Vietnam Women's Memorial Project, a nonprofit, nongovernmental group.

December 6 / The Soviet press agency, Tass, announces that Florence Griffith Joyner was voted athlete of the year in its survey of 36 news agencies in 32 countries. Griffith Joyner won three gold medals for the United States in track and field at the Summer Olympics.

December 8 / Wilma L. Vaught (Brig. Gen. USAF, ret.) president of Women in Military Service for America Memorial Foundation, Inc., announces the design competition for a memorial to women in military service to be built at the gate of Arlington National Cemetery. Authorized by Congress in

1986 with the proviso that the foundation raise nonfederal funds to pay for it, the memorial will honor all the women living and dead who have served in the U.S. military and will include a register listing them. However, since no complete list now exists, members of the public are urged to come forward with the names of women they know to have served.

December 12 / The Secretary's Commission on Nursing of the U.S. Department of Health and Human Services issues a final report recommending that the federal government take steps to ease the shortage of registered nurses—a shortage the commission attributes "primarily [to] increased demand as opposed to contraction in supply." Among the commission's recommendations: authorizing a temporary, one-time increase in Medicare hospital rates for the sole purpose of increasing nurses' pay; increasing federal financial aid to nursing school students; and giving nurses a larger role in decisionmaking.

December 24 / President-elect George Bush announces that he will nominate Elizabeth Hanford Dole to be Secretary of Labor in his administration. Dole, who was Secretary of Transportation for nearly four years during the Reagan administration, is the second woman Bush has nominated for a cabinet-level position. The first was Carla Hills, nominee for Special Trade Representative.

1989

January 1 / Federal laws taking effect today include a provision of the Tax Reform Act of 1986 that requires faster vesting in employer-provided pension plans. According to a spokeswoman for the Employee Benefit Research Institute (EBRI), the change should be particularly beneficial to women workers because "they tend to be in the workforce or with the same employer for shorter periods [than men]."

January 1 / The U.S. Supreme Court holds unconstitutional a city affirmative action ordinance that reserved a fixed percentage of city contracting business for minority contractors. Technically, the Court's decision in *City of Richmond v. J.A. Croson Co.*, which involves race, does not necessarily determine the constitutionality of affirmative action plans based on gender; nevertheless, the decision does indicate that the Court considers proof of past discrimination essential in justifying city-initiated, voluntary affirmative action plans.

January 3 / With the swearing-in of newly elected U.S. Representatives Nita Lowey (D-NY) and Jolene Unsoeld (D-WA), the total number of women in Congress reaches a record high of 27 (two senators, 25 representatives).

January 3 / The Equal Rights Amendment is reintroduced in the House of Representatives as H.J. Res. 1 by Rep. Don Edwards (D-CA) and 133 cosponsors.

January 5 / The DuPont Company announces the results of a survey of its workers showing that family obligations are increasingly important in the career choices of both men and women. One finding: more than half of the male employees surveyed said they were using or were planning to use child care. The survey also indicated that women employees bearing the major responsibility for raising children and running households found it difficult to progress in their careers at the same pace as men.

January 5 / Portia Porter Mittelman accepts the position of staff director of the Senate Special Committee on Aging. Appointed by the committee's chair, Sen. David Pryor (D-AR), Mittelman will be the first black woman ever to serve as staff director of a Senate full committee.

January 7 / At the 1989 Women's Agenda Conference in Kansas City, Missouri, a Bush/Quayle polling consultant tells a panel: "The major accomplishment of Bush/Quayle was the closing of the gender gap, which we measured in late spring as 15 to 20 percentage points, to a more reasonable level of six to eight [percentage points] by the conclusion of the campaign . . . [This accomplishment] was critical to winning."

January 9 / In a letter to President Reagan, U.S. Surgeon General C. Everett Koop says that he will not issue a report that the president had requested on the health risks arising from abortion because a comprehensive study conducted by the Public Health Service found little scientific evidence that abortion causes women significant physical or emotional harm.

January 10 / In a settlement described by the Labor Department as the "largest back-pay amount ever obtained by the federal government from a single employer in a sex or race discrimination case," Chicago's Harris Trust and Savings Bank agrees to pay employees $14 million in back pay to settle federal charges of sex and race discrimination dating back to 1973. The charges, brought under presidential Executive Order 11246, were based on a complaint filed by the Chicago-based Women Employed, which—represented by the National Women's Law Center—was a party to the case and to the settlement. While the settlement does not include any admission of discrimination by the Harris Bank, the bank agrees to revise its affirmative action policies and to provide special training to women and minority workers.

January 11 / A law intended to make working conditions healthier for video display terminal (VDT) operators goes into effect in Suffolk County, New York. Thought to be the first such initiative by a local government in the United States, the law includes provisions requiring work breaks and special training for employees who spend at least 26 hours a week at VDTs in private workplaces with more than 20 terminals. Court challenges have blocked implementation of a section of the law that would require employers to pay most of the cost of eye exams and glasses for their employees who use VDTs.

January 15 / Survey findings released today show that employed males in low-income neighborhoods are twice as likely as their unemployed counterparts to marry the mothers of children they have fathered out of wedlock. According to the researchers at the University of Chicago who conducted a study of nearly 2,500 Chicagoans in low-income neighborhoods, the male's employment acts as an incentive in a low-income couple's decision to marry, regardless of whether the mother stands to lose AFDC eligibility.

January 18 / President Bush nominates Constance Berry Newman to head the Office of Personnel Management and Susan Engeleiter to head the Small Business Administration. Newman, who began her career in 1961 as a clerk typist in the Interior Department, has held important management positions, including Assistant Secretary of Housing and Urban Development and Director of VISTA. She has most recently served on the Bush transition team. Engeleiter, the first Republican woman ever to be elected to the Wisconsin State Senate, has been its minority (Republican) leader since 1984. She ran unsuccessfully for the U.S. Senate last year.

January 25 / The Equal Rights Amendment is reintroduced in the Senate as S.J. Res. 1 by Senator Edward Kennedy (D-MA).

January 26 / The National Research Council (NRC) reports that women constituted only 21 percent of the 363 U.S.

citizens who earned doctorates in mathematics at U.S. institutions in 1988. Non-Hispanic whites heavily predominated among both male and female degree recipients. The NRC says that women and members of minority groups, particularly blacks, Hispanics, and Native Americans, are disproportionately affected by poor mathematics education which keeps them out of programs leading to vital scientific and professional careers.

January 30 / Effective today, employees of the Tennessee Valley Authority (TVA) will be allowed up to 10 weeks of unpaid leave to care for a new baby or for a family member who is ill. The TVA is a corporation wholly owned by the U.S. government.

January 31 / The National Research Council, releasing a survey of doctorate recipients from U.S. universities, reports that 448 U.S. black women earned doctoral degrees in U.S. institutions in 1986, 16 (four percent) more than in 1977, although 21 percent fewer than in 1982 (the decade's high point for U.S. black female recipients). The number of U.S. black males awarded doctorates in 1987 was, however, less than half the number in 1977 (317 vs. 684); the annual number of U.S. black male doctorate recipients has declined steadily over the decade.

February 2 / Lt. Cmdr. Evelyn J. Fields of the National Oceanic and Atmospheric Administration (NOAA) takes command of the research ship McArthur. According to NOAA, Fields is the first woman to be placed in command of a commissioned sea-going ship in one of the seven U.S. uniformed services.

February 2 / Karen Thompson visits her lover, Sharon Kowalski, for the first time in more than three years. Kowalski was severely disabled in an automobile accident in 1983; in 1985 her father, as legal guardian, forbade Thompson to visit her. Thompson fought successfully in court for the right to visit Kowalski.

February 3 / Awarding scholarships solely on the basis of Scholastic Aptitude Test (SAT) scores discriminates against girls, rules federal Judge John M. Walker in a case challenging New York State's criteria for awarding state scholarships. While boys consistently do better than girls on these tests, which are intended to predict students' ability to succeed in college, opponents of the tests assert that girls typically do better in college than their SAT scores seem to predict.

February 5 / Judith Richards Hope is elected to serve on the Harvard Corporation, the 353-year-old university's chief governing board. Hope is the first woman ever to be named to the corporation.

February 11 / The Reverend Barbara Clementine Harris is consecrated bishop in the Episcopal Church—that church's first woman bishop in history. In accordance with church law, Harris's election by the diocese where she will serve as suffragan bishop (the Diocese of Massachusetts) was ratified by a majority of all the Episcopal dioceses in the United States. However, because some Episcopalians continue bitterly to oppose the ordination of women as priests and bishops, Harris's consecration is marked by protest and controversy as well as by joy and celebration.

February 24 / Women hold 150 appointed cabinet-rank state positions in 1989, up from 70 in 1981, according to a study released today by the National Women's Political Caucus. Of the 39 states where cabinet officers are appointed, Virginia has the highest percentage (three out of seven) of females among its cabinet appointees. Maryland is second with seven out of 18.

March 3 / Laurie Shields, cofounder with Tish Somers of the Older Women's League (OWL) and founder of the Alli-

The Reverend Barbara Clementine Harris, first woman bishop in the history of the Episcopal Church. *Courtesy The Episcopal Times*

ancc for Displaced Homemakers (later the Displaced Home-makers Network), dies of breast cancer at age 67.

March 8 / The House Education and Labor Committee approves H.R. 770, the Family and Medical Leave Act of 1989. Like its 100th Congress predecessor (H.R. 925, as amended and approved by the same committee in 1987), the bill would require employers to allow employees up to 10 weeks of unpaid, job-protected family leave over a two-year period and up to 15 weeks of personal medical leave over a one-year period. II.R. 770 would exempt some employers—initially, those with fewer than 50 employees; later, those with fewer than 35.

March 15 / A child care initiative proposed by President Bush is introduced in Congress. H.R. 1466/S. 601 would en-title families with at least one working parent and an annual income below $13,000 to a refundable tax credit for each child under age four, whether or not the family incurred child care expenses. The bill would also make the existing dependent care tax credit refundable to low-income families, although those eligible for both credits would have to choose one or the other; they could not claim both.

March 16 / Gilda Oliveros is sworn in as mayor of Hialeah Gardens, Florida. She is believed to be the first Cuban-born woman to be elected mayor of a U.S. city.

March 17 / For the first time in its 229-year history, the New York City St. Patrick's Day parade is led by a woman—Grand Marshal Dorothy Hayden Cudahy.

March 22 / On the "op ed" page of today's *New York Times*, Felice N. Schwartz defends her controversial article in the *Harvard Business Review (HBR)*. In "Management Women and the New Facts of Life" (*HBR*, January/February 1989) Schwartz began by asserting that "the cost of employing women in business is greater than the cost of employing men," called for employers to distinguish between "career-primary" and "career-and-family" women managers, and recommended that employers devise policies that would allow women in the latter category "to trade some career growth and compensation for freedom from the constant pressure to work long hours."

In the lively debate about her *HBR* article, critics have not only questioned the adequacy of the data on which Schwartz based her assertion of the relative costs of employing women and men but have also raised the fundamental objection that she singles out mothers and ignores fathers in her call for corporate policies allowing work/family tradeoffs. Schwartz's critics hold that her approach would result in a "mommy track," reinforcing and perpetuating the assumption that it is always the responsibility of women to bring up children.

Dorothy Hayden Cudahy, the first woman to serve as grand marshal of the New York City Saint Patrick's Day parade. *John Sotomayor/New York Times*

Schwartz's response in today's *Times* ("The 'Mommy Track' Isn't Anti-Woman") does not address the questions raised about her data, but says that "acknowledging that there are costs associated with employing women will not lead companies to put women in dead end jobs" because the costs "pale beside the payoffs." In any case, according to Schwartz, "whether or not men play a greater role in child rearing, companies must reduce the family-related stresses on working women. The flexibility companies provide for women now will be a model in the very near future for men—thus women will not be forced to continue to take primary responsibility for child care."

March 22 / The gap between the richest and poorest Americans has been widening, according to a report released today by the Ways and Means Committee of the House of Representatives. Real (inflation-adjusted) average family income increased by 5.6 percent between 1979 and 1987, but the average for the poorest fifth of American families dropped by 6.1 percent between 1979 and 1987, while the average for the richest fifth increased by 11.1 percent.

March 26 / Hospitals seeking to recruit and retain skilled nursing staff increased nurses' maximum salaries in 1988 by the largest real (i.e., inflation-adjusted) percentage in history, the American Nurses Association (ANA) announces today. However, says the ANA, in inflation-adjusted dollars, the average maximum salary ($32,160) in 1988 remained below the average in 1981.

March 28 / Indiana's Fourth Congressional District elects Jill Long to the U.S. House of Representatives, where she will increase the number of women members to 26. Long, a professor of business and a Democrat, was chosen in a special election held to fill the vacancy left by the appointment of Rep. Dan Coats to serve out Vice President Quayle's term in the U.S. Senate.

April 6 / The Census Bureau reports that divorced white women are almost twice as likely as their black counterparts to be awarded alimony, and more likely than black women to get property settlements.

April 6 / The House Education and Labor Committee completes hearings on child care legislation, particularly H.R. 3, the Child Development and Education Act of 1989, and H.R. 30, the Act for Better Child Care (ABC).

April 9 / Hundreds of thousands of women, men, and children march in Washington, D.C., to demonstrate support of women's rights, especially the right to legal abortions.

Officially estimated at 300,000 strong, this is one of the largest Washington demonstrations on record.

April 12 / The House Post Office and Civil Service Committee approves the segment (Title II) of H.R. 770, the Family and Medical Leave Act of 1989, that applies to federal employees (who would be entitled to up to 18 weeks of unpaid, job-protected family leave over a two-year period and up to 26 weeks of personal medical leave per year). (See March 8, 1989, above, for the provisions that would apply to employees in the private sector.)

April 20 / The Senate Labor and Human Resources Committee approves S. 345, the Senate version of the Family and Medical Leave Act of 1989. The Senate bill would require employers to allow workers up to 10 weeks of unpaid, job-protected family leave in a two-year period and up to 13 weeks of personal medical leave over a one-year period. Employers with fewer than 20 employees would be exempt.

April 20 / The U.S. Department of State confirms that it is acting to comply with court orders to end sex discrimination in the Foreign Service and to remedy the effects of past sex bias. In notices acknowledging that it discriminated against female Foreign Service officers (FSOs) between 1976 and 1985, the department is advising hundreds of women FSOs that they may be entitled to remedy, including reassignment to better jobs. The court orders arise from a 1987 federal court finding (in *Palmer v. Shultz*) that the State Department discriminated against female Foreign Service officers in job evaluations, job assignments, and honor awards. In a related case, the court found that the Foreign Service entrance examinations in 1985, 1986, and 1987 discriminated against women.

April 26 / The Supreme Court hears oral arguments in *Webster v. Reproductive Health Services*, a case involving a Missouri state law that seeks to limit access to abortion. Declaring in its preamble that life begins at conception, the Missouri statute prohibits abortions in public institutions, bars the use of public funds for abortion counseling, and requires physicians to test for fetal viability if a woman seeking an abortion appears to be at least 20 weeks pregnant. The case could provide the high Court with an opportunity to modify or overturn *Roe v. Wade*, the 1973 decision that legalized abortion.

April 26 / The House Administration Committee approves an amendment to H.R. 770, the Family and Medical Leave Act, to allow employees of the House of Representatives the same family and medical leave guarantees as the bill would afford employees of the federal government.

April 27 / A spokeswoman for the Food and Drug Administration (FDA) announces that an FDA advisory committee has voted unanimously to recommend FDA approval of a contraceptive implant (Norplant) for women that would prevent pregnancy for up to five years.

May 1 / The U.S. Supreme Court rules in *Price Waterhouse v. Hopkins* that if a woman charging sex discrimination under Title VII of the Civil Rights Act of 1964 presents direct evidence that illegal sex stereotyping was a motivating factor involved in denying her the promotion, the burden is on the employer to prove that the promotion would have been denied even if sex stereotyping had not been a factor.

May 9 / Federal funds for vocational education will continue to include special set-asides for sex equity and single-parent and displaced-homemaker programs under legislation overwhelmingly approved today by the House of Representatives. The Carl Perkins Applied Technology Education Program Act (H.R. 7), a five-year reauthorization of federal vocational education programs, will also strengthen the role of sex equity coordinators.

May 10 / Females account for no more than 37 percent of this year's National Merit Scholarship semi-finalists, according to a study conducted by FairTest, a Cambridge, Massachusetts, research group which charges that the Preliminary Scholastic Aptitude Test (PSAT) is biased against females. National Merit Scholarship semi-finalists are chosen entirely on the basis of their PSAT scores, although other factors are taken into account in selecting the finalists from the pool of semi-finalists.

May 12 / A five-year study of sex differences in writing skills in 14 countries finds that girls write better than boys do because they receive more encouragement to develop their writing skills. According to a spokesman for the International Association for the Evaluation of Educational Achievement, which sponsored the study, "sexual stereotypes are very strong in the classroom."

May 14 / A study released today by the Equality Center reports that three-quarters of all high schools violate Title IX of the Education Amendments of 1972 by engaging in such practices as not allowing excused absences for prenatal or postnatal care and not reinstating students returning from pregnancy leave to the status they held when the leave began. Over 40 percent of all girls who drop out of school give pregnancy or marriage as their reason.

May 16 / The Coalition for Women's Appointments reports that 17 of its recommendees are among the 41 women appointed so far to high-level positions in the Bush administration.

May 17 / Both Houses of Congress approve legislation which would increase the minimum hourly wage to $4.55

over three years. (The current minimum wage, which has not been increased since 1981, is $3.35.) The bill would also allow a subminimum training wage of 85 percent of the minimum for first-time jobholders during the first 60 days of their employment. President Bush, who supports a $4.25 minimum and a six-month subminimum wage period, is expected to veto the bill.

May 27 / Suzie Azar is elected mayor of El Paso, the fourth largest city in Texas. The state now has the distinction of having women mayors in its four largest cities (three of which—Houston [Kathy Whitmire], Dallas [Annette Strauss], and San Antonio [Lila Cockrell]—are among the 10 largest cities in the United States).

May 28 / AT&T, the Communications Workers of America, and the International Brotherhood of Electrical Workers agree on a ground-breaking new three-year contract that includes many provisions to help AT&T's workers—the majority of whom are female—meet work/family responsibilities.

Among the components of the agreement: establishing a $5 million AT&T-financed fund, administered jointly by the company and the unions, to furnish seed money to help establish community-based child and elder care programs; doubling (to one year) the previously allowable job-protected parental leave for the care of a newborn child and allowing a similar leave for the care of a seriously ill family member (although the leaves would be unpaid, company-paid health insurance coverage would be provided for up to six months and life insurance coverage for one year); company reimbursement for up to $2,000 of an employee's costs for adopting a child; and special accounts that allow workers to set aside up to $5,000 tax free for dependent care. The contract must be ratified by union members.

May 30 / The Supreme Court rules that under the Uniformed Services Former Spouses Protection Act, a military veteran's spouse is not entitled to a share of the veteran's disability benefits if the couple divorces, even if the veteran has elected to receive the disability benefits rather than an equal amount of military retirement pay, which the act requires to be shared. Justices O'Connor and Blackmun, the two justices dissenting, call on Congress to "address the inequity created by the Court."

May 30 / San Francisco's Board of Supervisors approves an ordinance giving legal recognition to the "domestic partnerships" of homosexual and unmarried heterosexual couples if they file a declaration of domestic partnership with the county clerk. To be eligible, a couple must live together and be jointly responsible for living expenses, and neither partner may be married to anyone else. The ordinance also prohibits future city and county policies that treat married couples differently from domestic partnerships. Among the practical effects of the ordinance: partners in a domestic partnership will be afforded the same hospital visitation rights as married couples.

June 4 / Playwright Wendy Wasserman receives a Tony Award for her play, *The Heidi Chronicles*. She is the first woman in the award's 41-year history to win a Tony as the author of an original play.

June 5 / The Supreme Court hands down a major decision revising previous standards for determining the legality of employment practices that have a disparate impact on women and minorities but are not motivated by an intent to discriminate. As a result of this 5-4 ruling (in *Wards Cove Packing Co. v Antonio*), employees seem likely to have increased difficulty in winning disparate impact employment discrimination cases; the Court's decision simultaneously increases the burden on employees to demonstrate that an employer's hiring and promotion practices have a disparate impact and reduces the burden on employers to defend those practices by showing their "business necessity."

June 12 / The Supreme Court hands down two more decisions that are considered setbacks for women and minorities seeking equity in the workplace. The high Court's 5-4 decision in *Martin v. Wilkes* opens long-standing affirmative action plans to legal challenges by allowing employees who charge that they are the victims of reverse discrimination under a court-ordered affirmative action plan, and who were not a party to the original lawsuit from which the plan arose, to bring suit to overturn the plan. In the *Martin* case, the aggrieved employees are white male firefighters who charge that their employer's eight-year-old affirmative action plan discriminates against white males.

In *Lorance v. AT&T Technologies*, the Court rules to limit the time during which an employee can sue to challenge a discriminatory seniority system. The Court holds that such suits must be brought during the period before the applicable statute of limitations runs out, and that the period begins on the date when the seniority system was adopted, not on the date that the employee becomes subject to the system and thus has reason to challenge it. This decision places potential victims of a discriminatory seniority system in the position of having to foresee that the system could eventually or possibly apply to them, and to bring suit before they suffer actual harm or risk forfeiting the opportunity to sue.

June 14 / The House of Representatives fails to override President Bush's veto of H.R. 2, the bill to increase the minimum wage to $4.55.

June 21 / In *The Florida Star v. B.J.F.*, the Supreme Court holds that the First Amendment protects a newspaper from liability for truthfully publishing a rape victim's name if the name was lawfully obtained.

June 21 / The Census Bureau reports that in 1988 more than half (54.4 percent) of childless married women age 30 to 34 were planning to have children in the future. The comparable proportion in 1975 was 33.5 percent.

June 23 / The full Senate approves S. 5, a compromise version of the Act for Better Child Care. As passed by the Senate, S. 5 authorizes $1.75 billion for grants to increase and improve child care services. Compromising on several contentious issues, the bill does not set federal minimum health and safety standards, requiring instead that states set standards, and it allows parents who receive child care vouchers to place their children in sectarian programs while barring religious bias in hiring program employees and admitting children. S. 5 also includes a package of tax credit provisions designed to assist low-income working families with children.

June 27 / The House Education and Labor Committee completes and approves an amended version of H.R. 3, the Child Development and Education Act. Like the Senate's child care bill, S. 5, H.R. 3 would authorize $1.75 billion for child care and would require states to implement minimum health and safety standards. H.R. 3 must also be acted on by the Ways and Means Committee before it can come before the full House.

June 27 / The Women's Research and Education Institute (WREI) presents U.S. Congresswoman Lindy Boggs (D-LA) with the first annual American Woman award.

July 3 / Ruling in *Webster v. Reproductive Health Services*, the U.S. Supreme Court upholds by 5-4 the right of a state to impose severe restrictions on abortion. The Court allows to stand a Missouri statute that begins by declaring that life begins at conception and that prohibits public hospitals or other facilities supported by taxpayers to be used for performing abortions not necessary to save the life of the mother, even if no public funds are spent on the procedure. The statute also prohibits public employees, including physicians and other health professionals, from performing or assisting with an abortion not necessary to save the mother and requires medical tests to determine the viability of any fetus thought to be at least 20 weeks old.

In its decision, the Court does not go so far as to overturn the constitutional right to abortion established in *Roe v. Wade*, but Chief Justice Rehnquist writes for the majority: "Nothing in the Constitution requires States to enter or remain in the business of performing abortions. Nor . . . do private physicians and their patients have some kind of constitutional right to access to public facilities for the performance of abortions." In his dissent, Justice Blackmun (who wrote for the majority in *Roe v. Wade*), writes: "I fear for the liberty and equality of the millions of women who have lived and come of age in the 16 years since Roe was decided."

The American Woman 1990-91

ONE A Portrait of African American Families in the United States

HARRIETTE PIPES MCADOO

Highlights

THERE IS NO SUCH THING as "the" African American family. Stereotypes about black people and black families are pervasive, encouraged by the media's apparent lack of interest in portraying black families as ordinary families. Yet black families, which are not confined to any single social class, economic status, lifestyle, or religion, are as diverse as white, Hispanic, Asian, and other families in the United States today.

- Regardless of race, family structure plays an important role in the economic situation of families in the United States. Whether a family consists of a married couple or is headed by a single parent has a significant impact on the economic well-being of that family.

- In 1987, married-couple families accounted for slightly over half of the 7.2 million African American families; 43 percent were headed by women, and six percent were headed by men.

- The high proportion of female-headed families is a major reason that the overall median income for black families was less than 60 percent of the median income of all U.S. families in 1987.

- Regardless of race, children in a female-headed family are at some risk of being poor; the risk is very great if the family is black. Over two-thirds of all children living in female-headed African American families had incomes below the poverty level in 1987. Children in female-headed black families are more than three times as likely to be poor as children in other black families.

- Yet, a common conception that most blacks are poor is a misconception, although the poverty rate among blacks is more than three times that of whites (33.1 percent vs. 10.5 percent in 1987).

- Because of wage and job discrimination against black men, black married women have always been more likely to work outside the home than have their white counterparts. The typical black married-couple family is a two-earner family: in nearly 60 percent, both the husband and wife are employed.

- A black family with both spouses working earns, on average, more than twice as much as those in which only the husband is employed.

- The majority of single black women who head families also work for at least part of the year.

- In the black population, females outnumber males by a considerably wider margin than is the case in the white population, a fact that has a direct bearing on the proportion of female-headed black families.

- Primarily because of the dearth of males, divorced or widowed black women have an average 13-year wait before remarriage, while black men remarry, on average, within two years.

- Categorizing the black poor as an underclass, with all that term suggests of a permanent and irreversible situation, may be tempting to some because it seems to provide a simple answer to a complex problem. But poverty is nothing new in the United States. What is different is that traditional avenues for upward mobility have become blocked, as the economy has slowed and the job skills demanded by the labor market have changed.

- There is a strong relationship between the high proportion of single-mother black families and the situation of black males. In general, society has shown relatively little constructive interest in the problems confronting African American males, problems which arise from a lack of viable alternatives. Particularly disturbing is the fact that the proportion of young black males in the educational system has been dropping.

- Despite formidable challenges facing young black males, the majority of them are law abiding, working, or in school. Many are overcoming great barriers to go on to achieve success.

- Despite the inequities faced daily by African Americans, they maintain a core of optimism and a feeling that things will get better eventually.

- Education is highly valued by many as an avenue to success, but, sadly, parents' dreams for the achievement of their children may not be realistic today. Real hope for

African American youth depends on facing the present reality of the educational system in the United States.

Introduction

Contrary to what many people seem to think, there is no such thing as "the" African American family. African American families are as diverse as white, Hispanic, Asian, and other families in the United States today. Black families are not all headed by single women. Nor are they predominantly poor. There are indeed many black families headed by women, but there are more black families headed by married couples. Far too many black families are certainly poor, but the majority of black families are not poor.

Yet stereotypes about black people and black families are pervasive, encouraged by the media's attention to black athletes and criminals and their apparent lack of interest in portraying black families as ordinary families with hopes, aspirations, and problems like other American families. The privileged Huxtable family on *The Cosby Show* is hardly typical of American families, either black or white.

Black families today are not confined to any single social class, economic status, lifestyle, or religion. Indeed, there have been African Americans at every economic level for generations. Certainly, a large proportion of blacks has experienced devastating poverty. But many blacks have achieved comfortable financial success, and many others have successfully maintained a stable working-class status (Frazier, 1939; McAdoo, 1988; Willie, 1988a).

Discrimination is, however, an experience that no people of color, whatever their economic or social status, escape. As former Secretary of Health, Education, and Welfare (HEW)

Joseph Califano has observed, "Racism haunts the American attic like a malevolent specter, denying peace to any who would live in the house." In recalling his years as secretary of HEW, Califano noted that "our vigorous enforcement of civil rights laws on behalf of women, Hispanics, and the handicapped met with relatively modest resistance." But "similar action on behalf of blacks often sparked fierce opposition" (Califano, 1989: 28). That opposition is the basis of the continuing victimization of African Americans and marks one of the most persistent problems black families face.

Cultural patterns have helped African Americans cope. Because experience showed that they could not depend on the support of society's institutions in times of need, blacks have traditionally relied heavily on their families. For example, extended families have provided care for the relatives' children and for nonrelated children as well (Billingsley, 1968; McAdoo, 1978). Religion has played an important part in family life (Hill, 1971).

African Americans have been a presence in the United States for over 300 years, and as of 1988, the estimated 30.3 million black Americans represented 12.3 percent of the U.S. population.[1] The South is home to a slight majority of blacks today, although their concentration in that region is much diminished from what it was at the beginning of this century, when 90 percent of all blacks resided in the South. Substantial migration northward began during and after World War I, when the war effort's economic expansion, accompanied by a shortage of white males and a decline in the number of immigrants, encouraged employers to look to southern blacks for labor. There was heavy black migration to the northern industrial states in the 1930s and during World War II.[2]

Many of the jobs available to black migrants were low-

wage and low-status jobs requiring few skills or little education. Nonetheless, they opened up opportunities and paid
better wages than were available in the South, thus enabling
many blacks to provide moderate economic security for themselves and their families. America's rising prosperity in the
1950s and 1960s brought unprecedented economic opportunity and upward mobility to many blacks. But when the U.S.
economy faltered in the 1970s and 1980s, the consequences
were severe for many African Americans, especially in the
northern industrial belt. Many jobs were lost as factories laid
off workers or closed for good. And when the overall economy began to recover, the new jobs often required different
skills and more formal training than the old jobs, or paid
relatively little.

Characteristics of African American Families

Regardless of race, family structure plays an important
role in the economic situation of families in the United
States. Whether a family consists of a married couple or is
headed by a single parent—and whether that parent is the
mother or the father—has a significant impact on the family's
economic well-being. In the American population as a whole,
the proportion of single-parent families has been growing, but
this trend began earlier among blacks than among other
Americans. In 1987, married-couple families accounted for
only slightly over half of the 7.2 million African American
families; 43 percent were headed by women and six percent
were headed by men (Table 1.1). The high proportion of female-headed families is a major reason that the overall median income for black families was $18,098 in 1987, less than
60 percent of the median income of all U.S. families.

Table 1.1 • AFRICAN AMERICAN FAMILIES BY TYPE, 1987
(numbers in thousands)

Family Type	Number	Percent
Married-couple	3,682	51.3
Female householder, no husband present	3,074	42.8
Male householder, no wife present	421	5.9
Total	7,177	100.0

Source: U.S. Bureau of the Census, August 1988b, Table 1.

Black married-couple families had a median income of $27,182, nearly triple the $9,710 median for black families headed by women. (Even families headed by black males alone, while not as well off as married couples, had a median income nearly twice that [$17,455] of female-headed families.) Although a family with an income at the median for black couples was not affluent, it was well above the poverty level, which stood at $11,611 for a family of four in 1987. (Average family size for a black married-couple family that year was 3.7.)

Clearly, then, a common perception that most blacks are poor is a misconception, although the poverty rate among blacks is more than three times that of whites (33.1 percent vs. 10.5 percent in 1987). However, as is the case among all ethnic groups, the poverty rate varies widely depending on family type and the presence of minor children. For example, among black families that included children under 18, those headed by women were over four times as likely to be poor as two-parent families—59.5 percent vs. 13.6 percent.

One of the obvious reasons for this disparity is that there are twice as many adult potential earners in married-couple families as in one-parent families. And, indeed, the typical black married couple is a two-earner family: in nearly 60 percent of these families, both the husband and wife are employed. A black family with both spouses working earns, on average, more than twice as much as those in which only the husband is employed (median weekly family earnings of $733 vs. $399 in 1988). And while black married-couple families are less likely than whites to fall into the very upper-income categories, nearly 10 percent of them had 1987 incomes of $60,000 or more, which was about twice the median income for all families in the United States.

It should be noted, however, that black married couples overall have not recently prospered to the extent that white couples have: taking inflation into account, the median income of black married couples dropped 1.4 percent between 1986 and 1987, although the median for white couples rose by 1.9 percent. Black families of all types were more vulnerable to the swinging economic tides of the 1970s and 1980s than white families overall, and while many African Americans have been able to maintain a relatively prosperous status, others have been less fortunate.

The Female-Male Gap

In the black population, females outnumber males by a considerably wider margin than in the white population, a fact that has a direct bearing on the proportion of female-headed black families. As of 1988, an estimated 15.9 million African Americans were female; only 14.4 million were male. This translates into a sex ratio of 110 females for every 100 males. (Among whites, there are 104 females for every 100 males.)

Age has a significant bearing on the sex ratio: as Table 1.2 shows, up until the late teens, black males outnumber females, but by age 20 to 24, women have definitely gained the edge. That there is an actual shortage of males in the adult black population has obvious implications for the marriage or remarriage prospects of young black women and older black women who become widowed or divorced—prospects made grimmer by such factors as the incarceration of an unhealthy number of black males and drug dependency.

Table 1.2 • SEX RATIO: ESTIMATED NUMBER OF
WOMEN PER 100 MEN IN THE AFRICAN
AMERICAN POPULATION BY AGE, 1988

Age	Ratio
Under 5	97
5–9	97
10–14	97
15–19	98
20–24	105
25–29	109
30–34	112
35–39	117
40–44	120
45–49	122
50–54	124
55–59	120
60–64	122
65 and over	149

Source: U.S. Bureau of the Census, January 1989b, Table 4.

Comparing the marital status of black males to that of black females is instructive. As can be seen from the data in Table 1.3, black women are more likely than black men ever to have been married (63 percent vs. 58 percent) but less likely than black men to be currently married and living with a spouse (32 percent vs. 39 percent).

Gender differences are particularly pronounced among

Table 1.3 • MARITAL STATUS OF AFRICAN AMERICAN
          WOMEN AND MEN, AGE 15 AND OVER, 1988 (in
          percentages)

Marital Status	Women	Men
Single (never married)	36.9	42.5
Married, spouse present	31.6	39.2
Married, spouse absent	9.5 ⎫	6.3 ⎫
Widowed	12.2 ⎬ 31.5	3.6 ⎬ 18.4
Divorced	9.8 ⎭	8.5 ⎭
Total percent	100.0	100.0
Total number (in thousands)	11,618	9,603

Source: U.S. Bureau of the Census, January 1989a, Table 1.

the previously married or separated. Black women are far
more likely than black men to be separated, divorced, or widowed (nearly 32 percent vs. 18 percent). Black men who are
not currently married are considerably more likely never to
have been married than are black women. Primarily because
of the dearth of males, divorced or widowed black women
have an average 13-year wait before remarriage, while black
men remarry, on average, within two years (McAdoo, 1987).
The economic implications of this difference are clearly important, since women single parents are economically very
vulnerable.

African American Children in Families

Contributing to the growing diversity among black families are major changes in the marital status of the parents
(McAdoo, 1987). There has been an increase in the proportion of divorced and separated persons, as well as in the percentage of parents who have never married. One consequence is a substantial increase in the number of children in
one-parent families.

In 1988, there were nine million black children under the age of 18 living with one or both parents. Forty-two percent of them were in two-parent families; 55 percent lived with their mothers only. As of 1988, some 600,000-plus black children under 18—six percent of all—lived with relatives other than their parents. This was more than twice as many as lived with their fathers only.

Regardless of race, children in a female-headed family are at some risk of being poor; the risk is very great if the family is black. Over two-thirds of all children living in female-headed African American families in 1987 had incomes below the poverty level; the comparable figure for children in black families not headed by women was one-fifth (Table 1.4).

The high poverty rate among children in female-headed African American families has no single explanation. At a

Table 1.4 • POVERTY RATES OF CHILDREN[1] IN AFRICAN AMERICAN FAMILIES BY FAMILY TYPE, SELECTED YEARS, 1959–87

Year	All Families	Female-Headed Families	All Other Families
1959	65.5	81.6	60.6
1966	50.6	76.6	39.9
1969	39.6	68.2	25.0
1970	41.5	67.7	26.0
1975	41.4	66.0	22.1
1980	42.1	64.8	20.3
1981	44.9	67.7	23.4
1982	47.3	70.7	24.1
1983	46.2	68.3	23.7
1984	46.2	66.2	24.3
1985	43.1	66.9	18.8
1986	42.7	67.1	17.0
1987	45.1	68.3	19.8

[1]Related children under age 18.
Source: U.S. Bureau of the Census, August 1988b, Table 16.

time when even white males are finding it difficult to support their families on their earnings alone, the problems facing black women—with median annual earnings roughly half the median for white males—are formidable. If they are divorced, black mothers are considerably less likely than their white counterparts to have been awarded a property settlement and only about half as likely to have been awarded alimony. As noted earlier, a black widow's or divorcee's chance of bettering her economic situation by remarriage while her children are young is very slim.

A black mother is likely to face job discrimination on account of her race as well as her sex. Her employment options may be further limited because she has total responsibility for the care of her children. If she is a never-married mother whose schooling was halted by too early parenthood, she may lack basic job skills. And cutbacks in "safety net" programs in the 1980s have also taken their toll.

Despite these obstacles, the majority of black female family heads had some work experience in 1987, and over one-third (1.1 million) of them worked year round, full time. The poverty rate for the families of these fully employed black women was far lower than for black female-headed families overall; nevertheless, about one in eight (12.3 percent) of the fully employed women had incomes below the poverty level.

To be sure, children living in female-headed families are less likely to be poor today than they were in 1959, when the poverty rate as it is currently computed was first defined. In that year, nearly 82 percent of the black children in these families were poor, compared to 68 percent in 1987.

Most of the improvement in the poverty rate occurred in the 1960s. Progress slowed during the 1970s, although the poverty rate continued to drop. After 1980, the poverty rate began to rise again, and as of 1987, the poverty rate for children in black female-headed families had returned to what it had been nearly 20 years earlier. Moreover, between 1969 and 1987, the *number* of children living in black female-headed families increased sharply. Consequently, as of 1987, there were nearly 1.3 million more poor children in black female-headed families than there had been two decades before.

Today, as in the late 1950s, the poverty rate for children in female-headed black families is higher than it is for children in other black families, but the trend in those rates has been similar for children in all family types. However, because the improvement in the rate has been far greater for children in two-parent families than it has been for children in single-parent families, the "poverty gap" between children in female-headed and other families has widened: 30 years ago, children in female-headed families were "only" 1.3 times as likely to be poor as children in other black families; in 1987, they were more than three times as likely to be poor.

Statistics like these have caused some to assert that African Americans have increasingly become divided into two groups, an "underclass" and a middle class (Wilson, 1988). Categorizing the black poor as an underclass, with all that term suggests of a permanent and irreversible situation, may be tempting to some because it seems to provide a simple answer to a complex problem. But poverty is nothing new in the United States. What is different is that traditional avenues for upward mobility have become blocked, as the economy has slowed and the job skills demanded by the labor market have changed.

Use of the term "underclass" does not convey the reality of social isolation and lack of adequate jobs in large northern urban centers. It does not explain the poverty that has existed for generations throughout the country (Farley and Allen, 1987). Nor does lumping the African American population into just two categories recognize the diversity among these families, the survival of a solid working-class community, or the generations of upwardly mobile black middle- and upper middle-class families who have succeeded despite barriers placed before them by the majority population (McAdoo, 1988; Willie, 1988b).

Studies have shown that young children, black and white, feel good about themselves and their abilities when they are young (Cross, 1978; Harrison, 1985; McAdoo, 1977). As they become older, however, the sense of control over their lives lessens. The early life experiences of black children form their sense of efficacy as adults. African American children—particularly poor children in poor neighborhoods—are faced early with restrictions that result from segregated housing, inferior schools, and lack of access to appropriate role models. These conditions limit opportunities to succeed. Moreover, a tendency in the white population to regard all blacks as basically poor and underprivileged tends to devalue all members of the race—even those who are not poor. As a consequence, many African Americans have internalized a devalued sense of self worth.

Problems of Adolescent Pregnancy

The increase in the number and proportion of children living in female-headed black families is not due to an increase in adolescent pregnancy. Adolescent pregnancy has been dropping among blacks, while the opposite has been happening among whites (Edelman, 1987; McAdoo, 1987).

What has increased, however, is out-of-wedlock pregnancy and childbearing among both teenage and adult women and divorce. About half of all black single mothers are divorced, separated, or widowed (Glick, 1988).

Even though the majority of out-of-wedlock births are to adult women over the age of 20, out-of-wedlock parenthood is a serious problem among black teenagers. It is one for which there is no single or simple explanation. Ignorance of contraceptives among sexually active teenagers is the most common reason: pregnancy is often an accident. In some cases, the out-of-wedlock pregnancy may be planned. Some girls need someone of their own to love and take no precautions against pregnancy (Dash, 1989). But again, one explanation is not sufficient. Sexual manipulation of young girls by adult men can be a factor: the fathers of teenaged mothers' babies tend to be in their twenties. The imbalance in the sex ratio also accounts for women's acquiescence to sexual advances (McAdoo, 1987).

Certainly of central importance is the large proportion of young black men with few opportunities of finding jobs that can support families. In the past, when a premarital pregnancy occurred, the young couple generally married. Furstenberg (1981) found that adolescent fathers tended to marry the mothers of their children when they were financially able to provide for the children. Young men without jobs tend not to marry (McAdoo, 1987), and the increasing vulnerability of these individuals continues the trend.

Whatever its cause, single parenthood imposes a significant financial burden on the custodial parent. But the long-term negative social and economic consequences of single parenthood are especially severe in the case of adolescents, particularly unmarried ones. Shorter-term problems (with long-term implications) that are associated with adolescent pregnancy include low birthweight and high infant mortality rates, and the interruption or termination of the mother's schooling.

It is clear that some of the negative consequences of adolescent pregnancy can be alleviated if an intensive effort is made. For example, programs promoting extensive early prenatal care for pregnant adolescents have had excellent results. In Washington, D.C., where a comprehensive prenatal care program for adolescents was instituted, teenage mothers were found to have the best pregnancy outcomes (Ahmed, 1987).

Attempts to deal with educational deficiencies have not been as successful. Educational programs geared to young urban teens have deteriorated over the past few years. This is unfortunate for many obvious reasons, but it has a less well-known impact on marital decisions. Mark Testa has found that as the educational attainment of a mother increases, especially if she finishes high school, the probability that she will marry also increases (Schmidt, 1989).

Yet a recent study of high schools' policies toward pregnant and parenting students found that schools too often stigmatize these young women and by various practices may hinder or discourage them from completing high school (Nash and Dunkle, 1989). However, the study did find that schools say they are trying harder to help keep pregnant and parenting teens in school by such means as counseling, flexible scheduling, and enrollment in special classes or programs.

When successful, such efforts can make a significant difference. A study of black single mothers found that those who gave birth out of wedlock as teenagers but who were able to remain within their extended families and complete high school fared as well emotionally, educationally, and financially in the long term as those who married before having children and then became single. In fact, the never-married mothers had higher educational attainment, obtained better jobs, and earned higher salaries than the women who married, became mothers, and then became single (McAdoo, 1987). The negative consequences of unmarried adolescent pregnancy can be overcome with the social support of families and communities.

But too often, the young unmarried mother drops out of school and spends the years which society expects her to use in acquiring skills for the future in caring for children. Programs that enable mothers to return to school, to arrange for care of their children, and to obtain good medical care for the children would prevent many of the problems that arise from too early parenthood.

Teenage mothers are not, however, the only young parents who can benefit from programs designed to help them complete their education. It is unfortunate that programs for expectant teenage parents rarely involve young fathers. It is extremely important that both young men and young women stay in school and/or enroll in promising job training programs. Not only would their doing so help prevent pregnancy, it would provide some hope for the future when pregnancy does occur. Most important, of course, is the fact that these young men and women would be better prepared for the world of work.

The Special Problems of African American Males

As has already been stated in this chapter, there is a strong relationship between the high proportion of single-mother black families and the situation of black males. For this reason, interventions that focus solely or primarily on women and girls are destined to have a only limited success. Yet in general, society has shown relatively little constructive interest in the problems confronting African American males. Many of these problems—poor education, unemployment, drug abuse, fathering out-of-wedlock children, and a high crime rate, for example—arise from a lack of viable alternatives.

The public school system does not prepare young black men to succeed in the workforce once they get out of school. Too many of them drop out before completing high school. The educational system also poorly prepares those who stay in school for the technical positions that are increasingly essential to making it in a world demanding more complex skills (Edelman, 1987; Wilson, 1988). Discrimination in the labor market further limits opportunities.

Young black men also suffer from a lack of male role models in the home and in school (Kunjufu, 1986). Boys growing up in single-mother families are often surrounded by females who may not understand the challenges faced by young black men. The employment of mothers means that young men do not always have the supervision they need. They may be left to acquire by chance the values and habits that must last for their lifetimes. In married-couple families, both parents are often forced to work, and adult supervision may be inadequate for young boys. This is a problem that is increasingly faced by parents of all racial groups.

It has been said that young black men are at high risk of not being able to move effectively into the next century. Too many young poor males are becoming involved in self-defeating and dangerous activities. The drop in life expectancy for black males in recent years—when white male life expectancy has been steadily increasing—is accounted for almost entirely by the high rate of violent death among males between 15 and 25 years of age. A system that should be preventing lawlessness is designed instead only to prosecute lawbreakers. Too many persons in positions to make a difference by developing and implementing policies to provide young black males with constructive and healthy alternatives have overlooked the crushing problems of these young boys.

Particularly disturbing is the fact that the proportion of young black males in the educational system has been dropping. Moreover, according to a recent report of the Joint Center for Political Studies, both schools and institutions of higher education persist in having too many barriers to achievement (Johnson, 1989b). They tend to have lower expectations of African American males than of other students, and they make assumptions of intellectual deficiencies. The result can be self-fulfilling prophecy. If young people are not expected to succeed, they will not be helped and encouraged to succeed, and they won't.

Black males' share of college enrollment fell from 4.3 percent to 3.5 percent between 1976 and 1986, while over the same period, black women retained their proportion at five percent (Vobejda, 1989). A growing male-female educational gap will make it even more difficult for black women of marriageable age to find suitable partners.

And even the college enrollment statistics for black males—as troubling as they are—may be somewhat misleading in terms of educational outcome. One of the few areas for which young black men receive adequate preparation and encouragement in school is athletics, a fact that predestines many young men for failure. Only a few particularly gifted or promising athletes receive college scholarships enabling them to move beyond secondary school, and too many of them are exploited for their athletic prowess and receive an inadequate education. The less gifted athletes, their academic skills neglected, are shut out of higher education.

Despite these formidable problems, one must nonetheless maintain a balance when examining the situation of young African American males. The majority of young black men are law abiding, working, or in school, and will go on to become married fathers. It is too easy to overlook the young men who maintain a sense of pride in themselves, their families, and their communities. In fact, many black youths are overcoming great barriers—societal indifference, poverty, and the like—to go on to achieve success. Research is needed on those young men who have prevailed to determine what it is that enables these men to succeed despite such odds.

Women's Roles in African American Families

Women have historically played important, strong roles in African American families, a fact that derives to an extent from African cultural traditions. The role of black women has often been misinterpreted by people of European heritage as a pattern of dominance. To the contrary, it reflects the basic strength of cultures in which all persons, regardless of gender, had important family roles to play.

Black families in the American diaspora have maintained some of their African traditions, although those traditions have been altered as a result of slavery, later poverty, time, and the influence of the western tradition of male dominance. Nevertheless, patterns of flexible roles within the family, shared child care, extensive involvement with extended kin and social networks, and shared decisionmaking within the home are characteristics that often distinguish the African American family to some degree from other families in the United States (Hill, 1971; McAdoo, 1978).

Women have an important economic function in black married-couple as well as female-headed families. Because of wage and job discrimination against black men, black married women have always been more likely to work outside the home than have their white counterparts. Generations of black women have had to cope with the double demands of paid work and family life. As a result, some of the adjustments white married women had to make when they began to enter the labor force in substantial numbers had long since been made by black married women.

The majority of single black women who head families work for at least part of the year; nearly 60 percent had some work experience in 1987. The importance of a steady full-time job on the economic well-being of a single-mother family is obvious from the comparison of poverty rates earlier in this chapter. But too many black women who head families are unable to work enough or earn enough to lift their families above the poverty level.

Difficulty in arranging for the care of their children is a factor. At one time, child care was provided within the network of family and shared community. But those resources are rapidly disappearing in many areas—especially urban areas—causing real child care problems for both married and single women.

Where Do We Go from Here?

One would think, given the problems outlined in this chapter, that African Americans would feel like giving up. But in spite of the inequities confronted daily by African

Americans, they maintain a core of optimism. There is a feeling that things will get better eventually. This optimism prevails despite centuries of economic isolation, racism, negative stereotypes, and long periods in which things have not been getting better for many black men, women, and their families.

In 1989, a survey sponsored by the NAACP Legal Defense and Educational Fund found that even members of the so-called underclass have aspirations for their own and their families' futures like the aspirations of more fortunate Americans. Poor single mothers responding to the survey were hopeful for their children's futures. Over half hoped that their children would go to college (Johnson, 1989a).

The desire for future advancement is shared by all races. Education is highly valued by many African Americans as an avenue to success. Sadly, however, their dreams for the achievement of their children may not be realistic today. In the past, education *was* a means of escape from poverty. This was at a time when black teachers were leaders of their communities, when teaching was an honored profession. Now, teaching has lost much of its status. Instead, there is a growing emphasis on making money. The most gifted African Americans are no longer going into teaching, and the loss of their talent has serious consequences for black children.

Real hope for African American youth depends on facing the present reality of the educational system in the United States. Parents must become active and demand better schools and improved services for young people. Leaders, both black and white, must recognize that more than cosmetic changes are needed to help black young people make it successfully through their pre-adolescent and adolescent years. Real change, however, costs money and must have the commitment of members of Congress, state and local legislators, school boards, parents, and communities around the country.

Pervasive racism is surely a key cause of the lack of a national commitment to see that African American families thrive and that American institutions really help black children succeed in school and prepare for the world of work. Certainly this country seems willing to spend energy and resources on trying to deal with the consequences—in crime, drug dependency, and unemployment—when black children fail because our institutions fail them.

The problems now facing African American communities in the United States dwarf most of those of the past. It is becoming increasingly difficult for black families to survive, much less to prosper. And even the families and individuals who have survived and prospered must struggle continually against institutional racism.

People of color are a sizable proportion of the total population, and their numbers are increasing. American society will continue to become more diverse. In some localities, "minorities" will be "majorities" by the year 2000. For this reason, if for no other, the concerns of African Americans must be the concerns of U.S. society as a whole. Americans must avoid the temptation to look for simple explanations of complex difficulties or easy solutions for problems that may arise from diversity. Many approaches to problem solving will be required. Concerted efforts at many levels, in many directions, and by many people will be necessary in order to move forward toward to decent and healthy life for all.

TWO Women and Affordable Housing

CUSHING N. DOLBEARE AND
ANNE J. STONE

Highlights

FROM MANY PERSPECTIVES, the United States is the best-housed nation in the world, but millions of Americans are unable to find decent housing that they can afford. The situation is especially critical for America's low-income households, the majority of which are maintained by women.

- Although U.S. families in general typically own their homes, those families maintained by women typically do not. Nearly three-quarters of all families maintained by women in their childrearing years (under 45) are renters. In contrast, two-thirds of married-couple families in that age range own their homes.

- Renters in general have a lower median income than owners; even so, the nearly seven million female-maintained renter families had a median income ($9,302) that was less than half that of married-couple renters and a poverty rate nearly three times as high—45 percent—in 1985.

- Women-maintained families with children are particularly disadvantaged in the rental market, where they often face illegal discrimination because of race, or sex, or the presence of children; those getting public assistance may face an additional barrier that remains legal: discrimination because of the source of their income.

• Single female renters are much more likely to be elderly than are single male or married-couple renters. Elderly single women tend to be economically vulnerable and those who rent particularly so: the median income in 1985 for the 2.7 million elderly single female renters was $6,446; their poverty rate was 40.2 percent.

• While the quality of America's housing in general has vastly improved in the last half century, some seven million occupied housing units were physically inadequate in 1985. Households maintained by women, especially minority women, were overrepresented in these units.

• The paramount housing problem today is not an absolute shortage of housing units but rather a severe and growing shortage of suitable units that low-income households can afford.

• The current federal rule of thumb is that a household should be expected to pay no more than 30 percent of its annual income for housing, including utilities. Yet of the 11.6 million renter households with annual incomes under $10,000 (61 percent of them female-maintained), more than five million spent at least half of their incomes on housing in 1985. More than two million spent 70 percent or more.

• In 1985, there were about four renter households with incomes of $5,000 or less for every unit costing $125 per month (30 percent of $5,000), and federally assisted units accounted for more than half of these very low-cost units.

- The private sector has historically provided the bulk of low-income housing, without subsidies, but in recent years millions of units have left the low-rent stock as landlords have been forced to raise rents to cover rising costs or have found conversion to higher-rent units more profitable.

- While the number of federally assisted units has continued to grow since federal housing programs began in the 1930s, far too few units have been added relative to the need, which has been accelerating even as the federal government has applied the brakes to low-income housing programs.

- Households that are eligible for assisted housing often have to wait for years to get it. Most low-income households are not in assisted housing.

- Half of the federally assisted low-income units that exist today could disappear from the low-income stock in the next 20 years as government-owner subsidy agreements expire.

- The federal government has spent less on low-income housing programs in the last half century than the Treasury lost in just two recent years due to homeowner tax deductions, which amount to indirect housing subsidies for middle- and upper-income owners.

- It should be recognized that a federal role is vital in (1) establishing the framework within which the private sector provides and finances housing and (2) assisting the very needy whom the private sector cannot accommodate unaided.

- Since women maintain the majority of low-income households needing assistance, measures to meet the housing needs of low-income households in general will obviously be of particular benefit to women. However, in all housing policy and planning, careful attention should also be paid to the special housing-related needs of homeless women with children, of battered women, and of displaced homemakers.

Introduction

From many perspectives, the United States is the best-housed nation in the world. In 1985, the latest year for which government housing data are available, more than half of this country's 88.4 million occupied housing units were less than 25 years old and over 90 percent of them were in good condition.[1] Ample space was the norm: median household size was 2.3 persons, while the median housing unit had 2.6 bedrooms and 5.3 rooms overall. Median monthly housing costs were a generally affordable 21 percent of income. And nearly two-thirds (63.5 percent) of all households owned their homes (U.S. Department of Housing and Urban Development and U.S. Bureau of the Census, December 1988). No other country has provided so well for such a large proportion of its population.

But this generally positive picture is marred by a serious and growing housing crisis that affects millions of Americans: there is nowhere near enough decent housing that they can afford. Moreover, much of the housing that is affordable to them today may become unaffordable in the next few years.

The housing crisis is a women's issue of major importance. This is not because most U.S. women are poorly housed; they are not. Rather, the housing crisis should be considered a women's issue on the same basis that poverty is a women's issue, and, indeed, there is a close connection between them. Women predominate among those American householders who are most likely to be in bad housing or who pay an inordinate amount of their incomes for housing, or both, largely because women predominate among the poor.

Certainly, women (and men) of moderate and middle incomes may have real problems in finding suitable housing that they can afford. But because the housing needs of low-income people are so urgent and their housing options so limited, the focus of this chapter is on affordable low-income housing. Evidence that it is women who have the most to gain, and the most to lose, from what happens to low-income housing in this country is to be found throughout government data about American households.

Table 2.1, which shows all households in occupied housing units in 1985, allows comparisons not only by type of household, sex of householder, and tenure (i.e., whether owner or renter), but by race and Hispanic origin.[2] It can be seen that 57 percent of households overall consist of married couples, with or without children or other family members. Families maintained by women account for about 13 percent of all households, one-person households maintained by women (more than half of them elderly) for about 15 percent. The remaining 16 percent are households maintained by men, whether as family householders or living alone. In fact, women are present as either householders or spouses in some 85 percent of all American households; the comparable figure for men is 72 percent.

The American Housing Survey found not only that households maintained by females outnumber those maintained by males by a factor approaching two to one, but that the elderly proportion of female householders (34 percent) is double that of male householders. And more than twice as many women as men maintain family households.

Table 2.1 • TENURE OF HOUSEHOLDS IN OCCUPIED HOUSING UNITS
BY TYPE OF HOUSEHOLD, RACE, AND HISPANIC ORIGIN,
1985 (numbers in thousands)

Household Type	Number	Percent Distribution			Percent Who	
		All	Owners	Renters	Own	Rent
All households						
Married couples	49,972	57	69	34	78	22
Female-headed families	11,806	13	9	21	42	58
Single females	12,845	15	12	19	52	48
Male-headed families	5,661	6	5	10	45	55
Single males	8,142	9	5	16	37	63
Total households	88,425				63	37
Total percent		100	100	100		
Black households						
Married couples	3,528	36	53	22	65	35
Female-headed families	3,071	31	20	39	29	71
Single females	1,393	14	13	15	39	61
Male-headed families	684	7	6	8	37	63
Single males	1,226	12	8	16	27	73
Total households	9,903				44	56
Total percent		100	100	100		
Households of Hispanic origin[1]						
Married couples	2,718	54	72	41	53	47
Female-headed families	1,058	21	11	27	21	79
Single females	431	8	7	10	32	68
Male-headed families	436	9	6	11	25	75
Single males	435	9	4	11	20	80
Total households	5,078				40	60
Total percent		100	100	100		

[1]People of Hispanic origin may be of any race.

Source: U.S. Department of Housing and Urban Development and U.S. Bureau of the Census,
December 1988, Tables 2-9, 5-9, and 6-9.

When households are broken down by tenure—owners
and renters—the distributions by household type are noticeably different. For example, married couples constitute a
larger proportion of owners (69 percent) and a smaller pro-

portion of renters (34 percent) than of households overall; the reverse is true for families maintained by women, who account for nine percent of owners and 21 percent of renters.

The desire for homeownership is so strong in this country that most families who can afford to do so own rather than rent. Income will be discussed in more detail below, but the tenure statistics in Table 2.1 hint at the differing financial circumstances of American households, depending on their type and race or origin. The great majority (78 percent) of married-couple families are homeowners. Homeownership is most typical of those 45 or older (88 percent); nevertheless, more than two-thirds of married couples under 45, whose families are most likely to include children, own their homes.

In contrast, not only are the majority of women-maintained families renters, but nearly three-quarters (73 percent) of those under 45—who constitute 61 percent of all women-maintained families—are renters.

While the tenure of single female householders overall is shown in Table 2.1, it is those over the age of 65 who are relevant to the focus of this chapter. More than three-fifths (62 percent) of all single women who own their homes are elderly (compared to 35 percent of single men who own, and 18 percent of married owners), and about 60 percent of single elderly women are homeowners. One might therefore assume that, as a group, elderly single women are fairly well off. In fact, however, single elderly female homeowners have the lowest median income of any group of owners (Table 2.2). Most are widows whose homes were acquired during their married years, and 90 percent of them are white. Slightly less than half of elderly single black women are owners; the proportion for those of Hispanic origin is 43 percent.

About 2.7 million elderly single women rent and again,

Table 2.2 • MEDIAN INCOME AND POVERTY RATES OF
HOUSEHOLDS BY HOUSEHOLD TYPE AND
TENURE, 1985 (income in dollars)

	Owners		Renters	
Household Type	Median Income	Poverty Rate	Median Income	Poverty Rate
All households	27,816	9.1	14,460	25.3
Married couples	33,315	5.4	21,160	16.6
Female-headed families	19,076	17.2	9,302	44.9
Under age 45	19,837	17.2	8,921	47.3
Age 65 and over	14,178	20.2	9,137	35.4
Single females	9,808	24.1	9,091	30.6
Age 65 and over	8,254	28.5	6,446	40.2
Male-headed families	28,472	6.9	16,680	13.4
Single males	19,509	12.4	14,748	18.7

Source: U.S. Department of Housing and Urban Development and U.S. Bureau of the Census, December 1988, Tables 3-1, 3-20, 4-1, and 4-20.

the elderly constitute a much higher proportion (44 percent) of single female renters than of single male or married-couple renters. Only about 14 percent of single male renters and less than 10 percent of married-couple renters are age 65 or over. Elderly female renters are at the rock bottom of the income scale: their median income in 1985 was less than half (45 percent) of the median income of renter households overall, which, in turn, was only about half (52 percent) of median owner income.

That owners enjoy a higher median income than renters holds true for all household types, although the relative size of the gap varies. Owner families maintained by women have a 30 percent lower median income than other owner families but it is still more than twice that of their renter counterparts. The difference is most pronounced for the women under 45—those most likely to have children in their households.

As these statistics make plain, women householders in general have lower incomes than other householders; particularly low are the incomes of women renters who are maintaining families, or who are aged and alone. And, as Table 2.3 shows, women-maintained households accounted for a large proportion of the households who were least likely to be able to afford decent housing. Not only did women-maintained households constitute the majority (58 percent) of all households with incomes below $10,000, but almost half (47 percent) of all female householders were in that income range. This compares to 10 percent of married-couple households and 27 percent of male householders. Disproportionately concentrated at the bottom of the income scale, women householders were sparse at the top: only six percent of the households in the top fifth of the income distribution—incomes over $40,000—had female householders.

Among renters—whose median income, it bears repeating, is only slightly over half that of owners—women householders were again concentrated in the lowest income range: more than half (54 percent) had incomes under $10,-000 and more than a quarter (28 percent) had incomes under $5,000. Women-maintained households accounted for two-thirds (67 percent) of all renter households with incomes under $5,000. The poverty rate for single, elderly female renters was 40 percent; for women-maintained renter families it was 45 percent.

Poverty persists and worsens for women-maintained families although it has abated for other family types. Between 1959 and 1985, the number of poor families in this country dropped 13 percent, from 8.3 million to 7.2 million, but the number of poor families maintained by women nearly doubled—from 1.9 million to 3.5 million (U.S. Bureau of the Census, October 1987). And that trend is continuing.

Table 2.3 • DISTRIBUTION OF HOUSEHOLD TYPES BY INCOME, 1985
(in percentages)

Household Type	Total	*Annual Household Income*			
		Under $10,000	$10,000 to $19,999	$20,000 to $39,999	$40,000 or more
All married couples	57	24	48	67	85
All female householders	28	58	34	18	6
Family householders	13	24	17	10	4
Single females	15	34	17	8	2
Age 65 and over	8	24	7	2	1
All male householders	16	18	19	16	10
Total percent	100	100	100	100	100
Total number (in thousands)	88,425	20,089	20,233	29,065	19,038
Married-couple owners	69	33	59	75	88
Female owners	21	53	30	15	5
Male owners	10	14	11	10	7
Total percent	100	100	100	100	100
Total number (in thousands)	56,145	8,514	10,812	20,205	16,614
Married-couple renters	34	17	34	40	62
Female renters	40	61	38	23	12
Male renters	25	22	27	28	26
Total percent	100	100	100	100	100
Total number (in thousands)	32,280	11,574	9,422	8,859	2,424

Source: U.S. Department of Housing and Urban Development and U.S. Bureau of the Census, December 1988, Tables 2-20, 3-20, and 4-20.

Women who maintain families that include children are five times as likely to be poor as other families with children: in 1985, 45 percent of female-maintained families with children under 18 were poor, compared to nine percent of other families with children. (Among women-maintained families with children under six, the poverty rate was a staggering 61 percent—again, five times the rate [12 percent] among other families with young children) (U.S. Bureau of the Census, January 1987). Although only 20 percent of all households

with children under 18 were maintained by women in 1985,
the latter accounted for over 70 percent of all such households with incomes below $5,000 and for over half of those
with incomes between $5,000 and $10,000. The proportion
of women-maintained families drops sharply as income increases, as Table 2.4 shows.

Table 2.4 • FEMALE HOUSEHOLDERS WITH CHILDREN UNDER
            18 AS A PERCENT OF ALL HOUSEHOLDERS WITH
            CHILDREN UNDER 18 BY INCOME, 1985
            (numbers in thousands)

Household Income	All Householders	Female Householders	Percent Female
Under $5,000	2,154	1,528	70.9
$5,000–$9,999	2,947	1,613	54.7
$10,000–$14,999	3,117	1,024	32.9
$15,000–$19,999	3,295	863	26.2
$20,000 and over	22,406	1,875	8.4
All households	33,918	6,903	20.4

Source: U.S. Bureau of the Census, January 1987, Table 1.

The typically low incomes and disproportionate degree of
poverty among women-maintained households provide
ample evidence that they constitute the majority of households most likely to need assistance in obtaining decent, affordable housing. Low income is the major barrier excluding
women from homeownership. Unless, like elderly widows,
they already own and have paid off their mortgages, lower-
income households are rarely able to purchase homes and
must seek their housing in the rental market—an environment where women-maintained families with children are
particularly disadvantaged. These women may find that there
is no housing at all to be had at costs they can afford.

Or, if the housing exists, many of them face discrimination, not only because of their sex or race or the presence of children, but because they are receiving public assistance. The Fair Housing Amendments enacted in 1988 address the subject of discrimination against children, at least on paper, but it is still perfectly legal for any landlord to refuse to rent to households who are welfare clients.

Not only are renters unable to build assets in the form of equity in their homes, they face the threat of rising rents and, often, displacement, as economic and market values change. A landlord can decide to move tenants out because more money can be made by selling the property, converting it to a condominium, or maybe even just making it a luxury rental. For low-income renters, who are so largely female, this means the likelihood of some kind of housing jeopardy all of their lives.

An Overview of Housing Issues

There is no single "housing problem." Rather, depending on the size and economic resources of their households, and on the supply and availability of housing in their locality, people encounter a range of housing problems. For some people, these may involve sacrificing amenities or extras in order to pay housing costs, or finding the location inconvenient, or the equipment outdated and maintenance poor. More acute are the problems of people who can manage to pay for their housing only by going without food, clothing, or other necessities. Because their economic margins are so narrow, these people are among those likely to face the most acute housing problem of all: the inability to obtain any housing at all.

Before discussing the critical nature of the low-income housing problems that, as has been demonstrated, have their major impact on women-maintained households, some general comments on contemporary housing issues are in order. In general, the decades since the end of World War II have seen a transformation in America's housing. Housing quality has improved enormously; actual housing shortages—severe right after the war—have been overcome. But as problems of quality and supply have receded, housing affordability has become an increasingly important issue.

Housing Quality

In 1940, when the first census of housing was taken, 46 percent of all occupied dwelling units in the United States either lacked basic plumbing facilities or were classified as "dilapidated." By 1985, less than two percent of all occupied units were classified as having "severe" physical problems; another seven percent had "moderate" physical problems.

Obviously, these proportions reflect remarkable improvement in housing quality overall. Nevertheless, the 1985 percentage translated into more than seven million physically inadequate occupied units—and a housing quality problem for women, in particular, because the occupants of the inadequate units were disproportionately female. More than one-fifth (22 percent) were occupied by women-maintained families. Another eight percent were occupied by single elderly women. Overall, family households maintained by women were more than twice as likely as married-couple families to be living in inadequate housing (14 percent vs. six percent). The problem was considerably worse for minority families and especially for those maintained by women: one in every four families maintained by black women, and one in five of those maintained by women of Hispanic origin, lived in physically inadequate housing.

Housing Supply and Housing Availability

It is important to distinguish between the overall *supply of housing* (that is, the number of units in the housing stock, regardless of their condition or cost) and *available housing*, which is the number of appropriate units (that is, units in decent condition at costs that are affordable to those who need them).

In most communities, housing supply is not the problem, that is, the quantity of housing units is sufficient to provide everyone with shelter of some sort. This is in sharp contrast to the situation at the end of World War II, when there were acute shortages in the housing supply in most parts of the country. Today, the problem is more likely to be that the housing that does exist is of poor quality, or that it costs too much, or, frequently, both. People often double up or sleep in cars or on the streets in the same communities and neighborhoods where housing has been abandoned or units are offered for rent or sale.

In other words, just because the physical housing units exist does not necessarily mean that they are *available* to those who need housing. Housing availability is difficult to measure, but it is a persistent problem for many households. In part, the problem is related to supply: in some communities there is a misfit between the size and type of housing that exists and what is needed. More commonly, housing availability is related to discrimination because of race, national origin, religion, household composition, presence of children, physical handicaps, or sexual preference. Generally speaking, those civil rights statutes that exist have not been effectively enforced.

But the paramount housing availability problem today is affordability. Even householders with incomes at or above the median may feel squeezed by high housing costs, which may prevent them from purchasing rather than renting, or from obtaining the size or type of housing they desire. The problem is far more acute for lower-income households. Very simply, housing costs more to rent or purchase than a growing number of households—particularly women-maintained households—can conceivably pay for it. Very low-income families must devote the bulk of their incomes to housing and often still miss rent payments.

Housing Costs

At the beginning of this chapter it was noted that American households overall pay a median of about one-fifth (21 percent) of their income for housing costs, which include rent or mortgage payments, utilities, fuel, maintenance, etc. But, reflecting owners' typically higher incomes, the median ratio of housing costs to income is somewhat lower for owners (18 percent) and considerably higher for renters (28 percent).

For many renters, housing costs are a heavy burden, indeed. Nearly one-fifth (19 percent) of all renters paid at least half of their incomes for housing in 1985. Eleven percent (nearly 3.6 million renter households) paid more than 70 percent; 95 percent of these households had incomes under $10,000 per year. At the bottom of the income scale, 43 percent of the 5.4 million renter households with annual incomes under $5,000 paid more than 70 percent of their incomes for housing. Table 2.5 highlights the extent to which both low-income renters and low-income owners are burdened by high housing costs. For example, 46 percent of the 11.6 million renters with incomes under $10,000 spent at least half of their annual incomes on housing; less than 10 percent spent less than one-

Table 2.5 • MONTHLY HOUSING COSTS FOR RENTERS AND OWNERS
AS A PERCENT OF INCOME, BY HOUSEHOLD INCOME, 1985

		Annual Household Income			
Costs as Percent of Income	Total	Under $10,000	$10,000 to $19,999	$20,000 to $39,999	$40,000 or more
Renters					
Less than 15 percent	13.1	1.8	6.9	21.9	59.4
15 to 24 percent	27.0	7.8	28.8	49.0	31.1
25 to 34 percent	19.6	14.0	31.5	18.5	3.8
35 to 49 percent	13.0	17.1	18.8	4.7	0.5
50 to 69 percent	7.9	16.7	5.9	0.7	0.2
70 percent or more	11.1	29.4	1.7	0.1	0.0
No cash rent	6.3	7.5	6.4	5.0	5.0
Zero or negative income	2.1	5.7	—	—	—
Total percent	100.0	100.0	100.0	100.0	100.0
Total number (in thousands)	32,280	11,574	9,422	8,859	2,424
Percent female-maintained	40.4	61.1	38.5	23.1	12.4
Owners					
Less than 15 percent	36.7	6.0	27.5	39.9	54.4
15 to 24 percent	26.6	19.1	31.5	28.4	25.0
25 to 34 percent	14.0	19.5	16.3	15.2	8.3
35 to 49 percent	7.3	16.7	10.8	6.0	1.9
50 to 69 percent	3.1	10.1	4.8	1.5	0.2
70 percent or more	3.5	17.8	2.7	0.8	0.1
Mtge. payment not reported	7.9	4.7	6.4	8.2	10.0
Zero or negative income	0.9	6.2	—	—	—
Total percent	100.0	100.0	100.0	100.0	100.0
Total number (in thousands)	56,145	8,514	10,812	20,205	16,614
Percent female-maintained	20.7	53.1	29.7	15.1	5.0

Source: U.S. Department of Housing and Urban Development and U.S. Bureau of the Census,
December 1988, Tables 3-20 and 4-20.

fourth. In contrast, 59 percent of the 2.4 million renter households with incomes of $40,000 or more paid less than 15
percent of their incomes for housing. Four-fifths of all renters

who paid less than 15 percent of their incomes for housing had incomes of $20,000 or more. Only five percent had incomes under $10,000. The pattern for owners is similar, although less extreme.

Households maintained by women were surely heavily represented among those with the highest housing cost burdens: 61 percent of renter households and 53 percent of owner households with incomes below $10,000 had female householders.

Yet the households who pay relatively the most for housing are those who can, in reality, afford the least: housing should not cost so much that people are unable to obtain other basic necessities. On the basis of a realistic concept of housing affordability, lower-income people would be expected to pay a smaller proportion of income for housing than would more affluent people. Embodying this concept, the "market basket" or "residual" approach to calculating affordability subtracts the cost of basic necessities, such as food, clothing, transportation, and health care, from income; the remainder (if any) is the amount affordable for housing.

Calculations based on this approach lead to the conclusion that in 1985 over one U.S. household in 10 really could not afford anything for housing and still meet other basic needs.[3] For female householders, the comparable proportion was one in five (see Table 2.6).

The results of applying the market basket approach to housing affordability highlight the serious shortcomings of the current rule of thumb that 30 percent of income is an appropriate amount for housing costs, including utilities. People without enough income to cover their essential non-housing expenses clearly cannot "afford" 30 percent of their incomes for housing.

The 30-percent-of-income standard cannot be ignored,

Table 2.6 • ESTIMATED HOUSEHOLDS WITH INCOMES BELOW
LEVEL NEEDED TO COVER CONSUMPTION NEEDS
OTHER THAN HOUSING BY HOUSEHOLD SIZE, 1985
(numbers in thousands)

Number of Persons in Household	Threshold Level	Total Number	Estimated Households Below Threshold	
			Number Maintained by Women	Percent Maintained by Women
One	$3,828	2,900	1,700	59
Two	$5,956	1,900	800	42
Three	$8,759	1,700	1,100	65
Four	$10,456	1,500	600	41
Five	$14,104	1,000	200	20
Six	$17,752	500	100	20
Seven or more	$21,399	500	100	20
Total below threshold		9,900	4,600	47
All households		88,458	24,463	28
Percent below threshold		11	19	

Source: Thresholds estimated by author from Bureau of Labor Statistics lower living standard data for 1981 (U.S. Department of Labor, 1982), updated by change in the Consumer Price Index. Income data from U.S. Bureau of the Census, January 1987.

however, both because it is the current payment standard for housing assistance and because the U.S. Department of Housing and Urban Development (HUD) and others use it to measure "cost burden."

Using the 30-percent standard, a household with an annual income of $10,000 would have $250 a month to spend on housing and $583 for all other needs. In 1985, 11.6 million renters (36 percent of all renter households) had incomes below $10,000. Two-thirds (7.7 million) of these were female-maintained households, nearly half (3.6 million) of which actually had incomes below $5,000. Thirty percent of $5,000 is $125 per month.

Yet rental housing costing less than $125 a month has

virtually disappeared from the housing stock. In 1985, there were an estimated 2.1 million rental units costing less than $125 a month but there were 5.4 million renters who, on the basis of the 30-percent of income standard, could afford no more than that (Leonard, Dolbeare, and Lazere, 1989). After taking into account that about one-third of all the units renting for less than $125 were occupied by households with incomes above $5,000 (ibid.), one finds that there were nearly four times as many very poor renter households (incomes under $5,000) as there were units available to them at 30 percent of income. Obviously, few options exist for households—whether individuals or families—who really cannot afford *anything* for housing without sacrificing other basic needs and who have less than one chance in five of obtaining housing at 30 percent of income.

The situation would be even more critical were it not for low-income housing assistance by federal, state, or other programs: units subsidized under such programs accounted for well over half of the units renting for less than $125. Indeed, it is the virtual disappearance of unsubsidized housing available at very low rents, combined with persistent poverty, that is the major cause of rising homelessness.

The private, for-profit sector has historically provided the bulk of low-rent housing in this country, without housing subsidies. But unless they can cover their costs, owners are forced to raise rents or abandon their units. Millions of units have disappeared from the low-rent stock as energy and other costs have risen. As a practical matter, the for-profit private sector cannot meet, and cannot be expected to meet, the housing needs of renters at the very bottom of the income scale.

This circumstance is not new, nor is the recognition that

government needs to address it. The federal government began to provide housing assistance to some low-income households in the 1930s and has been doing so ever since. But, while millions of households have been helped, the federal commitment to low-income housing has been weakening in recent years, even as the number of households needing assistance has been increasing. The housing "safety net" is already badly frayed and, as will be shown, could largely give way in the next two decades.

Federal Housing Subsidy Programs

The federal government is the source of two types of housing subsidies: assistance for low-income renters and income tax deductions to homeowners. Female householders get short shrift from both. First, because women householders predominate among the low-income renters most likely to need assistance, they suffer disproportionately from the generally inadequate level of federal low-income housing assistance. This is true even though women-maintained households constitute a majority (61 percent) of households in subsidized rental housing. Second, because women who maintain families are unlikely to be homeowners, they are far less likely than other family householders to benefit from the major federal housing subsidies, which are provided in the form of income tax deductions to homeowners affluent enough to itemize deductions on their income tax returns.

Low-Income Housing Subsidies

The federal government has provided housing assistance to low-income people (and some with moderate incomes, as well) under a variety of programs for more than half a century. The primary responsibility for federal housing programs is lodged in the Department of Housing and Urban Development (HUD). (A separate set of programs for rural areas—primarily focused on home ownership—is operated by the Farmers Home Administration at the Department of Agriculture.)

It was not until 1970 that the number of households living in HUD-assisted housing reached one million. Since then, the number of households living in housing with federal subsidies has more than quadrupled, reaching 4.1 million in 1985. Until 1980, most federal housing subsidies were project-based, with the subsidy going to the owners of units rented to low-income households. Since then, most of the increase in housing assistance has been through tenant-based subsidies, by which a recipient household is given a certificate or voucher and must seek a unit (which is required to meet federal quality standards) in the private market.

The first low-income housing was provided during the early years of the Depression; this early public works project was formalized as the public housing program in 1937. Following World War II, public housing was both expanded and augmented by a series of other programs, most of which involved reducing the owners' effective mortgage interest rates (one of the major components of total housing cost).

In 1974, most of the earlier programs were supplanted by a new and more flexible program (known as Section 8) which subsidized the difference between 25 percent of tenant income (at that time the "affordability" rule of thumb) and market rent for the housing occupied, with separate subsidy levels for existing units rented as-is from private landlords ("Section 8 Existing") and more expensive rehabilitation and new construction ("Section 8 New Construction/Substantial Rehabilitation"). Section 8 was to become the largest direct federal housing subsidy program.

The foregoing is a highly simplified description of the evolution of often abstruse federal programs. Their complexities are less important than two critical facts. First, with the exception of Section 8, no federal housing program has in fact provided adequate subsidy to cover the gap between what very low-income tenants themselves could or were required to pay and the cost of debt service and operating expenses for the buildings or units. Second, as described above, the total number of housing units provided with subsidy under all federal programs has been unable to keep up with the rapidly worsening affordability crisis.

Except for units with monthly housing costs below $150 per month, only a small fraction of rental units with low monthly housing costs are subsidized, but, as mentioned earlier, millions of units have disappeared from the low-rent stock as energy and other costs have risen or because conversion to higher-income housing has become more attractive. Expansion of the subsidized housing stock has been insufficient to offset this trend.

And, it is important to understand that, unlike other safety net programs such as Aid for Families with Dependent Children (AFDC) and food stamps, under which assistance is provided as a matter of right to all applicants who meet eligibility standards, federal housing assistance for low-income people is not an entitlement. Households who apply and are eligible for housing assistance must wait until it becomes available. Even those who need housing aid urgently may have to wait years to get it. This is the major reason why only 28 percent of renter households with incomes below the poverty level lived in subsidized housing in 1985, while 50 percent of such households received food stamps and 48 percent were covered by Medicaid (U.S. Bureau of the Census, January 1987).

Threats to the Subsidized Housing Stock

Fully half of the present stock of federally subsidized housing is threatened over the next two decades. Most of these losses are expected to occur between 1991 and 1996, but the attrition has already begun. Subsidized housing will be lost (1) by owners' decisions to opt out of low-income housing and convert their units to other uses, (2) by default or foreclosure because rising costs have outstripped the subsidies provided, or (3) through expiration of subsidy contracts. (Under a number of federal programs, subsidized housing has been provided by for-profit owners, who have agreed to keep their rents low for a specified period in return for receiving the subsidy. Some of these so-called use restrictions have already expired and an increasing number will expire during the next decade.) Furthermore, many older subsidized housing developments have not been adequately maintained and need major repairs and renovation. This situation has come about primarily because federal subsidy programs have not in the past been designed or administered to pay for the full costs of providing decent housing for low-income people. Instead, as utility costs rose far more rapidly than tenant incomes during the 1970s, needed operating subsidies were either not provided at all or came too little and too late. (Beginning in 1986, the U.S. General Accounting Office [GAO] released a series of reports relating to potential reductions in the low-income housing stock. [See U.S. General

Accounting Office 1986, 1987, and 1988; National Low Income Housing Preservation Commission, 1988].)

Housing advocates, Congress, and the administration are
all aware that subsidized stock is at grave risk, but differ on
what to do about it. The administration's budget projections
assume that vouchers will be given to tenants affected by the
loss of subsidized units. Congress is wrestling with the problem, having included some stopgap provisions in legislation
approved in 1987. Advocates are, for the most part, pressing
for extension of present contracts for the remaining useful life
of the properties involved, or, in the case of Section 8 Existing, for another 15 years.

The prospect for the future is grim. Substantial federal
funding commitments will be required just to avoid losing
ground over the next 15 years. Yet unless the trend of rising
costs and lower real renter incomes is reversed, even if the
existing subsidized stock is preserved, we will fall farther and
farther behind because the need for additional subsidized
housing will grow. There is every reason, therefore, to believe
that the number of homeless families will double or treble by
the end of the century.

Patterns of Federal Housing Assistance

It is widely believed that for decades the federal government has poured major resources into massive low-income
housing programs and that our present low-income housing
crisis is a result of the failure of these programs. The truth is
that direct spending for housing assistance has never been
more than a tiny fraction—less than 1.5 percent—of the federal budget. Moreover, the cost of housing assistance for low-
and moderate-income households is dwarfed by the cost to

the Treasury of housing assistance provided through the tax code, primarily to middle- and upper-income households.[4]

There are three major categories of federal spending for housing: *budget authority*, which is the total federal financial commitment over the life of the subsidy; *outlays*, which are the actual cash payments of these subsidies; and *tax expenditures*, which represent the cost to the Treasury of various special provisions of the Internal Revenue Code that provide exemptions, deductions, credits, or deferral of income for tax purposes. Those provisions that relate to housing are referred to as housing-related tax expenditures.

Budget authority (often referred to as BA) for housing is the amount committed each year for the sum of housing payments to be made over the life of the subsidy contract. It is figured as the maximum possible subsidy under the program in question, multiplied by the number of years in the term of the contract. Housing *outlays* are the payments made each year for all the units currently receiving subsidy, regardless of when they were first occupied. Housing *tax expenditures* are the total cost to the Treasury of the various housing-related tax deductions or other tax-reducing provisions of the Internal Revenue Code during the year. The major housing-related tax expenditures arise from homeowner deductions of mortgage interest and property taxes.

Outlays for federal housing assistance were less than one percent of the total federal budget until 1981 and have only once been more than 1.5 percent. Indeed, all federal spending for low-income housing payments plus public housing operating subsidies, from the beginning of the programs in the 1930s through fiscal year 1987, totaled $97 billion. This was $5 billion less than housing-related tax expenditures in 1986 and 1987 alone. In other words, the cost to the Treasury of special housing-related deductions was more in two years than the outlays for subsidized housing over 50 years.

Despite a series a cutbacks under the Carter administration from the level of additional assisted housing units provided during the Ford administration (which provided the highest annual number of subsidized units ever), over $30 billion in budget authority for HUD-subsidized low-income housing had been approved for fiscal 1981 when President Reagan took office. That amount was estimated to support an additional 250,000 low-rent units (that is, 250,000 units beyond those already subsidized under previous budget authority). Further, over half (55 percent) of the added units were to be new or substantially rehabilitated, thus increasing the nation's stock of rental housing.

In the previous year (1980), 81 percent of all of HUD's incremental reservations had been for new or rehabilitated units under programs that tied the subsidy to the unit.[5] But federal housing assistance has since shifted away from subsidizing buildings that then become part of low-income stock to subsidizing units selected by recipient households who find their own housing, which must meet cost and quality requirements, in the private sector. In 1987, only 35 percent of incremental reservations were for new or rehabilitated units; the remainder were for Section 8 Existing certificates or vouchers, which lower the cost of housing to the tenant, but do not add to the stock. (Unlike the food stamp program, where the household receives the subsidy, the federal housing subsidy payment under the voucher and certificate programs goes to the owner of the unit.)

Since 1981, there has been a sharp decline in the number of additional low-income households assisted each year. Budget authority dropped from $26.9 billion after the 1981 Rea-

The following analogy may help clarify the federal budget terms used in this chapter. Suppose you are buying a house for $100,000. You pay 20 percent down and obtain a 25-year mortgage at an interest rate of 10 percent. In addition to your monthly mortgage payments of $727 for principal and interest, you figure you will spend an average of $100 monthly for property taxes, and $200 for utilities, maintenance, insurance, and other housing costs. Thus, your total monthly housing costs will be $1,027.

Applying the federal budget concepts to this example, your *budget authority* for this purchase will be your total costs over the 25-year period, or $328,088 ($20,000 down, plus $80,000 principal, plus $138,088 interest, plus $30,000 property taxes, plus $60,000 in other costs). Your *outlays* for the first year would be your actual expenses that year—$32,324 (your $20,000 down payment, plus your other costs which total $12,324). In succeeding years, your outlays would not include the down payment and would be $12,324 each year.

But your actual net housing costs would be less than that because you would receive a subsidy in the form of federal tax deductions—your share of federal housing-related *tax expenditures*—which would be $1,375 the first year if you were in the 15-percent tax bracket, and $2,566 if you were in the 28-percent tax bracket. As the interest portion of your monthly mortgage payment drops, your benefit from the mortgage interest tax deduction will decline; in the fifth year, for example, (assuming your property tax has not changed) your housing-related tax deduction would be $1,319 for the 15-percent bracket and $2,463 for the 28-percent bracket.

Please note that, in this example, your tax deductions are an entitlement; that is, you are entitled to take these deductions regardless of whether you need them to be able to afford your housing. In contrast, if your income were so low that you were forced to rent and to pay more than half of your income for housing, you would almost certainly be eligible for subsidized housing, but you would probably have to wait for years to get it if you applied.

gan rescissions to $10.5 billion in 1988. Meanwhile, housing-related tax expenditures rose from $33.3 billion in 1981 to $53.7 billion in 1988.

The pattern of federal housing assistance is highly regressive when federal housing subsidies are considered as a whole—that is, including both direct subsidies and housing-related tax expenditures. Far more federal housing help goes to affluent people than to low-income people, mostly because such a large proportion of federal housing assistance is provided through the tax code and primarily benefits well-off taxpayers. In 1985, mortgage interest deductions and real estate tax deductions accounted for $81 of every $100 in federal housing-related tax expenditures. Congressional analysts have estimated that 57 percent of the mortgage interest deduction dollars and 62 percent of real estate tax deduction dollars benefited taxpayers who had adjusted gross incomes above $40,000 (U.S. Congress, 1985). Many married women were no doubt among these lucky beneficiaries, but very few women who maintained households were likely to have been among them: in 1985, only six percent of all women-maintained households had incomes of over $40,000.

Addressing Low-Income Housing Needs

Major changes in our nation's approach to housing subsidies will be required to deal with the housing needs of low-income women. The most critical need is to provide all low-income households with an entitlement to housing assistance if they otherwise cannot obtain decent housing without sacrificing other basic needs. This could be done for less than the cost to the Treasury of the upper-income homeowner deductions.

Close the Affordability Gap

Since affordability is the major housing problem facing low-income women, the primary solution is to close the gap between what decent housing costs and what they can afford to pay for it.

Instead of rationing housing assistance to fit within arbitrary budget and appropriation levels, it should be made an entitlement, available automatically to all households with incomes below 50 percent of median who can demonstrate that they are homeless, facing the immediate threat of homelessness (e.g., subject to eviction or foreclosure), living in physically inadequate housing, or unable—based on the market basket approach—to afford other necessities after paying rent and utilities.

The capacity to pay the initial rent deposit, continuing housing assistance through rent certificates or vouchers, and counseling and related assistance in the search for housing would, if available for all homeless households, enable them to make use of the housing in their communities that now is often underused or abandoned not because it isn't needed, but because those who need it cannot afford it.

Protect Presently Subsidized Housing

This country cannot afford to lose either the units themselves or the investment it has made in the present subsidized housing stock. Even though a relatively small proportion of low-income women live in assisted housing, it is their only reliable source of decent, affordable housing.

It should be a basic principle of public policy that subsidized units will be retained unless replacing them with other units in the same locality is less expensive. Retaining existing units can usually be accomplished through a combination of additional subsidies, incentives to keep the housing subsidized, and disincentives to convert (such as a windfall profits tax).

In all but a few instances, it will be cheaper to retain the present subsidized housing than to replace it. A study by the National Low Income Housing Preservation Commission (1988) found that the cost of retaining almost all of the assisted stock would be less than providing its residents with vouchers. Moreover, where retaining existing subsidized units is more expensive than replacing them, the reason is usually some factor—such as neighborhood gentrification— that makes retaining some low- and moderate-income housing in the neighborhood an important social objective. Expiring subsidy contracts should be renewed or extended. Public and other subsidized housing that needs major repairs should be brought up to decent standards.

Expand the Supply of Affordable Housing

In the long run, the solution to the low-income housing problem lies in a combination of increasing the incomes of poor households (a subject beyond the scope of this chapter) and reducing the cost of housing to consumers. The supply of affordable housing should be expanded through purchase of satisfactory existing buildings in "as-is" condition to prevent conversion or demolition, through acquisition and rehabilitation of substandard units, and through new construction.

An expanded low-income housing supply program would benefit women both by providing them with a reliable source of affordable housing and also—if designed with this end in view—by affirmative efforts to assure that women play a substantial role in the provision and operation of the housing. Involving women as active participants in programs to better their own housing conditions has proved to empower women in many ways that have broad implications for their futures and the futures of their children. The confidence gained in learning construction and/or management skills and in seeing that their efforts and ideas can help bring about concrete improvements in their own living circumstances can—and often does—enhance their ability to improve their other circumstances as well.

The best approach would be to expand the supply of low-rent housing through programs that would favor nonprofit housing developers and operators—those who see their task as providing decent housing at the lowest possible cost. Neighborhood-based community development corporations, tenant cooperatives, churches and synagogues, labor unions, and others are capable of playing a major role in providing decent, affordable housing *if* they are furnished the necessary capital and operating subsidies, and technical assistance and support.

Along with programs to increase the supply of affordable rental housing, initiatives to increase the supply of housing affordable for low-income buyers should be vigorously supported. Such housing should be financed primarily by capital grants, to be repaid with interest only if and when the housing is converted to upper-income or commercial use.

Encourage Homeownership for All Households With Children

The inequity of federal housing assistance is nowhere more clearly demonstrated than in federal support for homeownership. The homeowner deductions in the tax code provide the greatest subsidies for the highest-income people—those who need them least. In contrast, with the exception of a tiny home repair program for elderly householders in rural areas, no federal housing assistance is provided to support homeownership for low-income households.

Providing low-income single parents (as well as two-parent households) with opportunities for homeownership would both improve their housing and provide a stable anchor for their lives. Subsidies would be needed to cover utilities, maintenance, repairs, and taxes (as they do for the low-income renter households receiving housing subsidies), as well as mortgage payments. To keep costs down and prevent windfall profits, the subsidies could be made at least partially repayable as incomes rose, or on resale of the units.

End Housing Discrimination

Federal fair housing laws have prohibited discrimination because of race, religion, or national origin since 1968, and because of sex since 1974. Enforcement tools have been weak, however. Discrimination against families with children is now prohibited under amendments enacted in 1988, which also strengthened enforcement procedures. Vigorous implementation will be required if the law is to have a major impact, especially on patterns of racial segregation. And discrimination because of source of income is still not covered by the law. Women-maintained households who receive part or all of their incomes from AFDC may still be legally discriminated against, and often they are.

Before . . .

And after rehabilitation by The Enterprise Foundation. *Courtesy The Enterprise Foundation/Ted Hoffman, photographer*

Strengthen the Federal Role

Although there is increasing involvement by state and local governments in addressing low-income housing needs, two basic roles for the federal government are critical. The first is to establish the economic and institutional framework within which the private sector provides and finances housing. Carrying out this role effectively can both add to and improve the housing stock and expand the number of people who can afford it. The second major federal role, and the context for the foregoing recommendations, is to furnish the help necessary to enable people who cannot be served by the unassisted private sector to obtain decent housing.

As noted above, there is simply no way that the private sector, unaided, can meet the minimum housing needs of those whose incomes are below or near the poverty level—a population that, as has also been noted repeatedly in this chapter, is disproportionately female. Utility and other operating costs have long been so high that a substantial number of poor households in this country find that these costs alone would be more than they could afford, even if their housing itself were provided free of charge. Moreover, the states and localities with the largest numbers of poor people are generally those least able to bear the substantial costs involved in providing access to decent, affordable housing. Solving the low-income housing crisis therefore requires far more in the way of federal funds than has previously been envisaged, even as the possibilities for administering housing assistance in partnership with state and local governments and the non-profit sector are being pursued.

Special Needs

There are a number of other issues—largely outside the scope of this chapter—that should be considered if the housing needs of low-income women are to be comprehensively served. One necessity is that women be involved as equal participants in the framing and implementing of the country's housing policy. Their perspective and experience are needed as never before if the design of housing programs is to respond to some of the special housing and housing-related problems that beset women particularly. Homeless women and battered women (some women are both), and displaced homemakers are among the women with special housing needs.

Homeless Women and Children

Homeless families with children, which are disproportionately single-mother families, are widely reported to be the fastest growing segment of America's homeless population. The consensus among those most knowledgeable about the circumstances of the homeless population is that the lack of sufficient affordable low-income housing is the root cause of family homelessness, which, it should be mentioned, is not limited to the unemployed. Low-income families who lose their housing because of accident (a fire, for example) or falling behind on (an often unaffordable) rent often simply cannot find another place to live.

Once families become homeless, the lack of adequate emergency housing too often forces them to split up, with the children put in foster care or sent to live with friends and relatives who may not even be in the same community or state. Many apparently childless homeless women are mothers whose children have been removed from their care, often *because* they are homeless (failure to provide a home constitutes child abuse in some jurisdictions). Split-up homeless families are often "invisible." So are the many intact homeless families who live in abandoned housing, chicken coops, or old cars.

Homeless families with children who are given shelter are often forced to move from one shelter to another; even the "transitional housing" provided by some jurisdictions is by definition temporary. The crowded, inhumane conditions characteristic of many shelters and temporary housing accommodations are highly detrimental to children's ability to function psychologically and in school.

Like all homeless people, homeless women with children need affordable, permanent housing. To have even the hope of finding such housing, and the long-term prospect of remaining in it, homeless single mothers responsible for children are particularly in need of child care services so that they can be free to undertake a housing search, and/or a job or job training.

Battered Women

Where they will live if they leave is one of the most basic issues battered women face when attempting to escape abusive relationships. In 1986, close to a million battered women and their children sought emergency shelter but only one-third of them received it (National Low Income Housing Coalition, Women and Housing Task Force, 1988). The rest were turned away because there was no shelter space for them. Even those who found emergency shelter were faced with homelessness because of time limits requiring that they leave in two weeks, a month, or, at most, three months.

For a battered woman, the availability of safe and afford-able housing can mean the difference between life-threaten-ing abuse and a life free from violence. Even homelessness may seem less perilous than the alternative of returning to an abusive situation. Moreover, because many homeless bat-tered women do not identify themselves as "battered," staff-ers in homeless shelters do not refer these women to available resources for battered women, such as counseling and legal advocacy. The staffers themselves may not know that such resources are available. Homeless battered women thus tend to be difficult to count and even more difficult to serve.

Displaced Homemakers

Displaced homemakers are women who have been full-time homemakers and have lost their primary source of in-come because of separation, divorce, widowhood, or because their spouses have become disabled or have been unemployed for a long time. Many displaced homemakers are forced to seek new housing arrangements.

Because displaced homemakers by definition usually have little or no income, they often cannot afford adequate hous-ing, especially if they have children. Displaced homemakers who are awarded the marital home in the divorce settlement often cannot keep up the mortgage payments. Even those who have some resources may lack credit histories of their own, or be saddled with poor credit ratings arising from ac-tions by their spouses over which they had no control. A blank credit history or bad credit rating can block access to either private or subsidized housing.

Conclusion

Whether they be the underlying housing needs of America's poor or the special needs of women who are homeless, or battered, or displaced, the housing needs of low-income women and their families will not disappear on their own. Fundamental to meeting these needs are economic resources, and the key to generating these resources is political will. Political will, in turn, is produced by informed and persistent advocacy, the broader-based the better. Success in addressing America's deepening housing crisis may well depend on how much attention is paid to housing by organized advocates for women and how much attention is paid to women by organized advocates for housing.

THREE Child Care in the United States

FERN MARX AND
MICHELLE SELIGSON

Highlights

CHILD CARE HAS MOVED into the national spotlight. During the 100th Congress, child care was the focus of more than 100 bills and the subject of congressional hearings, government reports, and planks in the platforms of both political parties. Escalation of public interest in the issue represents a convergence of factors, including the sharp increase in the employment of mothers with young children and changing attitudes about the appropriateness of mothers working outside of their homes.

- Providing more public and private resources for quality early childhood programs, including child care, is regarded by many as one of the major agenda items for the 1990s.

- Beyond the importance of child care in supporting maternal labor market participation, the demand for early childhood programs is currently driven by a desire in both the public and private sectors to intervene in the cycle of poverty at an earlier and more efficient point.

- Unfortunately, there are significant limitations in the available data on child care in the United States. No single national child care data base exists. Census data for 1984-85 show that 37 percent of the 8.2 million children of working mothers were cared for in someone else's home by relatives or nonrelatives. Thirty-one percent were cared for in their own homes by relatives or nonrelatives. Twenty-three percent were in day care centers or preschools, and eight percent were cared for by their mothers while they worked.

- Among young, dual-earner married couples, 30 percent of full-time workers and nearly 40 percent of part-time workers used some type of shift schedule that enabled the spouses to share the care of their children.

- Whether their children are cared for by relatives or by non-relatives has important implications for the costs of care to families: parents relying on nonrelatives are about twice as likely to pay for care as those using relatives for care.

- Quality, location, and price, in that order, were the most common reasons mothers in one survey gave for selecting their current child care arrangements.

- The supply of different types of child care has increased considerably in response to rising demand. Nonetheless, depending on the community, there may be a mismatch between supply and demand, and parents may not be able to get the quality or type of care they want.

- There is a shortage of licensed or regulated care for very young children in most parts of the country. Child care resource and referral agencies report that parents most frequently request help in locating care for children under age three.

- Care for children between the ages of three and five appears to be more widely available, but much of the care for these children is half day, and parents are increasingly seeking full-working-day care.

- After-school programs for school-age children also remain in short supply.

- Today there is an active attempt to broaden the definition of child care. An important recent development has been the initiation of a public dialogue connecting the need for child care and the need for early childhood education. Quality of care has also become a focus of the discussion.

- Current debate over the cost and quality of child care and the appropriate public role in its provision often neglects what many consider to be the most serious crisis in the early childhood field: the low pay, high turnover rates, and acute shortage of qualified staff to provide care and education to young children.

- The unsubsidized cost of child care, particularly full-time care, is burdensome for many parents and prohibitive for some. In 1984-85, women who paid for child care had median child care expenditures of $38 per week, which works out to $1,976 per year. This sum may appear modest, but considered in relationship to women's median earnings, it represents a significant expenditure.

- One study found that a single parent earning 100 percent of the median income for a single parent and requiring full-time care for a preschooler and a toddler could pay as much as 36 percent of gross income on care.

- Several studies have indicated that the availability of affordable child care leads to greater labor force participation

by women, which in turn contributes to greater tax revenues and reduced welfare dependency.

• But the affordability/availability issue is not simply a matter of making increased funds available to low- and moderate-income families. Parents have repeatedly indicated that
quality is a major concern in selecting care for their children.

• Present federal government involvement with child care
takes the form of direct and indirect expenditures through
the tax system.

• The 1980s began with many states facing growing demand
for publicly subsidized child care. Federal support for child
care did not keep pace with inflation during the 1970s, and
in the early 1980s, the federal government enacted measures that produced funding cuts and changes in some
child care programs. The cuts had a profound effect on the
supply of child care for low-income families in many states.

• Although a few states were able to mitigate the effect of
federal cuts, by 1987, only 18 states had managed to create
new child care programs and increase the number of children served over 1981.

• Many of the state initiatives were targeted to special populations, but others were more broadly conceived to improve the availability, quality, and supply of child care.
Some states have experimented with measures to secure
funds for child care through increased fees, increased cigarette taxes, or use of state lottery funds.

• Local governments are also becoming involved in child
care. A small but growing number of municipalities and
counties have established child care offices or appointed

child care coordinators whose activities may include developing services and administering child care subsidy programs for municipal employees, directing city-run child care programs, and working with local business and developers to expand the availability of child care for employees.

- Some school districts have also made significant commitments to child care. There are, however, few indications that public schools can afford to expand their child care efforts—whether for preschool or school-age children—without significant additional funding to meet such expenses as salary and benefits for added staff, renovation of facilities, and new classrooms.

- A growing number of employers are becoming involved in offering child care resource and referral services to their employees, but public funding is necessary if such services are to be made available to all parents in a community.

- Employer involvement also includes operating or contracting for work-site or off-site child care services, seminars to inform parents on how to choose child care, cafeteria benefit plans allowing the choice of child care as a tax-free benefit, and salary reduction plans permitting employees to use pretax dollars for child care.

- Workplace studies have shown that problems with child care can reduce productivity, increase absenteeism, and contribute to low morale and high levels of stress among workers. Research also indicates that benefits such as dependent care, flexible work schedules, and parental leave help employers attract and retain workers.

Introduction

Child care moved into the national spotlight in 1988, when it was the focus of more than 100 congressional bills and the subject of congressional hearings, government reports, and planks in the platforms of both major political parties. Escalation of public interest in child care represents a convergence of factors:

- Growing political and public awareness that women in their childbearing years and the mothers of young children are in the workforce to stay and that the demand for child care has increased as a result;

- Changing attitudes about the appropriateness of mothers working outside of their homes;

- Increasing reliance on out-of-home child care arrangements by working parents at all socioeconomic levels;

- Growing involvement in child care on the part of employers who are increasingly sensitized to the need for measures to attract and retain competent employees; and

- Longitudinal research showing that participation in high quality early childhood programs has a positive impact on future adult development, especially in the case of disadvantaged children.

Recent surveys and public opinion polls indicate that Americans now recognize the need for public investment to increase the availability of child care and that they are willing to make that investment through the tax system (Harris, 1987). In recent years, there has been wider public discussion about the costs of child care, the ways of paying for care, the uneven quality of available child care, and the federal government's role in regulating care and setting standards. This chapter discusses some of these issues and offers an overview of the broad range of recent public and private responses to child care.

The Demand for Child Care

The increased demand for child care reflects two demographic trends: (1) the growth in the total number of young children as the large baby boom cohort has begun to reproduce, and (2) the sharp increase since 1970 in the employment of mothers with young children, the group that traditionally has been least likely to enter the labor force. As of 1988, 56 percent of mothers with children under the age of six were in the labor force. Assuming that present labor force trends continue, Hofferth and Phillips (1987) predict that by 1995, two-thirds of all preschool children and three-fourths or more of all school-age children will have mothers in the labor force. If Hofferth and Phillips are right, by 1995, 15 million preschool children and 34 million school-age children may have mothers who work outside the home at least part of the time. Clearly, the demand for child care shows no sign of lessening.

Today, the probability that a mother will be employed and that she will work full time varies considerably by such factors as race, age of youngest child, marital status, and income. Black mothers are more likely than white mothers to be employed. Mothers of very young children are more likely to work part time than are employed mothers of older children. Divorced mothers have higher rates of employment than married or never-married mothers. Very low-income mothers are less likely to be employed than those with higher incomes (Hofferth and Phillips, 1987). By the mid-1990s, however, it is anticipated that the labor force participation rates for white and black mothers, and for single and married mothers will be the same (Family Impact Seminar, 1989).

Beyond the importance of child care in supporting maternal labor market participation, the demand for early childhood programs is currently driven by a desire in both the public and private sectors to intervene in the cycle of poverty at an earlier and more efficient point. Providing more public and private resources for quality early childhood programs, including child care, is regarded by many people as one of the major agenda items for the 1990s.

Of singular importance to the public policy debate have been such studies as the Perry Preschool Project (Berrueta-Clement et al., 1984) and other longitudinal studies (e.g., Honig et al., 1986), which have found that children in good quality child care show no signs of harm and that children from low-income families may show improved cognitive and social development as a result of such care (see, e.g., research cited in Phillips and Howes, 1987). In addition there is evidence that both children and their parents receive long-term benefits from comprehensive early childhood programs like Head Start, which provide health and social services and parental involvement as well as early education (Lazar et al., 1977).

These findings appear to have had an impact on leaders in the private as well as the public sector. National organizations have developed policy statements and set goals which were very much influenced by evidence from the controlled study of the Perry Preschool Project. That project showed that there are long-term benefits from participation in early childhood programs: reduced delinquency, less use of intervention programs later in life, less special education placement, higher rates of school completion, and greater employment among adults who had been enrolled in quality preschool programs.

It is important to note that the Head Start and Perry Preschool programs were designed as part-day programs modeled after the middle-class nursery school. "Day care" was not their purpose. Yet, even though it is becoming increasingly clear that both the education and child care needs of families with young children must be addressed, most state-supported prekindergarten programs are part-day programs. Few of them—especially if they were enacted during the early to mid-1980s—address the need for child care among parents who are working or seeking work.[1]

Business leaders have become increasingly concerned about some of these issues, as evident in *Children in Need: Investment Strategies for the Educationally Disadvantaged*, a report published by the Committee on Economic Development (1987) and widely disseminated. This report recommends profound changes in public and private funding policy for young children and urges policymakers to adopt a strategy for improving the prospects for disadvantaged children that focuses on children from birth to age five and on teenagers who are most at risk for premature parenthood.

In 1986, the National Governors' Association issued an important policy paper, *Focus on the First 60 Months*, that calls for investment in programs serving young children and their families. Similar policy statements have been issued by the Council of Chief State School Officers, the National Conference of State Legislators, and the National Association of State Boards of Education. These organizations have been joined by unions, religious and civic groups, parents' organizations such as the national PTA, business and professional organizations, youth-serving agencies, and others in an alliance that represents the emergence of child care as a mainstream issue and that may ultimately result in the passage of national child care legislation.

Where Are Children Cared For?

Unfortunately, there are significant limitations in the available data on child care in the United States. No single national child care data base exists. Rather, statistics are collected by a variety of federal, state, and local organizations, including the Census Bureau, the Department of Education, and advocacy groups such as the Children's Defense Fund. These data collectors lack a common set of child care definitions, which makes it difficult to determine precise utilization patterns or to estimate demand for care. Information on the supply and nature of formal, regulated care or of informal care by family day care providers, relatives, neighbors, and others is still inadequate, although current research efforts funded in part by the federal government should provide better data of this type in the near future.

Nevertheless, the Census Bureau provides some important information on how working women care for their young children (U.S. Bureau of the Census, May 1987). Census data for 1984-85 show that 37 percent of the 8.2 million children of working mothers were cared for in someone else's home by relatives or nonrelatives. Thirty-one percent were cared for in their own homes by relatives, including their fathers, or nonrelatives. Twenty-three percent were in day care centers or preschools, and eight percent were cared for by the mother herself at work. Among mothers with preschool children, those who worked full time relied more heavily on child care arrangements outside the child's home than did mothers working part time.

Whether their children are cared for by relatives or by nonrelatives has important implications for the cost of care to families: parents relying on nonrelatives are about twice as likely to pay for care as those using relative care (ibid.).

Fathers provide the care for about one-third of the 48 percent of preschool children who are cared for by relatives in the child's or a relative's home. According to Presser (1988), "father care" has remained essentially stable over the past two decades. Not surprisingly, however, there are major differences between married and unmarried women's use of this arrangement. Nineteen percent of the preschool children with married mothers, but only two percent of those with unmarried mothers, were cared for by their fathers while their mothers worked. Unmarried women rely far more heavily on grandparents in the child's home than do their married counterparts (16 vs. three percent) (U.S. Bureau of the Census, May 1987).

The important role that fathers play in child care is underscored by Presser's finding that among young, dual-earner married couples, 30 percent of full-time workers and nearly 40 percent of part-time workers used some type of shift schedule that enabled the spouses to share the care of their children (Presser, 1988).

Use of organized child care facilities (nursery schools, day care centers, kindergartens) by employed women has increased substantially and sharply—from 16 percent in 1982 to 25 percent in 1984-85. Care by nonrelatives, whether in or outside the child's home, accounted for over half of the primary arrangements used by employed mothers of children under age five.

The shift toward nonrelative care and out-of-home care may not, however, indicate a move toward licensed or regulated care. Given that an estimated 80 to 90 percent of what is termed family day care is unregulated, it is clear that the dominant mode of child care in the United States in 1988 remained informal, unlicensed care in a home setting, at least for preschool children (Family Impact Seminar, 1989).

The majority of child care consumers appear to be satisfied with their child care arrangements, according to the preliminary results of a survey of child care supply and needs by Mathematica Policy Research, Inc. (Family Impact Seminar, 1989). The most common reasons mothers gave for selecting their current arrangements were quality, location, and price, in that order. However, if cost were no object, 25 to 50 percent of mothers of one- and two-year-olds said they would switch to center-based programs with an education component. Nearly half of the mothers of children age three to five, and a quarter of the mothers of infants, also stated that they would like an education component in their child care.

The Supply of Child Care

As noted earlier, while information on maternal employment and child care arrangements can be obtained from government surveys, information on the nature and supply of regulated and unregulated care is less adequate. At present we can only estimate whether there is a good match between supply and demand by type of care and geographic distribution. According to Hofferth (as cited in Family Impact Seminar, 1989), the supply of different types of child care has increased considerably in response to rising demand. Slots in center-based care are estimated to have doubled in the last 10 years, and licensed or regulated family day care may have

"Child care resource and referral agencies report that parents most frequently request help in locating care for children under age three."
© *Gail Troussoff/Woodfin Camp, Inc.*

increased by as much as one-third over the same period.

However, depending on the community, there may be a mismatch between supply and demand, and parents may not be able to get the quality or type of care they want. A shortage of licensed or regulated care for very young children in most parts of the country has been noted by Kahn and Kamerman (1987).

According to child care resource and referral agencies, parents most frequently request help in locating care for children under age three. Care for children between the ages of three and five appears to be more widely available, but much of the care for children in this age group is half-day, and parents are increasingly seeking full working-day care. After-school programs for school-age children also remain in short supply. Where programs do exist, they are often difficult for parents to locate and evaluate. Initial findings from Mathematica's survey of child care supply and needs confirm that lack of information is seen as the biggest problem facing both consumers and providers (Family Impact Seminar, 1989).

Expanding the Definition of Care

Today there is an active attempt to broaden the definition of child care. An important development in 1988 was the initiation of a public dialogue connecting the need for child care and the need for early childhood education. Quality of care has also become a key focus of the discussion. It is this nexus of quality care and education that will have to be addressed in legislation and in national, state, and local responses.

The quality of early childhood programs is a major concern not only for parents, who often list it first in importance in selecting care for their children, but also for policymakers, educators, advocates, and legislators struggling to define "quality" and to assign responsibility for developing useful standards or indicators.

The many child care bills introduced in the 100th and 101st Congresses address issues of quality to varying degrees and place responsibility for defining and monitoring quality variously—and in some instances simultaneously—in the hands of parents, state or local jurisdictions, or the federal government. Similarly, sponsors of the various bills use different strategies (grant-based, tax-based, or a combination of the two) to address another major and connected issue, affordability. Responsibility for paying for child care is assumed by some to rest with families, by others to belong to state or federal governments or employers, or some combination thereof.

Current debate over the cost and quality of child care and the appropriate public role in its provision often neglects to take into account what many consider to be the most serious crisis in the early childhood field: the low pay, high turnover rates, and acute shortage of qualified staff to provide care and education to young children. Gwen Morgan of Work/Family Directions and Wheelock College refers to the tradeoffs between affordability and quality, and between quality and caregiver wages as the "day care trilemma."

The Affordability, Availability, and Quality of Child Care

The unsubsidized cost of child care, particularly full-time care, is burdensome for many parents and prohibitive for some. In 1984-85, women who paid for child care had median child care expenditures of $38 per week, which works out to $1,976 per year (U.S. Bureau of the Census, May 1987). This sum may appear modest, but considered in relationship to the median earnings of working women ($12,869 for full-time working women in 1985), it represents a significant expenditure. Hofferth, compiling data from several consumer surveys in 1985, found that among mothers who paid for the care of one child under age five, the average weekly payment was $37 for about 30 hours of care (Family Impact Seminar, 1989).

In examining the costs of child care, it is important to take into consideration such factors as the age of the child in care, how many children a family has in care, type of care (relative care, family day care, center-based care, etc.), and regional variations in costs. The Children's Defense Fund

(1987) has published estimates of the average cost of child care in seven major cities in late 1985. These data provide some indication of the great variations in the cost of care for children under the age of three. Family day care costs ranged from an average of $50 per week in Atlanta to $115 per week in Boston; for center-based care, costs ranged from $55 per week in Atlanta to $120 in Boston. Across the seven cities, the average cost for a child in full-day, family day care was $75 per week or $3,900 per year (calculated for full-time, full-year care). Center-based care for a child of the same age averaged $91 per week or $4,732 per year. Full-time care for a child age three to five, while slightly less expensive, averaged $68 in family day care and $71 per week in center-based care. Annualized, the costs would be, respectively, $3,536 and $3,692.

These Children's Defense Fund estimates were based on 1985 costs. More recent estimates for Massachusetts indicate that infant and child care costs may be substantially higher.

Are such costs affordable, or are they unreasonable? Does the cost of care constitute a barrier to women's labor market entry? According to Kahn and Kamerman (1987), families cannot manage the full costs of care except at very high incomes. There is no unanimity regarding how much parents should spend on child care, but there does appear to be some agreement, based on several studies of family expenditure patterns, that families should probably not spend more than 10 percent of their income on child care if undue strain on their capacity to afford necessities such as food, shelter, and clothing is to be avoided.

Using the 1984-85 Census data, Hofferth has shown that families who had paid for care for a child under five spent 11 percent of their income on child care (Family Impact Seminar, 1989). This figure, however, does not account for the wide variation in the proportion spent on child care by different income groups. Poor families pay from 20 percent to 26 percent of their incomes on child care, while families with incomes over $40,000 typically spend less than five percent (ibid.). A recent study found that over half of the low-income families in Massachusetts paying for care spend more than 10 percent of their annual income for child care, and many pay more than 15 percent (Commonwealth of Massachusetts, 1988). Moderate-income families in the state also faced an affordability problem: 13 percent paid 15 percent or more of their income for child care.

The impact of the costs of caring for more than one child is illustrated by estimates in 1984 by the City of Madison (Wisconsin) Day Care Unit (Marx, 1985). A single parent earning 100 percent of the median income for a single parent and requiring full-time care for a preschooler and a toddler could pay as much as 36 percent of gross income on care. Clearly, for poor and moderate-income parents who must pay for it, child care can represent a significant proportion of the family budget.

For some poor single-parent families the high cost of care may constitute a significant barrier to employment, particularly if more than one child is involved. Concerns about poverty and welfare dependency among female-headed families over the past decade have created growing interest (1) in examining the extent to which absence of child care constitutes a barrier to labor force participation and (2) in the efficacy of subsidized child care as an income-enhancing strategy for low- and moderate-income families.

Several studies have indicated that the availability of affordable child care leads to greater labor force participation by women, which in turn contributes to greater tax revenues and reduced welfare dependency. Blau and Robins (1988) found that unemployed mothers in areas with higher child care costs were less likely to enter the labor force than were mothers in areas with lower child care costs. Census data for 1982 indicated that if satisfactory child care had been available at a reasonable cost, 21 percent of part-time employed mothers with preschool children would have increased their labor force participation (U.S. Bureau of the Census, 1983). This finding suggests that part-time employment may be a response to difficulty in locating good, affordable child care.

In this same survey, 26 percent of mothers who were not in the labor force indicated that they would look for work if child care were available at a reasonable cost. This response was especially common among unmarried women (45 percent), low-income women (36 percent), black women (55 percent), and women with less than a high school diploma (38 percent).

A recent Massachusetts study found that 11 percent of nonemployed parents who had at least one child under the age of 13 said they would look for work if satisfactory child care were available at a reasonable cost (Commonwealth of Massachusetts, 1988). While not all respondents in these studies would actually increase their labor force participation even if "satisfactory, reasonably priced" child care were available, the data suggest that many more mothers of young children would work if quality child care services were expanded and made more affordable.

The efficacy of child care in enabling low-income families, especially families receiving welfare assistance, to increase their incomes has received attention in both the federal welfare reform legislation and in those states involved in similar efforts. Reports on the results of demonstration programs have repeatedly cited the critical importance of child care to welfare recipients' success in the labor market, but published findings on this topic are few.

A 1979 study by the University of Central Florida reported that the availability of child care on a sliding-fee scale resulted in an almost 50-percent reduction in welfare recipiency, a 123-percent improvement in employment, and a 117-percent increase in family income. It also found that once AFDC recipients left welfare, they remained self-sufficient over the two years of the study (Marx, 1985).

In Massachusetts, as in many other states where welfare reform efforts have been undertaken, child care is deemed a critical component in the transition from welfare to work. The state's Employment and Training Choices (E.T. Choices) program is considered by many to be a successful model and a good example of a program that has put considerable resources into child care. While it is difficult to disaggregate child care from other support services provided by E.T. Choices, one evaluation found that participants considered the increased affordability of child care as one of the major benefits of the program. There are also indications that the availability of child care has enabled more women with very young children to participate in the program (Gray et al., 1984).

But the affordability/availability issue is not simply a matter of making increased funds available to low- and moderate-income families. Parents have repeatedly indicated that quality is a major concern in selecting care for their children. Thus, day care may be available but the quality may be unacceptable or, conversely, quality care may be available but unaffordable. In the case of infant day care, it may be both unaffordable and unavailable. In some communities adequate day care may exist but parents may lack knowledge about it or have no means of transporting their children to the facility.

Efforts to improve the quality of care by raising the traditionally low salaries of child care workers have, in some instances, made day care less affordable for moderate-income families. Problems like these have led some to contend that more federal spending is needed to support program expansion, to permit more low- and moderate-income families access to care, to support better training and higher wages for child care providers, and to promote higher day care standards. Others argue that except in the case of very low-income families, additional federal intervention in child care is unwarranted at this time and that by and large the child care market is performing well (Family Impact Seminar, 1989).

Policy and Program Responses

Present federal government involvement with child care takes two forms: (1) direct expenditures (primarily via the Social Services Block Grant to the states) and (2) indirect expenditures through the tax system, which allows various child care-related tax deductions and/or credits to employers as well as to parents.

Those who agree on the need for additional investment in child care by the federal government often disagree on the most appropriate form of that investment. Some believe that the answer is to increase the supply of day care by increasing direct federal spending. Others see the solution in providing indirect support to parents through the federal tax system. Advocates of these two different approaches are further divided on the issue of regulation, anathema to those seeking to keep direct government involvement to a minimum, imperative to those advocating large-scale investment strategies to improve the quality of care (Besharov and Tramontozzi, 1988; Lindsey, 1988; Rector, 1988; Samuelson, 1988).

Advocates for program expenditures argue that the existing child care delivery system needs a direct infusion of dollars to strengthen a child care labor supply severely strained by low wages and low status. Day care staffing is unstable—not surprising, considering that the work demands a good deal of skill but offers meager monetary rewards in return. On average, child care workers have nearly two years more education than U.S. workers overall, but earn about half of what the total workforce earns. Staff turnover in day care is about twice the national average and promotes concern about the quality of care (Hartmann and Pearce, 1989). Yet parents are hard pressed to pay the increasing costs of a child care system attempting to attract and retain good staff.

Advocates of a "demand-side" solution through the tax system see improvements to the child care system deriving from parents themselves, as they make their own evaluations and choices about the best care for their children—whether to use formal or informal services or to stay out of the paid labor force to be with their children at home. Arguments against large-scale direct funding for child care services include a concern that parents who do not pay for child care (e.g., those who elect to stay at home with their children) would be penalized because they would neither benefit from federal child care subsidies nor be eligible for the dependent care tax credit as presently constituted. This argument also turns on the belief that current tax credits actually benefit middle-class families rather than poor or low-income families.

The failure of the 100th Congress to approve the Act for Better Child Care (ABC), which called for $2.5 billion in federal direct spending for child care, appears to have resulted largely from these fundamental differences between what could be described as "supply-side" vs. "demand-side" approaches, although other issues also played a part. There were concerns about maintaining the separation of church and state if federal funds were to be used for care in religious institutions, concerns about discrimination against women who elect to stay at home, and concerns about the federal role in regulation of day care. Other factors included the appropriateness of spending $2.5 billion at a time when Congress needs to cut the federal deficit; refusal by the bill's sponsors to compromise on national child care standards (Pekow, 1988); business opposition to the parental leave bill that had been attached to ABC; and opposition by the public education community to the idea of using vouchers to pay for day care.

Other significant child care-related legislation introduced in the 100th Congress, but not passed, included the Child Care Services Improvement Act and Smart Start. The Child Care Services Improvement Act was similar to the ABC, but completely departed from it on the matter of national regulations, preferring to leave regulation up to the states. Smart Start focused solely on children age four, half of whom had to be from low-income families. The bill included provisions for full-working-day programs and would have allowed participation by agencies other than public schools.[2]

In approving the Family Support Act, the 100th Congress did pass one bill with a child care component. This welfare reform package, now law, requires education, training, job search, and work in return for income, health, and child care benefits. States are required to establish and operate a Job Opportunity and Basic Skills Training Program (JOBS). JOBS participation is mandatory for most single welfare recipients with children over three (and, at state option, for those with children over the age of one for up to 20 hours of work per week).

The law requires that child care and transportation assistance be provided on a sliding-fee basis for JOBS participants; for those who become employed, transitional child care is available for up to one year. All states must permit services for up to six months per year to two-parent families if the principal wage earner is unemployed.

Critics of the Family Support Act point out that it pays scant attention to the inadequacy of the present child care supply, or to the quality of the care provided to children of welfare recipients, and that it makes relatively little attempt to link its child care requirement to the need of these at-risk children for education and development (O'Connor, 1988). Some speculate that unless Congress approves a funding bill for child care soon, the Family Support Act may founder.

State, City, and County Initiatives

The 1980s began with many states facing growing demand for publicly subsidized child care. Federal support for child care had not kept pace with inflation during the 1970s, and in the early 1980s, the federal government enacted measures that produced funding cuts and changes in some child care programs.

The cuts had a profound effect on the supply of child care for low-income families in many states—especially those unable or unwilling to allocate state funds for child care. Although a few states were able to mitigate the effect of the federal cuts and, in some instances, actually to expand services, the Children's Defense Fund estimated that as of 1987,

23 states were still serving fewer children than they had been serving in 1981; 28 states were spending less for subsidized child care. Only 18 states had managed to create new child care programs and increase the number of children served over 1981 (Children's Defense Fund, 1987).

Many of the state initiatives were targeted to special populations, (i.e., school-age children, the children of teenage parents, or the children of welfare recipients in state welfare-to-work programs). Other initiatives were, however, more broadly conceived to improve the availability, quality, and supply of child care. Some states have experimented with measures to secure funds for child care through increased fees, increased cigarette taxes, or use of state lottery funds. Some local governments have attempted to use "linkage" agreements that require developers to build on-site child care facilities or to donate funds for community child care.

Massachusetts is one of the states that have managed substantially to expand commitment to child care. Considerable attention and new resources have been brought to bear on both improving the subsidized child care system and increasing the supply of care. Acting on the recommendations of the Governor's Day Care Partnership, a task force with a broad-based and diverse membership, Massachusetts has more than doubled real (i.e., inflation-adjusted) expenditures for child care since 1981. In addition, it has created and expanded a state-wide network of resource and referral agencies, and greatly expanded the day care voucher program for the state's voluntary workfare program, E.T. Choices.

Child care workers in programs receiving state funds received a 32-percent salary increase and family day care providers received a rate increase. A special Affordability Scholarship Assistance Program was developed for moderate-income families who required partial assistance in affording child care. The state also developed a loan fund to stimulate employer investment in child care programs. Not forgetting its own employees, the state set aside funds and created a labor-management committee to address the child care needs of state employees.

Other states have also acted on child care initiatives:

- Twelve states and the District of Columbia have earmarked funds to provide child care for teen mothers who are in high school, working toward a diploma or GED, or in a job training program.

- Several states have concerned themselves with child care workers' salaries. Connecticut, for example, has raised its reimbursement rates for family day care by 150 percent, and for child care centers by 66 percent.

- In at least three states, Hawaii, Massachusetts, and Pennsylvania, new state funds have been provided for training child care workers.

- Several states are expanding the child care supply by establishing start-up and/or renovation funds, or by providing tax incentives for that purpose. Oregon, for example, has established a 50-percent employer tax credit for building child care facilities or for reimbursing parents' child care costs (Children's Defense Fund, 1987).

- At least 14 states have enacted legislation to develop more school-age child care. These enactments range in size; the largest is California's $30 million "latchkey" program which supports the development and delivery of services, many of them in public schools.

Local governments are also becoming involved in child care issues. A small but growing number of municipalities and counties have established child care offices or appointed child care coordinators whose activities may include developing services and administering child care subsidy programs for municipal employees, directing city-run child care programs, and working with local businesses and developers to expand the availability of child care for employees.

Madison, Wisconsin boasts one of the older municipal initiatives in the country. The city provides general revenue funds for child care tuition assistance to low-income residents who are working or are in job training and who meet income eligibility guidelines. Funds may be used only in programs that meet city certification standards for quality, which are more stringent than state standards. Small grants are also available for capital improvements, and training and technical assistance is available to city-certified programs (Marx, 1985).

State Involvement in Early Childhood Education

Reflecting the national interest in education reform and the results of longitudinal studies demonstrating the efficacy of early education programs, particularly for poor, high-risk children, the states have initiated a variety of state-funded prekindergarten programs in the 1980s (Marx and Seligson, 1988). Today, a majority of states invest in some type of early education program. Various mechanisms are used: 26 states and the District of Columbia provide direct funding for prekindergarten programs; two states provide extensive parent education; and 10 states plus the District of Columbia supplement federal Head Start funds in order to expand and improve services to eligible children. Two-thirds of all state-funded prekindergarten programs are targeted to low-income or high-risk children. Nearly all these programs are administered by state departments of education, and in about half of the states, programs must be operated by public school systems. In the remaining states, public schools are permitted to subcontract with community-based programs, and/or private agencies are permitted to contract directly with the state.

It is heartening to see the rapid increase in the number of states involved in prekindergarten efforts, but it is important to note that most state efforts are small, and often are funded as pilot or demonstration efforts. In fact, expenditures for state prekindergarten programs, Head Start, and parent education programs totaled just under $300 million in 1988. The states alone clearly cannot meet the need for expanded services, particularly in light of increasing state fiscal constraints. Nevertheless, much can be learned from the states' efforts.

For example, despite assertions that new state-funded prekindergarten programs are necessary to assist the increasing number of working mothers, only a handful of states permit the new funds to be used for full-working-day programs. The limitations of part-day programs are reflected in recent interviews with 75 low-income women with preschool children in half-day (two and one-half to three hour) prekindergarten programs in New York City. Ninety percent of these mothers were not employed (Porter, 1988). They were waiting for their children to enter full-day school before pursuing their own education and training. Not only did having their children in prekindergarten for only a few hours limit the mothers' opportunities to improve their own economic status, but the programs did not provide the mothers with information on education or training for themselves or on child care options.

While half-day programs may serve the educational and developmental needs of high-risk children, it is questionable whether they serve the best interests of low-income parents seeking work. This issue will demand greater attention as states begin to implement the Family Support Act with its work requirement for mothers of preschool children receiving welfare benefits.

Although the Family Support Act does include a specific requirement that child care be coordinated with Head Start and other existing early childhood education programs, it will take major efforts on the part of states to link this new funding source for child care with the largely part-day prekindergarten and Head Start programs targeted to a similar population.

The added thrust toward combining care and education does not address the differences in salaries between child care workers and those of prekindergarten/kindergarten workers. Success in integrating these services will depend, in part, upon raising the salaries of child care workers, but the Family Support Act goes no further than permitting states to pay market rates for care, which means that most states will not have the option of significantly improving child care workers' salaries and working conditions.

Fewer than a third of the states have requirements for coordination efforts at the local level. As a result, there has been some indication of increased competition between programs for limited public funding, space, staff, and children. Experienced staff are reported to be leaving Head Start and child care programs for the better salaries and working conditions in public school-based prekindergarten programs funded by the states (Goodman and Brady, 1988; Marx and Seligson, 1988).

A few states have tried to minimize this kind of competition by establishing detailed requirements for local level coordination, including needs assessments, before awarding funds to local programs. New Jersey's newest program has attempted to minimize competition at both the state and local levels by having the Department of Education and the Department of Human Services jointly administer a pilot program designed to provide a full-working-day program based on Head Start standards. These are encouraging signs that states are becoming more sensitive to the need for coordination to prevent battles over "turf" and limited staff and dollar resources.

Child Care Resource and Referral Programs

Finding high quality, affordable child care can be a long and arduous process for parents. Resource and referral programs can facilitate this process by linking parents and child care providers and offering other valuable services to a community's child care system. Child care resource and referral agencies (CCRRs) can also help policymakers develop a rational child care system in a state or community. Because the child care system in the United States has grown in response to demand and without the benefit of centralized planning, it is made up of a bewildering array of public and private programs.

The data collected by resource and referral programs on the need for and the supply of specific types of child care can provide policymakers with important information as they consider various child care options. Resource and referral agencies can also aid in building the supply of child care by recruiting and supporting new family day care providers.

A growing number of employers are becoming involved

in offering resource and referral services to their employees, but public funding is necessary if such services are to be made available to all parents in a community. Increasingly, states are earmarking funds for resource and referral services (14 states and the District of Columbia did so as of 1987). The Dependent Care Block Grant has made a small amount of federal funding available for resource and referral in each state over the past four years. The growing interest nationwide in CCRRs has led to the development of a national organization, which publishes a directory of child care information and referral agencies as well as a quarterly magazine.

In an era characterized by federal emphasis on privatization, decentralization, and deregulation in the child care field (Kahn and Kamerman, 1987), the expansion of CCRRs during the 1980s began to fill an important gap. While their services vary tremendously, many CCRRs not only provide information and referral, but administer public funds such as child care subsidies under vendor/voucher arrangements and provide coordination and supportive functions for child care providers.

California not only has the largest child care budget of any state but also has been in the forefront of innovation in child care services. The California CCRR program, which covers all of the state's 58 counties, was funded by the state at $7.3 million in 1987-88 (Blank et al., 1987). The 67 CCRR agencies vary both in their auspices (some are free standing; others are part of schools or social service agencies; some are part of agencies delivering child care services) and in the services they provide.

A unique feature of the California system is a statewide network that advocates for child care issues at the state and national levels and provides statewide supply and demand data for policymakers. Overall, California provides the most extensive array of early childhood and child care services in the country, but as is the case elsewhere, there is little coordination at the state level.

State-funded central coordinating agencies may provide an important tool with which to rationalize the funding and delivery of child care services throughout a state (Marx, 1985). The state of Florida is unique in that it has nurtured the development of 17 umbrella agencies to cover all districts in the state. They are modeled on Orlando's Community-Coordinated Child Care for Central Florida, Inc., which began in the 1960s under the federal Community Coordinated Child Care Program (4C) and, with the help of state legislation, evolved into a central coordinating agency in the early 1970s.

Florida's central agencies are required by state law to provide social and health services and training and education for parents and providers. They are also required to administer day care subsidies (thus relieving the state from having to deal with multiple small contracts to local child care programs) and create visibility for day care in the community in order to generate a local match for state funds (Marx, 1985).

While these examples of outstanding state child care initiatives are by no means exhaustive, they do suggest the range of services provided by resource and referral agencies and the important function these agencies can perform in planning and expanding the current child care system in the United States.

Public Schools

As the nation struggles to match the supply of child care with the demand, public schools have been identified as another potential resource. Several congressional proposals on child care have included public schools as agencies that could receive additional federal funds for child care (e.g., the Act for Better Care, the New Schools Demonstration Act, the Child Development and Education Act).

As noted earlier in this chapter, a majority of states now fund special programs for young children. Most of those created in the 1980s target funds primarily to public schools, and most are part-day programs that were conceived as early intervention, educationally focused prekindergarten programs. They typically do not operate on a full-day schedule that would provide care for the children of parents who are working, in job training programs, or seeking work.

In addition to state funded programs, school districts operate a variety of prekindergarten programs, a majority of which are federally funded, including Head Start, Chapter I programs of the Education Consolidation and Improvement Act (ECIA), and state and federally funded special education programs. Nearly all are part-day programs; a 1986 survey found that only about six percent of public school early childhood programs were full-working-day child care programs. The norm was a three-hour session offered each school day during the regular school year. And, when asked to predict future trends for early childhood programs in their school districts, 85 percent of the school superintendents surveyed anticipated no changes in the age (typically four) of the children served, or in the daily hours of operation and months per year, or in the types of programs offered (Mitchell, 1988).

Nevertheless, some school districts have made significant commitments to child care. The Pomona, California, school district offers programs supported by parent tuition and government subsidies. The district has put together a financial and programmatic package that makes an array of early childhood and parent support services available.

A similar approach is used by the Affton-Lindbergh school district in St. Louis, Missouri, which offers flexible scheduling in both part-day and full-working-day programs and which has a reputation among parents for its responsiveness to the needs of working families (Mitchell, 1988).

School-age children as well as preschoolers may need care while their parents are working, but programs for school-age children are not widely available, nor are they used by a majority of parents. By the time children reach age eight, reported use of "self-care" rises sharply. However, the demand for before- and after-school care has increased considerably in recent years.

A 1988 survey of elementary and middle school principals found that 22 percent reported having some form of before- or after-school child care programs in their schools, up from seven percent in 1972. These programs operated largely on parent tuition, with school districts providing eight percent of the funding. More than four out of five of the principals surveyed said that before- and after-school programs should be offered in their communities. Lack of funding was seen as a major obstacle (National Association of Elementary School Principals, 1988).

There also appears to be growing public and teacher support for school involvement in before- and after-school programs; a recent national poll of teachers and parents found that more than half of both groups thought that the absence of supervision and lack of after-school activities ranked first in a list of factors contributing to children's poor performance in school. Many parents wanted schools to provide after-school programs for their children and said they would pay for them (Harris Poll, 1987).

There are, however, few indications that public schools can afford to expand their child care efforts—whether for preschool or school-age children—without significant additional funding to meet such expenses as salaries and benefits for added staff, renovation of facilities, new classrooms, and training and retraining for public school employees who lack early childhood training or experience.

School districts tend to offer an array of child care services only if there are sufficient state and/or federal financial resources. Federal Dependent Care Block Grant dollars have provided states with modest start-up and improvement funds mainly used by public schools or by private agencies and groups in conjunction with the schools. While these federal funds are important as a source of support for getting services started, by law they may not be used for operating costs or to subsidize parents' fees.

Absent a significant increase in state or federal funds, local taxpayers may resist efforts to increase property taxes in order to fund child care in the schools. This reluctance, and caution on the part of public education officials against extending the boundaries of schools too far beyond their primary mission, are two factors that may keep school involvement in child care at a relatively modest level in the immediate future.

Workplace Issues

Increased demand for out-of-home child care combined with the decline in federal subsidies for child care has encouraged exploration of alternative funding sources and strategies, including the involvement of business and industry (Kahn and Kamerman, 1987).

Industry faces a shrinking labor pool, and the costs of

employee recruitment and retention are increasing. Some industries, such as banking, finance, insurance, and services, employ large numbers of women in their prime childbearing years. Benefits such as dependent care, flexible work schedules, and parental leave help employers attract and retain workers.

An early 1980s study of 391 employees of companies that offered child care services found that 38 percent of these workers selected their employer because of the child care assistance, and 69 percent were encouraged to stay because of it (Bureau of National Affairs, 1984). Employers were surveyed in a 1982 study; two-thirds of the companies providing child care assistance reported that it reduced employee turnover (Burud, 1984).

Workplace studies have also shown that problems with child care can reduce productivity, increase absenteeism, and contribute to low morale and high levels of stress among workers. For example, 58 percent of the female workers, and 33 percent of the male workers, in five midwestern corporations felt that child care concerns hurt their productivity (Galinsky and Friedman, 1986). Yet despite mounting evidence of the benefits of employer support for child care, it has been estimated that only 4,000 of the nation's six million employers were providing any form of child care assistance in 1988 (Friedman, 1988).

Employer involvement in child care ranges from operating or contracting for work-site or off-site child care services (in 1988, there were about 600 on-site day care centers, of which 400 were located in hospitals), seminars to inform parents about how to choose child care, cafeteria benefit plans allowing the choice of child care as a tax-free benefit, salary reduction plans permitting employees to use pretax dollars for child care, scholarships and discounts for use of community-based child care, and child care resource and referral services.

In the past five years, some corporations have undertaken child care initiatives that go well beyond the companies' own employees. The BankAmerica Foundation launched the California Child Care Initiative in October 1985, using six of the state's network of child care resource and referral agencies to recruit and train new child care providers. During the pilot year, over 200 licensed providers were recruited and trained, which resulted in services to an additional 1,000 children. The success of the pilot project led the Initiative to serve other areas in the state. Over the first two years of this project, more than $700,000 was raised from other corporations and from state and local governments.

IBM contracted with a private Boston-based consulting firm, Work/Family Directions, Inc., in 1984 to identify and develop community-based child care resource and referral agencies for its more than 200,000 employees. But IBM also made a commitment to strengthen child care services for others in the community. The local agencies in the network have used IBM program funds to establish new family day care homes and day care centers. IBM has also furnished funds to train child care workers (Galinsky and Friedman, 1986).

The American Express Company Foundation, in collaboration with Child Care, Inc., established the Neighborhood Child Care Initiative Project in New York City. Funding ($395,000) was raised from large corporations and foundations. The project was designed to support four new neighborhood networks of family day care providers and improve the services of two existing networks. Community-based organizations sponsor each of the networks, help providers obtain licensing, training, and other needed support, and provide referral services for parents seeking child care.

Experts observe that companies tend to become involved in child care in communities where there is already a reasonably well-developed child care system. However, the business sector is also seen to contribute to the development of that system by assessing the community's supply of child care.

Increased employer involvement in child care is anticipated: half of the companies represented in a large 1988 survey of personnel managers were reported to be in the "planning stage," and 86 percent of 71 Fortune 500 companies also surveyed in 1988 said they would do more about child care in the future (Galinsky, in press).

Conclusions

None of the approaches to providing high quality, affordable child care that have been reviewed in this chapter will, by themselves, address the complex interaction between supply, demand, and parental preference. However, each of them holds promise as one component in a coordinated system.

As this chapter is written, federal lawmakers appear ready to approve some type of child care legislation which will most likely combine a supply-side with a demand-side approach. Whatever the final outcome, however, it is clear that reliance on the federal government alone cannot solve the urgent need of many American families for high quality, affordable child care.

The variety of approaches to child care that have evolved in both the private and public sectors reflect both the impact of research studies showing positive long-term outcomes from good early childhood programs and growing awareness of the shared responsibility of all sectors for a meaningful investment in our children's futures. While employers may fund child care to reduce employee turnover or enhance recruitment, there are strong indications that corporate America is also recognizing the need to invest in future productivity by investing in children.

Public schools and municipalities are becoming increasingly convinced that supporting quality programs for young children prevents future expenditures for remediation. Particularly encouraging is the development of state and local resource and referral agencies to improve parental access to, and choice among, the variety of existing programs, and to provide resources for improving the quality of these programs.

Ensuring that in the decades to come there will be access to affordable, high quality child care for every parent who needs it will certainly require money, but money alone is not the answer. Coordination and cooperation will be vital to strengthen the nascent child care partnership of government at all levels, the public education system, and the corporate sector.

FOUR Gender Equality and Employment Policy[1]

DEBORAH L. RHODE

Highlights

OVER THE LAST QUARTER CENTURY, changes in ideological, economic, and demographic patterns have all contributed to major transformations in the roles of women and men. Law has both reflected and reinforced these changes. The result has been an unprecedented equality in formal treatment of the sexes, but a continued disparity in actual status.

- Law has helped break barriers to entry for persons seeking nontraditional employment, but most occupations remain highly segregated or stratified by sex. Most female workers remain segregated in relatively low-status, low-paying, female-dominated occupations.

- Although women have made substantial inroads in a number of male-dominated occupations, it has been estimated that at current rates of change it would take between 75 and 100 years to achieve complete occupational integration in the workforce.

- Even in gender-integrated occupations, women's jobs, pay, and promotion opportunities are likely to differ from men's.

- Given the low wages of women and barriers to advancement, it has been economically rational for working couples to give priority to the husband's career, to relocate in accordance with his job prospects, and to assign wives a disproportionate share of domestic obligations.

- Women's continuing workforce disadvantages stem in part from the law's traditional focus on gender differences rather than gender disadvantages. The law's primary objective has been to secure similar treatment for persons similarly situated; less effort has centered on remedying the structural factors that contribute to women's disadvantaged status.

- Gender differences in the workforce are dismissed by defenders of the equal opportunity approach to employment discrimination as artifacts of cultural lag or employee choice and beyond the scope of legitimate legal concern. Yet, most research suggests that the obstacles confronting women are more entrenched than the equal opportunity approach acknowledges.

- Individual career choices often represent preconceptions about "women's work," which are shaped by cultural stereotypes, family and peer pressure, and the absence of alternative role models. Individual choices have also been constrained by unconscious discrimination and workplace structures.

- According to human capital models of labor force participation, gender differences in earnings and occupational status are largely attributable to differences in career investments. Research has concluded, however, that characteristics such as education and experience cannot account for more than half of the current gender gap in earnings. Moreover, on the whole, women who make comparable investments in time, preparation, and experience still advance less far and less quickly than men.

• Competitive market forces, some economists argue, do not necessarily discourage deliberate bias against women or minorities.

• Unconscious bias affects not only opportunities for individual workers but also reward structures for women as a group. Men's tasks are rated as more valuable than women's no matter what those tasks entail. Women in a wide range of employment settings also remain outside informal networks of support, guidance, and information exchange that are critical to advancement.

• Workers who seek to balance work and family commitments confront barriers, the most obvious of which involve the length and rigidity of working schedules, the absence of adequate parental leave provisions, and the lack of child care.

• Affirmative action and pay equity are two methods of dealing with occupational inequities.

• Affirmative action opponents argue that singling out women for special assistance can reinforce the very assumptions that society strives to dispel. From this perspective, de facto quotas will encourage selection of those who cannot succeed by conventional criteria. However, virtually all preferential treatment programs assist only candidates who are basically qualified for the jobs at issue.

• The primary objective of pay equity or comparable worth has been to challenge pay disparities between male and female jobs that cannot be justified by factors relevant to employment performance and conditions. Critics raise many objections to pay equity, one of which is cost. Although comparative long-term data are lacking, it does not appear that the growing number of employers who have implemented comparable worth reforms have triggered the kinds of problems critics have raised. When phased in over a period of years, typical costs of American reforms have been around five to 10 percent of employers' total wage rates.

• If occupational equity is to become a serious national commitment, expressed in social policy as well as in political rhetoric, an array of strategies expanding beyond antidiscrimination, affirmative action, or comparable worth mandates is needed.

Introduction

In surveying the current occupational landscape from the perspective of women, it is possible to give two accounts. One alternative is an uplifting *Pilgrim's Progress* narrative, which stresses women's recent advances and increasing opportunities. By contrast, there's a competing *Myth of Sisyphus*, which compiles figures on occupational segregation and stratification and concludes that we're still pushing the same rocks up the same hills. The following overview sketches a third possibility that borrows from the story lines of both tales, but leaves the final script somewhat more open-ended.

Over the last quarter century, changes in ideological, economic, and demographic patterns have all contributed to major transformations in gender roles. Laws have both reflected and reinforced these changes. Since the early 1960s, the United States has developed a broad array of legislative, administrative, and judicial mandates against gender discrimination. The result has been unprecedented equality in formal treatment of the sexes, but a continued disparity in actual status. Enacted legislation has helped break barriers to entry for those seeking nontraditional employment, but most occupations remain highly segregated or stratified by sex. While legal mandates have entitled men and women to equal pay for the same work, relatively few males and females have in fact performed the same work. If domestic and paid labor are combined, the average woman works longer hours and receives substantially less income than the average man. Although women have entered elite professions in substantial numbers, they have tended to cluster at the lowest levels. Most female workers have remained in relatively low-status, low-paying, female-dominated occupations.

The following discussion explores the major institutional and ideological forces underlying these disparities. It begins with a brief overview of occupational inequality and the most commonly accepted strategies for coping with it: requirements of equal opportunity and equal treatment. Although these strategies have been of vital importance in raising the cost of and consciousness about sex-based discrimination, they have not adequately addressed the full range of factors that contribute to women's unequal workforce status.

In part, the difficulty stems from the law's traditional focus on gender differences rather than gender disadvantages. Statutes have been enacted to secure similar treatment for persons similarly situated; less effort has centered on remedying the structural factors that contribute to women's dissimilar and disadvantaged status. A related difficulty involves the individualist premises that have restricted legal policies. All too often a focus on maximizing individual choices has deflected attention from the social forces and workplace values that constrain such choices. Enforcement of equal opportunity, pay equity, and affirmative action laws has been hampered by a preoccupation with individual villains, with a demand for evidence of intentional discrimination, and a reluctance to penalize innocent third parties. Too much concern has focused on the conscious motivations of decisionmakers and too little on the cumulative disadvantages that their actions impose.

Significant progress toward social justice will require alternative frameworks. Equal opportunity is inadequate as a means and an end; what is needed are fundamental changes in workplace practices, premises, and priorities.

Patterns of Inequality

Despite an increase in antidiscrimination mandates, wide disparities have persisted in the vocational status of men and women. In 1955, the median annual wages of full-time female workers were approximately 64 percent of the annual wages of males. Over the next several decades, that figure declined and then climbed back to 64 percent in 1986 and to 65 percent in 1987 (70 percent of weekly wages) (National Committee on Pay Equity, 1989).

However, the above wage ratios do not capture the full extent of gender differences in earnings, since only about half of all employed women work full time for the full year, and disproportionate numbers lack employment-related benefits such as health and pension coverage (Kamerman and Kahn, 1987). Even among full-time workers, the average female college graduate still earns less than the average white male with a high school diploma. The average black female college graduate in a full-time position receives less than 90 percent of her white counterpart's salary (which is equal to the earnings of a white male high school dropout). Women, particularly minority women, are also disproportionately represented among the unemployed and among involuntary part-time workers.

These salary and unemployment disparities reflect broad patterns of occupational segregation and stratification. Most women employees are crowded into a small number of job categories, and about half are in occupations that are at least 80 percent female (Reskin and Hartmann, 1986: 7). Even in gender-integrated occupations, women are likely to hold different jobs and have different pay and promotion opportunities. Most jobs still tend to be stratified by race and ethnicity as well as by sex, and women of color remain at the bottom of the occupational hierarchy.

Despite significant progress toward greater integration, some projections suggest that at current rates of change, it would take between 75 and 100 years to achieve complete occupational integration (Beller, 1984). Some of the more dramatic improvements have been in formerly male-dominated professions such as law, medicine, and management, where women's representation ranged between three and 14 percent in the early 1960s and increased to levels of 20 to 40 percent in the late 1980s (U.S. Bureau of the Census, 1964; U.S. Bureau of Labor Statistics, 1989). However, at the highest levels of power, status, and financial reward, significant disparities remain that cannot be explained solely by women's recent entry into those professions.

For example, in the late 1980s, female lawyers comprised 25 percent of all associates but only six percent of the partners in law firms; studies of lawyers with comparable education qualifications have also found that women are substantially less likely to reach partnership (Abramson and Franklin, 1986; American Bar Association Commission, 1988). At all professional levels, underrepresentation of women of color is even greater than that of white women.

Gains in blue-collar employment have also been limited. For example, although the absolute number of women in the skilled trades increased fourfold between 1960 and 1980, women still hold only about 20 percent of those positions (Marano, 1986). Nor has women's increasing interest in "men's work" been matched by a comparable increase in men's enthusiasm for "women's work." Within the most heavily female-dominated job sectors, such as clerical work, male representation has not significantly changed (Bielby and Baron, 1984).

Defenders of the conventional equal opportunity approach to employment discrimination typically dismiss these asymmetries as artifacts of cultural lag or employee choice and, in either case, as matters beyond the scope of legitimate legal concern. From their perspective, formal prohibitions on gender bias in educational and employment practices will, in time, prove sufficient to guarantee equal opportunity; any remaining disparity in occupational status can be attributed to individual choice, capabilities, and commitment, and is not a ground for further legal intervention.

Yet most research suggests that the obstacles confronting women workers are more entrenched than the equal opportunity approach acknowledges. In identifying these obstacles, it is important to note at the outset certain complexities in the concept of occupational equality. It is not self-evident that proportional representation in all employment sectors is the ultimate ideal. To assume that, under conditions of full equal-

"Although the absolute number of women in the skilled trades increased fourfold between 1960 and 1980, women still hold only about 20 percent of those positions." *Courtesy AFL-CIO News/Images Unlimited*

ity, women will make precisely the same occupational choices as men is to accept an assimilationist perspective that many feminists renounce. Yet one can remain agnostic about the precise degree of gender differentiation in the ideal society without losing sight of the disadvantages confronting women in this world.

In assessing those disadvantages, it is useful to distinguish two sorts of problems. Workforce inequalities reflect both the relatively low status and pay scales in female-dominated occupations and the factors discouraging women's entry and advancement in alternative employment contexts. These phenomena in turn depend on complex interrelationships among individual choices, social norms, discriminatory practices, and institutional structures.

Individual Choice and Socialization Patterns

Although individual choice plays an important role in virtually all theories of occupational inequality, the nature of that role is a matter of considerable dispute. According to human capital models of labor force participation, gender differences in earnings and occupational status are largely attributable to differences in career investments. In essence, these models assume that women seek to balance work and family commitments by selecting female-dominated occupations that tend not to require extended training, long hours, inflexible schedules, or skills that deteriorate during absence from the workforce.

Under this theory, the solution to women's workplace inequality lies with women themselves. In their crudest form, human capital approaches lead to a kind of Marie Antoinette response to occupational stratification. If women want positions with greater pay, prestige, and power, let them make different career investments; if female nurses want pay scales equivalent to male hotel clerks, let them become hotel clerks (G. Becker, 1975; Blau, 1984).

This theory is questionable on several levels. Most studies have concluded that characteristics such as education and experience cannot account for more than half of current gender disparities in earnings (Duncan, 1984; Treiman and Hartmann, 1981). On the whole, women who make comparable investments in time, preparation, and experience still advance less far and less quickly than men. Even in their most sophisticated forms, human capital approaches leave a vast range of questions unanswered. Why is it that females choose to be nurses rather than hotel clerks—or, for that matter, truck drivers, where job skills are even less likely to deteriorate with absence? Why don't male employees with family responsibilities disproportionately choose jobs requiring shorter hours? Answers to these questions require a more complex account of cultural norms and institutional constraints.

For many individuals, career decisions have been less the product of fully informed and independent preferences than the result of preconceptions about "women's work" that are shaped by cultural stereotypes, family and peer pressure, and the absence of alternative role models. Women who have deviated from traditional norms in job selection have generally received less social approval than those who have not. Many families also have discouraged career choices that would conflict with domestic duties, require geographic mobility, or entail greater prestige or income for wives than for husbands (Bernard, 1976; Kaufman and Richardson, 1982; Mednick, 1982; Reskin and Hartmann, 1986). Such patterns can be especially pronounced among some minority groups, where males' education may carry greater priority than females' (Mirande and Enriquez, 1979). Job training, counseling, and recruitment networks have often channeled women toward conventional occupations, and socioeconomic barriers have limited employment aspirations (Reskin and Hartmann, 1986; Roos and Reskin, 1984).

These constraints are reinforced by the mismatch between characteristics associated with femininity and characteristics associated with vocational achievement. The aggressiveness, competitiveness, dedication, and emotional detachment thought necessary for advancement in the most prestigious and well-paid occupations are seen as incompatible with the traits commonly viewed as attractive in women: cooperation, deference, sensitivity, and self-sacrifice. Despite substantial progress toward gender equality over the last several decades, these sexual stereotypes have been remarkably resilient.

Women remain subject to the familiar double bind. Those conforming to traditional definitions of femininity have often appeared lacking in the assertiveness necessary for occupational success, while those conforming to masculine models have appeared "bitchy," aggressive, or difficult to work with. A "third sex" in vocational contexts has yet to emerge (Epstein, 1988; Larwood and Wood, 1977; McBroom, 1986).

Different socialization patterns have also led women to arrange their priorities in ways that mesh poorly with occupational structures. Although society's commitment to equal opportunity in vocational spheres has steadily increased, it has not extended to equal obligations in domestic spheres. Most contemporary studies have indicated that women still perform about 70 percent of the family tasks in an average household. Employed wives spend about twice as much time on homemaking tasks as employed husbands (Rhode, 1989b; Roos, 1985).

As subsequent discussion in this chapter suggests, individual choices have also been constrained by unconscious discrimination and workplace structures. The result is a convergence of self-perpetuating social signals that reinforce occupational inequalities. Males' and females' different career investments have been heavily dependent on their perceptions of different opportunities.

Women have long faced relatively low wages in traditional vocations and substantial barriers to advancement in nontraditional pursuits. Under such circumstances, it has been economically rational for working couples to give priority to the husband's career, to relocate in accordance with his job prospects, and to assign wives a disproportionate share of domestic obligations. The gender division of labor in the home and workplace has been mutually reinforcing. Women's subordinate occupational status has encouraged them to make more modest career investments and to assume greater domestic responsibilities, both of which help perpetuate that subordination. To break this cycle will require treating individual choices not as fixed and independent phenomena, but as responses to cultural forces that are open to redirection.

Discriminatory Practices and Occupational Dynamics

Efforts to move beyond human capital explanations of occupational inequality have proceeded on several levels. One approach has focused on occupational segregation. Some commentators, drawing on dual labor market theories, have stressed men's concentration in the primary and women's in the secondary sector of the workforce. Others have emphasized more general effects of occupational crowding, i.e., since women have remained clustered in a relatively small number of female-dominated occupations, the resulting oversupply of labor in those fields has depressed wage rates and increased unemployment.

Such approaches, while useful to a point, have left fundamental causal questions unaddressed. Why, for example, have women remained crowded in certain sectors of the labor market? Why have those sectors commanded relatively low status and economic reward, and why do males and females with comparable qualifications have different opportunities for advancement?

In seeking answers to such questions, researchers have

accumulated increasing evidence on discrimination of various forms: deliberate, statistical, and unconscious. On the most overt level, economists such as Gary Becker (1971) have argued that competitive market forces do not necessarily discourage deliberate bias against women or minorities where employers have developed a "taste for discrimination." Such tastes, founded on personal prejudice, customer or coworker preference, or favoritism toward male "breadwinners," have been identified in a wide range of contexts (Matthaei, 1982). Litigation in the late 1980s revealed claims such as those advanced by owners of tuna fishing boats that excluded women. According to these owners, the presence of female employees would destroy morale and distract the crew: their boats would "catch fewer fish with women on board" (*Caribbean Marine Services v. Baldridge*, 1988).

The more insulated the labor market is from competitive forces, the more persistent these biases may prove. Even reasonably competitive markets will also permit what economists label "statistical discrimination," that is, discrimination premised on generalizations that are inaccurate in a large percentage of cases but that are nonetheless cheaper to indulge than refine. Long after statistical patterns erode, the effects of statistical discrimination often linger.[2] Once jobs become typed as male or female, socialization processes tend to perpetuate those labels (Treiman and Hartmann, 1981).

A final, and in contemporary society perhaps a most intransigent, form of discrimination operates at unconscious levels. Employer decisionmaking has reflected the same stereotypes about male and female capabilities that have constrained employees' vocational choices. For example, surveys of a wide variety of decisionmakers have revealed that identical resumes or scholarly articles are rated significantly lower if the applicant or author is thought to be a woman rather than a man. Men's success is more likely to be attributed to ability and women's to luck (Lott, 1985; Rhode, 1988; Shepela and Viviano, 1984).

Such unconscious bias affects not only opportunities for individual workers but also reward structures for women as a group. This point was well illustrated by a survey of the federal government's *Dictionary of Occupational Titles*, which rates the complexity of tasks in some 30,000 jobs (and which has influenced many public and private compensation plans). Among the occupations rating lowest in the 1965 *Dictionary* edition were foster mother, nursery school teacher, and practical nurse, all of which were thought equally or less demanding than parking lot attendant and "offal man," whose respective responsibilities were to park cars and "shove[l] ice into [a] chicken offal container" (Howe, 1977; Steinberg and Haignere, 1987). Although repeated criticisms prompted substantial revisions in a later *Dictionary* edition, the legacy of earlier biases has been difficult to eliminate.

Anthropological studies suggest the pervasiveness of the problem. While cultures vary considerably in the tasks they allocate to each sex, their valuation patterns have been consistent. As Margaret Mead once noted, there have been villages in which men fish and women weave and villages in which women fish and men weave, but in either type of village, the work done by men is valued more highly than the work done by women (Mead, 1968).

More overt, although often unintentional, forms of bias by colleagues and coworkers have comparable consequences. Women in a wide range of employment settings remain outside the informal networks of support, guidance, and information exchange that are critical to advancement (Aisenberg and Harrington, 1988; American Bar Association, 1988; Kanter, 1977). All of these problems are especially acute for women of color, who face unconscious discrimination on two fronts, and whose small numbers make finding mentors and role models especially difficult (Fernandez, 1981; Lawrence, 1987). Related problems involve sexual harassment, which not only impairs performance and restricts advancement but also discourages women from entering male-dominated environments (MacKinnon, 1979; Walshok, 1981).

The last decade has, to be sure, witnessed significant improvement in these areas. Court decisions banning sex-based discrimination by certain all-male clubs where key professional contacts are made, and decisions establishing legal liability for sexual harassment, have enabled more women to function effectively in the workplace (*Meritor Savings Bank, FSB v. Vinson* [1986]; *Roberts v. United States Jaycees* [1984]; *New York State Club Association v. City of New York* [1988]; *Rhode,* [1986]).

However, as long as women constitute small minorities in nontraditional employment contexts, substantial obstacles will remain. The presence of a few token females may do little to alter underlying stereotypes, and the pressures placed on such individuals make successful performance less likely.

Given these barriers and biases, women must work harder to succeed and when they do, they must deal with the envy and anxiety that success arouses. Those who do not advance under such circumstances, or who become frustrated and opt for different employment, confirm the adverse stereotypes that worked against their advancement in the first place. The perception remains that women can't make it by conventional standards, or are less committed to doing so. In either event, they do not seem to warrant the same investment in training, assistance, and promotion opportunities as their male counterparts (Epstein, 1988; Kanter, 1977; Menges and Exum, 1983).

Again, the result is a subtle but self-perpetuating cycle in which individual choices are constrained by discriminatory practices. Not only has gender bias shaped employment opportunities and salary patterns, it has also affected the way workplace structures have adapted to women's participation.

Institutional Constraints

Just after the turn of the century, the Supreme Court in *Muller v. Oregon* acknowledged the "obvious" respects in which performance of a women's "maternal functions place[d] her at a disadvantage in the struggle for subsistence" (1908: 421). Three-quarters of a century later, the most fundamental of those disadvantages remain. Most women work in occupational environments designed by and for men. The way in which the workplace has been structured, advancement criteria defined, and domestic responsibilities allocated, have all tended to perpetuate gender inequalities.

In contemporary American society, any individual who seeks to balance significant work and family commitments confronts substantial barriers. Since, as noted earlier, women continue to assume the greater share of homemaking obligations, they also experience the greater share of workplace difficulties. The most obvious problems involve the length and rigidity of most working schedules, the absence of adequate parental leave provisions, and inadequacies in child care services. Despite increasing innovation, the vast majority of workers lack opportunities for flexible schedules or meaningful part-time work.

As of early 1989, America still failed to guarantee maternity benefits. A still more chronic problem involves the inadequacies of child care arrangements. Although by the late 1980s, over half of mothers with children under the age of three were in the workforce, few employers were providing any child care assistance (Employee Benefit Research Institute, 1988). Government support has been far too limited to fill the gap (Strober and Dornbush, 1988: 340).

For women, the lack of flexible scheduling options, temporary leave provisions, and child care services carry significant occupational consequences. Short-term losses result when a female employee finds it necessary to forgo promotional and training opportunities, or leaves a particular job, together with its seniority and benefit provisions. Long-term costs result from a woman's discontinuous work history, which makes advancement within the best-paying job sectors more difficult. Those with substantial family commitments are rarely able to reach positions with greatest decisionmaking power in either the public or private sector. As a consequence, policies governing parental leave, working schedules, child care, and related issues are made by those individuals who are least likely to have experienced significant work-family conflicts. The solution is not "mommy tracks" that risk becoming mommy traps. If our concern is both promoting equality between the sexes and improving the quality of life for both of them, more fundamental gender-neutral initiatives are needed.

The details of more effective strategies for dependent care have been addressed elsewhere and need not be rehashed here. Rather, what bears emphasis is the importance of both public and private sector initiatives in these areas. A useful first step would be federal legislation guaranteeing temporary

leave for childbirth or dependent care, with wage replace-
ment by employers or unemployment compensation packages. More incentives should be available for development of
child care programs, flexible scheduling alternatives, and
meaningful part-time work.

The Legal Response

As in other contexts, the law's primary approach to these
occupational issues has focused on gender differences rather
than gender disadvantages. The goal has been to prevent
those with comparable abilities from experiencing different
and unequal treatment because of sex. Under the equal protection guarantee of the Fourteenth Amendment, courts
have prohibited various forms of intentional discrimination.
Title VII of the Civil Rights Act bars both intentionally discriminatory actions and certain conduct that, while neutral
on its face, has a disproportionate, adverse impact on women
and is not justified by business necessity. Various legislative
and administrative regulations have also required those receiving governmental contracts or assistance to implement
affirmative action programs.[3] Taken together, these remedies
have played a critical role in expanding women's employment
opportunities. This approach has not, however, adequately
confronted some of the deeper institutional and ideological
forces that contribute to gender disadvantage.

Part of the problem stems from the law's frequent focus
on individual intent and its reluctance to scrutinize conduct
that does not seem specifically designed to discriminate
against women. Given the unconscious level at which much
gender bias operates, together with the costs—both financial
and psychological—of initiating legal action, such a frame-

work is highly limited. Similar limitations follow from the inadequacy of governmental and private employer support for strong forms of affirmative action or pay equity. Although the latter two issues have generated a vast literature that cannot be fully summarized here, a few general observations bear attention.

Affirmative Action

Affirmative action strategies take a variety of forms, ranging from largely process-oriented requirements (such as special recruitment and training procedures) to preferential treatment for those individuals who are basically qualified for particular positions and who are members of underrepresented groups. The strongest requirements have typically grown out of court orders or litigation settlements; weaker forms have resulted from voluntary employer action or federal executive orders requiring government contractors and grantees to establish goals and timetables for employing underrepresented groups. Although such programs have been critical in securing progress for women and minorities, their implementation has been hampered by difficulties in evaluating compliance[4] and by opposition based on moral principles and practical consequences.

As a matter of principle, critics contend, gender- or race-based remedies subvert the premise they are seeking to establish; to assign preferences based on immutable and involuntary characteristics is to reinforce precisely the kind of criteria that society should seek to eliminate. Such preferences, opponents believe, also compromise fundamental concepts of individual merit and entitlement by penalizing white male job applicants who were not responsible for prior invidious treatment. To many observers, the case for preferential treatment for white women is particularly weak because they have not been subject to the same economic, educational, and cultural deprivations as racial and ethnic minorities (Block and Walker, 1982; Goldman, 1979).

It is, of course, true that affirmative action disregards claims to be treated as an individual, not as a member of a particular racial or sexual group. But arguments that hold such claims preeminent come several generations early and several centuries late. Group treatment has been a pervasive feature of America's social, economic, and political landscape, and has exposed women as well as minorities to systematic deprivations. To equate a limited and temporary form of discrimination against a privileged group with pervasive and lasting discrimination against unprivileged groups is to obscure the most basic cultural meanings and consequences that flow from such treatment.

Differential treatment of white male employees neither reinforces cumulative disadvantages nor infringes on any right to treatment solely on the basis of individual merit. Most employment decisionmaking already incorporates some factors that do not represent merit in any objectively measurable sense, such as personal connections and unconscious stereotypes. Particularly in upper level positions, what job qualifications are most critical and which candidates possess them are often open to dispute. The increased representation of women and minorities, whose experience differs from their white male colleagues, may enrich the standards by which merit is measured. To take an obvious example, female academics may offer different perspectives on traditional intellectual paradigms than their male counterparts. The contributions of women's studies programs over the last two decades underscore the point.

Comparable difficulties surround critics' pragmatic objections to affirmative action. According to opponents, singling out women for special assistance can reinforce the very assumptions that society strives to dispel. From this perspective, de facto quotas will encourage selection of those who cannot succeed by conventional criteria and thus compromise organizational efficiency and entrench adverse stereotypes. Or, if women do perform effectively in a context of preferential treatment, their performance will be devalued. As long as the beneficiaries of affirmative action appear unable to advance without special favors, prejudices will remain unaffected.

Such claims are problematic on several levels. Since virtually all preferential treatment programs assist only those candidates who are basically qualified for the jobs at issue, the extent of efficiency losses is difficult to measure. Objective qualifications such as grades in school have notoriously poor predictive value. Nor has any systematic evidence demonstrated significant declines in job performance as the result of affirmative action programs (Citizens' Commission on Civil Rights, 1984; Fallon, 1980).

Although the stigma some individuals attach to affirmative action beneficiaries should not be discounted, neither should it be overvalued. The current underrepresentation of women and minorities in positions of influence is also stigmatizing. Former Assistant Attorney General Barbara Babcock put the point directly when asked how she felt about gaining her position because she was a woman. As she noted, "It feels better than being denied the position because you're a woman" (Rhode, 1988: 1200).

To attain a social order in which wealth, power, and status are not distributed by gender, it is first necessary to dispel the stereotypes contributing to this distribution. Affirmative action advances that effort by placing a critical mass of women and minorities in nontraditional positions. More than a few isolated role models are necessary to counteract the latent prejudices and socialization processes that have perpetuated occupational inequalities (Gutek, 1982; Marini and Brinton, 1984).

Such considerations argue for strengthening affirmative action at all levels. But neither should the limitations of this approach be overlooked. A fundamental concern is that preferential treatment will secure only entry- or token-level representation for the most upwardly mobile women and thus help more to legitimatize than to challenge existing organizational values. In order to secure not just access to but alteration of existing workplace structures, other strategies are also essential.

Pay Equity

As a conceptual framework, comparable worth or pay equity has historical analogues in the medieval notions of a "just price." As a practical strategy, the concept gained support in this country during the late 1970s and 1980s. Its primary objective has been to challenge pay disparities between male and female jobs that cannot be justified by factors relevant to employment performance and conditions. As pay equity advocates have noted, current wage scales reveal hosts of examples not readily squared with merit principles: public school teachers who earn less than state liquor store clerks, nurses who earn less than tree trimmers or sign painters, and librarians who earn less than crossing guards and water meter readers (Kirp, Strong, and Yudof, 1985; Savage, 1983).

Most alternative approaches rely on forms of job evaluation and are often lumped under the generic title of comparable worth. One type of job evaluation involves a "policy-capturing" technique. This approach focuses on the *relative* worth assigned to particular positions under existing wage scales, either the employer's own rates or those of similarly situated employers. Under this approach, employers identify factors relevant to compensation and score jobs in terms of those factors (such as skills, responsibility, and working conditions). Then, statistical regression techniques are used to assess the relative importance of such factors in predicting current wages and to establish a weight for each factor. Each job receives a rating based on its weighted characteristics.

This ranking can serve as the basis for adjusting pay scales or setting salaries for new jobs, although employers may make further modifications in response to market forces. To pay equity advocates, the policy-capturing approach is primarily useful in identifying racial or gender biases in application of the employer's own evaluation system. For example, statistical analysis can identify the importance an employer attaches to particular factors in male-dominated or gender-integrated jobs and then can determine whether the same factors command the same financial reward in female-dominated positions.

From a pay equity standpoint, the strength of this system is also the source of its limitation. By relying on the employer's own standards for establishing relative value, a policy-capturing technique avoids more subjective and divisive issues about the intrinsic value of particular jobs. It demands only that employers be consistent in application of their own weighting system across job categories, regardless of the gender, race, and ethnicity of employees and the pay at which they are willing to work. However, since a policy-capturing system uses existing wage rates to assess the relative importance of job characteristics, it will reflect gender and racial biases that have traditionally affected those rates (Clauss, 1986; Killingsworth, 1985; Steinberg, 1984).

A more fundamental challenge to current salary-setting procedures is possible through techniques that focus on *intrinsic* worth. Under this approach, employers generally begin by defining the set of factors and factor weights that ought serve as the basis for pay differentials. Typically, this system will rank job characteristics such as skill, effort, responsibility, and working conditions, and then assign points to particular jobs based on their weighted characteristics. Compensation levels can then be adjusted to ensure parity between different jobs with similar ratings. By valuing job characteristics without explicit reference to employers' existing salaries or market rates, such techniques often expose underpayment of predominantly female occupations. Although employers can adjust their compensation structures to reflect market pay rates as well as their own rankings, an a priori system has the advantage of making such adjustments visible (Clauss, 1986; Remick and Steinberg, 1984).

To varying degrees, both these relative and intrinsic worth approaches can call into question current wage structures. By the mid-1980s, one or both frameworks were influential in shaping comparable worth litigation, legislative lobbying, and collective bargaining strategies. For some, however, these approaches present a range of problems. The primary difficulty centers on how to define worth. In this society, salaries are not based solely on relatively objective factors such as the skill, responsibility, and working conditions a job entails; the most cursory comparison of income levels for cabinet officials and fashion models makes the point directly. Pay structures also reflect the scarcity of labor supply and subjective judgments about merit.

Such subjectivity is especially visible in a priori intrinsic worth approaches. Gender biases can enter at any number of points: in the choice and weighting factors to be compensated, in their application to a given job, and in the standards for determining exemptions. How much weight should evaluators accord to particular skills and working conditions? By what criteria should skill be determined?

Some of the difficulties became obvious in one reevaluation study for salaried New York public employees. That study concluded that acquired (and hence compensable) abilities were necessary for zoo keepers in charge of baby animals, but that only innate (and hence noncompensable) abilities were necessary for day care attendants responsible for human infants (Lauter, 1984). To critics, the fuzziness surrounding concepts of job value becomes particularly troubling if comparable worth becomes a major litigation tool in securing occupational equality. Experts using different evaluation systems often come up with quite different rankings for the same job. For courts to preside over battles among experts with no principled basis for choosing between them could impose substantial uncertainties, inconsistencies, and legal costs.

Moreover, to the extent that job reevaluation calls for major upward adjustments in women's salaries, opponents raise further objections. Business leaders typically argue that comparable worth will increase inefficiency and unemployment, decrease competitiveness with foreign manufacturers, encourage women to remain in predominantly female-dominated occupations, and redistribute limited salary resources in favor of white middle-class women at the expense of lower-class minority men (Gold, 1983; Fishel and Lazear, 1986; Weiler, 1986).

However, both the magnitude and the distribution of

such adverse consequences are open to question. Criticism of the "subjectivity" of comparable worth procedures tends to ignore the biases reflected in current wage structures, biases that already distort responses to labor supply and demand. Subjectivity is what we now have; the fact that it is embedded in existing market dynamics does not render it morally just or economically essential. Estimates of the aggregate price of pay equity have ranged between $2 billion and $150 billion, and projections of efficiency and gross national product losses reflect similar variations (Remick and Steinberg, 1984).

On the whole, available research suggests that the costs of pay equity have often been overestimated and the potential benefits underestimated. While comprehensive long-term data are lacking, it does not appear that the growing number of employers here and abroad who have implemented comparable worth reforms have triggered the kinds of inflation, inefficiency, unemployment, or regressive distributional consequences that pay equity opponents generally claim. The typical costs of American reforms, when phased in over a number of years, have been around five to 10 percent of employers' total wage rates (Hartmann, 1987).

Moreover, the same job-evaluation procedures that have exposed evidence of gender bias often have revealed evidence of racial bias as well, and the resulting adjustments have benefited groups disadvantaged on both counts (National Committee on Pay Equity, 1987; Scales-Trent, 1984). Although evidence concerning class is more mixed, some broad-scale comparable worth initiatives have suggested that job evaluation procedures are more likely to reveal overcompensation in male-dominated white collar, not blue collar, jobs (Clauss, 1986). Whatever short-term costs some workers sustain as a result of job reevaluations must also be measured against the potential long-term gains of making compensation criteria explicit and a subject for collective bargaining and organizing strategies.

Much of the objection to pay equity could be minimized if implementation occurred gradually, with some sensitivity to its costs and to the respective competencies of various decisionmakers: courts, legislatures, and participants in collective bargaining. It is well within judges' capabilities and statutory authority to enforce principles of relative worth and to hold employers accountable for salary discrimination that cannot be justified by their own evaluation criteria. Issues of intrinsic worth—that is, judgments about what criteria are most important and how those judgments should be made—can be addressed primarily through political and collective bargaining processes.

Enough public and private sector initiatives are now in place to allow a more comprehensive review of different job reevaluation procedures and their effects on unemployment, inflation, turnover, occupational segregation, worker satisfaction, and income distribution. If adverse consequences of pay equity have emerged, further analysis of policies that might best cushion such effects, such as job retraining, affirmative action, and expanded unemployment compensation, is needed. The research agenda should also explore broader questions surrounding markets, merit, and money. How much consensus is there concerning the relative importance of factors that influence compensation? How closely do public attitudes about what salaries should be correspond to what salaries actually are? What evaluation procedures are most likely to seem fair to the greatest number of constituencies?

As with affirmative action, the most substantial risks of comparable worth are not those that conservatives invoke.

The danger is less that it will prove too radical than that it will not prove radical enough. One disquieting possibility is that some narrow vision of pay equity will prevail, and that concerns about gender will overshadow concerns about race, class, and ethnicity. Narrow incremental reform strategies could result in a modified compensation hierarchy under which the haves still come out far ahead but with more women among them. A related concern is that short-term political objectives could obscure broader normative issues. By cloaking job evaluation with a mantle of seemingly "scientific" objectivity, comparable worth adjustments could insulate wage hierarchies from more searching review.

A more hopeful alternative is that pay equity initiatives will focus attention on fundamental questions not only of gender equality but of social priorities. How should various job and worker attributes be rewarded and how much differentiation across salary levels is appropriate? Are we comfortable with a society that pays more for jobs such as parking attendant than for those such as child care attendant, whatever their male/female composition? Exploring the dynamics of comparable worth can enrich our understanding of class and gender inequalities and of the strategies best able to reduce them.

Inspired by a social vision that emphasizes collective responsibility rather than individual competition, job reevaluation could become a strategy for narrowing economic inequality. It could also prompt a reassessment of paid and unpaid work traditionally done by women. From that vantage, comparable worth is potentially a radical concept, but not in the sense most critics claim. It need not invite the kind of centralized planning reflected in current state-run economies, which have scarcely dispensed with wage hierarchies or ensured gender equality. Rather, pay equity initiatives could help spark a rethinking of the scope of inequality and the ideologies that sustain it.

Employment Policy and Structural Change

If occupational equity is to become a serious national commitment, expressed in social policy as well as in political rhetoric, an array of strategies extending beyond antidiscrimination, affirmative action, or comparable worth mandates is needed. Women's subordinate labor force status is a function of various factors, including sex-role socialization, workplace structures, and domestic constraints. Effective policy responses will require an equally varied set of public and private sector initiatives and a more systematic attempt to assess their relative success.

Although law has limited influence on socialization processes, it could play a more constructive role. Government-funded education, counseling, and vocational and job training programs often affect occupational choices. Yet despite formal mandates of gender equality, such programs have often served more to perpetuate than to counteract sex-role stereotypes.

Vocational education remains highly gender segregated, as do placements under government-sponsored job training programs (Reskin and Hartmann, 1986; Roos and Reskin, 1984). Efforts to improve women's math and science skills and to interest men in traditionally female vocations have been at best sporadic. Too few financial incentives have been available to private employers for programs that challenge occupational segregation through recruitment, training, counseling, and restructured promotion ladders that bridge male- and female-dominated job sectors. All of these areas require greater governmental resources and more systematic study (Reskin and Hartmann, 1986).

Finally, and perhaps most fundamentally, employment-related issues must be conceived as part of a broader political agenda. Men's and women's positions in the labor market are affected by a wide array of public policies concerning education, housing, welfare, tax structure, and social services. Too many of these policies reflect outmoded assumptions about women's secondary labor force status; too few address the structural problems that still confine many women to that role. For almost a century some feminists have sought programs that were better designed to accommodate public and private life: cooperative residential housing, child care and homemaker services, and integrated urban planning sensitive to the needs of single parents and dual-career couples. Current demographic trends have invested such policies with new urgency, not only to promote gender equality in this generation, but to provide decent environments for the next.

Women
in
Brief

Women and Contingent Work

ELIZABETH CONWAY

TEMPORARY, PART-TIME, AND CONTRACT work has a long history in the American labor market, particularly among women workers. Economic uncertainty and changing business practices during the past decade have made these employment patterns increasingly common. Workers on short schedules or under contract now make up one-quarter to one-third of the labor force, and the vast majority of those workers are female.

Economists often use the term "contingent" worker to describe temporary and contract personnel, as well as most part-time and part-year employees. The term refers to the weak bond that exists between these individuals and their employers, often manifested in a lack of job security or employee benefits. Counting the contingent workforce is a difficult task because employment categories overlap, job turnover is high, and labor force statistics do not account for the informality of some work relationships. Admittedly inexact estimates put the number between 29 and 35 million workers and suggest that the contingent workforce has grown more rapidly than the labor force as a whole during the 1980s (Belous, 1989).

Part-time and part-year workers make up the majority of the contingent workforce. In 1987, an average of 19.5 million people worked part time each week, defined by the Bureau of Labor Statistics (BLS) as less than 35 hours per week; 23

million people worked full time for less than a full year. A short schedule does not necessarily consign the person who holds it to the contingent workforce—many teachers, for example, work for only nine months of the year yet receive the same job security and benefits as full-year workers, and some "permanent part-time" workers are treated similarly. A disproportionate number, however, report far lower compensation and less stable working conditions than their counterparts who work full time all year.

Individuals working as temporaries or on contract are contingent workers by nature of their employment arrangements, which explicitly place them outside of the typical employer-employee relationship. Statistics on these workers are not very reliable. The federal government collects data on the temporary help service industry (e.g., Kelly, Manpower, and other suppliers of temporary help), but it does not record the number of temporary workers hired directly by employers. People who take summer or holiday jobs, or who simply fill in for absent employees, no doubt far exceed the 900,000 workers employed as agency temporaries on any given work day.

A great deal of contract work is concentrated in self-employment and the business services industry. An unknown number of the nation's 8.5 million nonagricultural self-employed individuals work as consultants, independent contractors, or subcontractors, selling their services to other individuals or firms. The business services industry, which employs some five million workers, also provides services to other businesses on a contract basis. Jobs in this industry range from janitorial work to trucking to highly skilled computer work. Although many workers in this industry are employees of business services companies, they work under contracts between their own employers and other firms.

The contingent workforce has historically been predominantly female. While men generally required more stable employment, informal work arrangements allowed women to balance their family responsibilities with a role in the market economy. Today, most working women hold permanent, full-time jobs, but women still comprise a majority of contingent workers. In 1987, two-thirds of part-timers and agency temporaries were women. Married women, in particular, frequently turn to part-time or part-year work during their childrearing years.

Contingent work, which is characterized by a lack of job security and low levels of compensation, is concentrated in low-wage service and manufacturing jobs, although different types of contingent work are found in different industries and occupations. Three-quarters of part-time jobs are in sales, clerical, service, and unskilled labor occupations, while only one-sixth are in managerial, professional, and technical fields. Just over half of all agency temporaries work in administrative support positions, and another one-fourth serve as operators, fabricators, or laborers.

Changes in the collection of government statistics make it impossible to analyze the growth of part-time professional employment over the past 10 or 20 years, but anecdotal evidence suggests that it is gradually becoming more common. Temporary help service agencies now hire nurses, accountants, and other professionals, although executives, professionals, and technical workers still account for less than 10 percent of all such temporary employment (Williams, 1989).

Pay and benefits for contingent workers are generally low. Part-time workers make up less than one-sixth of the labor force but account for two-thirds of those receiving minimum and subminimum wages. In 1988, part-time workers had a median wage of $4.68, compared with $7.70 for full-time workers. The concentration of part-timers in low-wage service jobs, as well as the comparative youth and short employment histories of the workers, accounts for much of the wage gap. But a study conducted in the late 1970s found that part-time workers received significantly lower wages even after controlling for these and other important characteristics (Owen, 1978).

Agency temporaries, as a rule, receive higher wages than part-time workers. A recent study found 1987 average hourly wages ranging from $3.72 for construction workers to $24.74 for engineers. Average wages in the administrative support occupations, where most female temporaries work, ranged from $4.74 for messengers to $9.46 for word processors (Williams, 1989). Comparable figures for temporary workers hired directly by employers are not available.

Compensation includes far more than wages. According to the BLS, voluntarily provided benefits (e.g., health insurance, pensions, vacation pay) comprised nearly 20 percent of compensation for an average worker in 1988. In contrast to full-time and permanent workers, however, contingent workers rarely receive benefits other than those required by law. Data from the Census Bureau's Current Population Survey show that only one-quarter of agency temporaries and less than one-third of part-time workers receive health insurance benefits through employment, compared with more than three-quarters of full-time, full-year workers. Similarly, less than 20 percent of part-time workers, but more than one-half of full-time, full-year workers participate in employer pension plans.

Contingent workers often obtain health insurance coverage through a parent's or a spouse's policy, by purchasing individual coverage, or by qualifying for Medicare or Medicaid. Still, more than 20 percent of all part-time workers have no health insurance coverage of any kind (Levitan and Conway, 1988).

Two groups of contingent workers—women moonlighters and independent contractors—are often particularly vulnerable to the absence of benefits. Moonlighting, traditionally undertaken by men with full-time work, is no longer a male preserve. The most recent data indicate that 4.7 percent of working women and 5.9 percent of working men hold second jobs (Stinson, 1986). Men who moonlight generally supplement full-time employment with part-time or second full-time jobs. Almost half of all women who moonlight, however, work at multiple part-time jobs. Although on average they work well over 40 hours per week, these women are treated as part-timers and often receive low wages and inadequate benefits.

Contract workers generally do not receive health or pension benefits from an employer, and the employer does not contribute payroll taxes on their behalf. Nonetheless, a significant number of women workers choose this arrangement because consulting or freelancing gives them control over the nature and conditions of their work. Employers also may prefer this arrangement because it enables them to obtain workers with special skills or to meet demand during busy periods. Some employers have taken this practice one step further, hiring as "independent contractors" workers who are neither independent nor on contract, although controversy exists regarding the extent of this practice (Christensen, 1988). An employee hired under such fraudulent arrangements not only forfeits current benefits but may also receive lower social security and pension benefits later in life.

The growth of dual earner and single-parent families and other social changes should drive more workers into the contingent workforce, but the opposite appears to be happening. The Bureau of Labor Statistics differentiates between voluntary and involuntary part-time workers, a useful distinction when looking at the contingent workforce. Voluntary part-timers are those who work short schedules for noneconomic reasons, generally because they do not want or cannot accept full-time employment. Involuntary part-timers would rather be working full time but are employed part time for a variety of economic reasons, primarily the inability to find full-time employment. In 1988, the labor force included an average of 14 million voluntary and five million involuntary part-time workers; 54 percent of the involuntary part-time workers were women. As women entered the labor force during the 1970s and sought work that did not conflict with homemaking responsibilities, the number of voluntary part-time workers increased greatly. During the 1980s this growth dropped off, as women increasingly accepted full-time jobs.

Involuntary part-time employment, which is a sort of partial unemployment, often foreshadows rising unemployment as employers reduce workers' hours before resorting to layoffs during economic downturn, and then restore full-time hours during economic recovery. Since the mid-1970s, however, involuntary part-time work has stabilized at higher rates during each recovery. After reaching a record high of 6.5 percent of all workers in 1982, it declined somewhat, but it still hovers around five percent, historically high for a recovery.

A most disturbing trend is a shift in the makeup of the involuntary part-time workforce. Until recently, the bulk of this group worked part-time because of slack work, usually a temporary condition. During the recession years of the early

1980s, the number of people affected by slack work increased but not as rapidly as the number unable to find full-time employment. This latter group grew from 38 percent of all involuntary part time workers in 1980 to 51 percent in 1984. Although their number has fallen during the recovery, people unable to find a full-time job still account for half of all involuntary part-timers.

Slack work primarily affects white men, while the inability to find full-time employment disproportionately affects women, minorities, teenagers, and persons without high school diplomas. Persons on reduced schedules because of slack work usually return to full-time status at their present job, but those unable to find full-time positions must change jobs to obtain full-time status. Thus, these workers remain on part-time schedules for longer periods of time than other people who work part time involuntarily, and experience higher levels of poverty and medical indigence (Levitan and Conway, 1988).

The factors that make alternatives to full-time, full-year work attractive to employers and to workers are different and often in conflict with one another. Employers generally look to the bottom line, attempting to reduce labor costs as far as possible, while workers seek to balance employment demands with other responsibilities and/or interests. In such an atmosphere, workers with rare or valuable skills may be able to negotiate acceptable short-time schedules, and secondary wage earners may value time more than career mobility or income and so find part-time work attractive. But many Americans simply cannot afford to work at contingent jobs under current conditions.

Employers traditionally viewed the contingent labor force as secondary earners working for "pin money." As fewer workers fall into this category, but as these jobs continue to become more prevalent, policymakers are beginning to address important issues associated with part-time and temporary jobs. Initiatives by individuals employers, state and federal governments, and advocacy groups offer hope for improved conditions for contingent workers.

The Provident Bank of Cincinnati, for example, originated a program known as "peak time." Part-time tellers at the bank receive higher hourly wages than their full-time counterparts, with the highest hourly pay going to tellers with the fewest or the least convenient hours (Bureau of National Affairs, 1986). Peak-time policies at the Provident Bank, as tends to be the case elsewhere, do not include fringe benefits, a factor that makes these jobs unacceptable for most primary earners. Improving the wages of contingent workers nonetheless represents an important step forward.

Other employers offer part-time or job-sharing options that include prorated wages and benefits. Under these policies, employers apply the same wage and benefit scales used for full-time workers, allotting them proportionally to hours worked. A worker employed half time, for example, would receive half the vacation time available to a full-time worker. The employer also pays a prorated portion of the premiums for insurance, pension, and other benefits, and the employee pays the remainder. The Association of Part-Time Professionals, an advocacy group, has taken a leading role in support of prorated benefits. Congresswoman Patricia Schroeder introduced a bill that would require employers to provide prorated health and pension coverage to part-time workers if they cover their full-time employees.

Congress included a section in the Tax Reform Act of 1986 that will force some employers to provide more benefits to their part-time workers. Under the new rule, employers who receive tax breaks for offering health, pension, and other fringe benefits will have to prove that higher-paid employees do not receive a disproportionate share of the benefits. Employers who deny benefits to a large number of part-time workers will face significant tax penalties as a result.

In 1987, the State of New Hampshire passed a law designed to alleviate insurance company discrimination against part-time workers. The law does not require employers to provide insurance benefits to part-time workers—states are prohibited from passing such laws—but it requires insurers to include part-timers in group policies when requested to do so.

Part-time, temporary, and other contingent workers also would benefit from many of the initiatives proposed for low-income workers in general. An increase in the minimum wage, efforts to extend health insurance to the uninsured, and tax breaks for low-wage earners are examples of such proposals. Perhaps the most fortuitous development of all would be the labor shortage that may emerge as a result of birth rates that have been falling since the 1960s. Such a shortage, if it materializes, could drive compensation to higher levels and enable more workers to negotiate better wage and hour packages with their employers.

In this time of tension between work and family demands, alternatives to full-time permanent jobs are more critical than ever, especially to women workers. A small but growing number of innovative workers, employers, and government bodies are attempting to create working arrangements that meet the needs of both workers and employers. These pioneers may point the way to improved treatment for all short-schedule or contingent workers.

Women in Medical School

IN FEW AREAS HAVE WOMEN'S changing educational aspirations
and opportunities been more apparent than in the field of
medicine. Barriers that women historically encountered in
attempting to enter medical schools have for the most part
been eliminated, and the results have been impressive. In
1985-86, women were awarded nearly one-third of all medical
degrees, up from just over 10 percent in the early 1970s. As of
1988, there were over 100,000 female physicians, or more
than double the number in 1975. Further inroads into this
traditionally male occupation can be expected if the proportion of women gaining admission to medical schools continues to rise.

Although a steady increase in women's representation
among entering medical students actually began in the 1920s,
progress was relatively slow until much later in the century.
The largest leap in the number of female medical school applicants occurred during the first half of the 1970s, when their
numbers nearly quadrupled, rising from under 2,300 to just
over 8,700. Women were less than nine percent of the applicant pool in 1970; within five years, they were over 20 percent. By 1988, more than 10,000 women—almost 40 percent
of the total—were applying to medical school.

Several forces were at work to explain this increase. An
overall change in women's aspirations was engendered by the
feminist movement. In addition, the enactment of Title IX of

the Education Amendments of 1972, coupled with the commitment of individual medical schools to grant equal opportunity for women, opened up the nation's medical classrooms
to women.

Although women have been less likely than men to apply
to medical school, in most years acceptance rates for women
have compared favorably to those of men. In fact, throughout
much of the 1970s, women were somewhat more likely than
men to be accepted. For example, in 1973, 40 percent of the
female medical school applicants, but only 35 percent of the
male applicants, were accepted. Since 1978, acceptance rates
for men have inched ahead.

The majority—six out of 10—of medical school applicants are relatively young, i.e., under 23, and differences by
sex are minor. Acceptance rates are higher for the younger
applicants, and younger male applicants are more likely to be
accepted than younger females are. However, in the "upper"
ages, the acceptance rate for women is greater. In 1988, for
example, 34 percent of the female applicants over the age of
38 were accepted into medical school; the comparable figure
for male applicants was 27 percent.

Overall figures obscure wide variations among medical
schools. According to data from the *Medical School Admission
Requirements 1990-91* (Association of American Medical Colleges, 1989), the proportion of new students who are women
ranges from 57 percent at the Medical College of Pennsylvania to 17 percent at the University of Utah. Women comprise less than 25 percent of new students at only two of the
nation's 127 medical schools and more than 40 percent of the
new students at 26 schools.

The sharp increase in acceptance rates (from about one-
third to three-fifths) for male and female applicants reflects

the fact that the total number of applicants has declined by over 30 percent in the past 15 years. In 1973, more than 40,000 hopefuls applied to medical school, but by 1988, there were slightly more than 26,700 applicants. All other things being equal, as an applicant pool shrinks, the probability of being accepted increases. The shrinking applicant pool is due to the fact that the number of men applying to medical schools is about half of what it was in the mid-1970s (see Table 25 in the statistical appendix to this book). Slightly fewer women are applying to medical school today than was the case from about 1980 to 1985, but the proportion of applicants who are female continues to climb.

There is considerable speculation over the reasons for the steady decline in the overall number of applications to medical school, which started 10 years before the country began experiencing a decline in the number of 22-year-old men. Currently, the proportion of male college students applying to medical schools is approaching four percent, which is lower than at any time since 1960. Women medical school applicants as a percentage of all college graduates rose above two percent for the first time in 1974; since then, that figure has remained fairly stable.

Clearly, many factors influence decisions about fields of study in general and medicine in particular. Not surprisingly, some potential male candidates, as well as some female candidates, are discouraged from pursuing medical careers by the well-publicized oversupply of specialists, high malpractice premiums, an increase in government regulations, high tuition costs, and the long, grueling internship and residency requirements needed to complete training. However, many women who at one time would have entered teaching or nursing now find becoming a doctor very attractive, despite those conditions that make it less attractive to some men.

Any guess about whether or when the proportion of medical school applicants who are women will level off would be just that—a guess. But as long as women's academic credentials continue to equal those of men, medical schools are likely to continue to welcome their applications.

Analyses of applicants' grade point averages (GPAs) indicate that women's overall college GPA is slightly above that of men, while their science average is slightly below. Women score higher on the reading skills subtest of the Medical College Admission Test (MCAT); men do better when it comes to biology, chemistry, physics, science problems, and quantitative skills (Tudor, 1988).

However, a recent study at a midwestern medical school suggests extra caution in interpreting women's GPAs and MCAT scores (Calkins, Arnold, and Willoughby, 1987). For men, cognitive characteristics, such as high school class rank, were the best predictors of clerkship grades and internship performance; for women, noncognitive characteristics, e.g., psychosocial qualities, were the best predictors. These noncognitive qualities were rated from letters of recommendation, the medical school interview, and previous work experience in health care.

Medical School Performance

Once women have enrolled in medical school, their academic performance is virtually indistinguishable from men's. They tend to outperform men in two areas—obstetrics/gynecology and patient interviewing skills (see Plauche and Miller, 1986; Preven et al., 1986; Weinberg and Rooney, 1973). However, studies also show that women medical students experience more depression and anxiety than men do (Lloyd and Gartell, 1981), and while medical training places a strain on the personal lives of both sexes, more women than men report that personal relationships come to an end because of the medical school grind (Clark and Reiker, 1986).

The reasons why women experience more stress are common to professional women in other fields. Fewer same-sex role models, less help at home, and lingering forms of discrimination are the chief culprits. A study of the gender climate at a midwestern medical school found that women students experience relatively little discrimination from patients, non-physician staff or peers, but that some faculty members still function on the basis of sex-role stereotypes. Interestingly, however, women students perceive that their male classmates experience more gender-based discrimination from patients than they do, especially during clerkships in pediatrics and obstetrics/gynecology (Grant, 1988).

A survey by the Association of American Medical Colleges (AAMC) sheds some light on differences in the way men and women experience medical school. As freshmen, women report less parental support for their decision to study medicine; perhaps reflecting this, only 61 percent of the female students, compared to 70 percent of the males, said they were very confident of their ability to succeed in medical school (Bickel, 1988). Male students also come from somewhat more affluent families. For example, mean parental income is higher among male students ($74,167 vs. $66,627 in 1987), which may partially explain the fact that women arrive at medical school with higher educational debts ($14,462 vs. $10,699). This debt gap continues through medical school, with the result that women who graduated in 1987 had an average debt of $37,400, compared to $34,700 for men. Debt is a greater problem for minorities; among black women, for example, the average debt was $7,000 more than it was for white women in 1987.

Female first-year medical students are more interested than men in the people-oriented and prevention-related aspects of medicine. Forty-three percent of the females and 34 percent of the males rated "working with patients to prevent illness" as the most important physician service. This finding sheds light on seniors' assessment of the adequacy of their medical school instruction. More often than men, women report that medical schools provide insufficient emphasis on patients' socioeconomic and emotional problems, public health, nutrition, and cost containment (ibid.).

Career Choices

Factors in addition to personal goals and aptitudes affect the choice of a particular career within medicine. These include changing predictions of physician supply and specialty needs. Decisions must be made about type of practice (health maintenance organization [HMO], group practice, etc.) and geographic location. Female graduates are somewhat less likely than men to predict that they will enter private practice (53 percent vs. 60 percent of 1987 graduates) and, conversely, are more likely to predict a salaried practice (14 percent vs. 10 percent). They are also slightly more likely to see full-time academic appointments in their futures (30 percent vs. 28 percent). These predictions correspond to existing patterns: female physicians practice more frequently than males in salaried positions in medical schools, clinics, and HMOs; men are more likely to choose office-based practices (Bowman and Gross, 1986). American Medical Association data also confirm that women physicians are playing relatively larger roles in ambulatory care clinics and HMOs. For example, in 1986, 22 percent of all women physicians with HMO contracts were full-time HMO doctors; this was true of only five percent of the men (Emmons, 1988).

When it comes to plans about specialties, male/female differences have changed relatively little in recent years. Women still prefer careers in primary care and obstetrics to a greater extent than men do; men, in contrast, more often prefer surgery. The proportion of both sexes who are interested in internal medicine, family practice, and pediatrics has been declining, but the decline has been steeper among men.

Plans on relocating to a socioeconomically deprived area are more common among graduating women than among men (20 percent vs. 13 percent in 1987). This is one area in which white and black students differ dramatically. Fifty-five percent of the 1987 black male and female graduates—but only 17 percent of white women and 10 percent of white men—intended to work in a deprived area.

Medical School Faculty

Despite the marked increase in the number and proportion of female medical students and physicians throughout the 1970s and 1980s, women are still finding it difficult to assume a proportional role in the administration of medical schools; the next battle might be to play a much more significant role in the running of the nation's medical schools.

The percentage of women medical school graduates joining medical school faculties has consistently exceeded the figure for men. For instance, 14 percent of the women and 10 percent of the men who graduated in 1961 are currently full-time medical school faculty members. Yet as of 1987, women were still only 19 percent of all medical school faculty members (up from 13 percent 20 years earlier). And only 53 per-

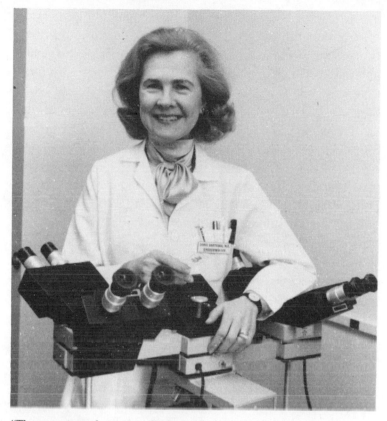

"The percentage of women medical school graduates joining medical school faculties has consistently exceeded the figure for men, [although] as of 1987, women were still only 19 percent of all medical school faculty members." One woman who has advanced in academic medicine is Dr. Doris G. Bartuska, professor of medicine and director of the Division of Endocrinology and Metabolism at the Medical College of Pennsylvania.
Courtesy American Medical Women's Association

cent of those women had M.D. degrees; the comparable figure for men was 70 percent.

As the number of women physicians keeps growing, this gender difference will narrow. But other trends, such as the gap remaining between men and women attaining the ranks of associate professor and professor, demand more consideration. Of faculty members holding M.D. degrees who were first appointed in 1976, 12 percent of the men, but only three percent of the women, held the rank of professor 10 years later.

This gap between the advancement of men and women into the upper echelons of academic medicine is the result of several factors, few of which have been systematically investigated. Studies show that women physicians' careers do not build in as sustained a way as men's do (Lorber, 1984) and that the average number of years of promotion to each faculty rank is greater for women (Wallis, Gilder, and Thaler, 1981). Women face particular challenges in the field of research, where productivity is a major prerequisite to academic advancement. They have more difficulty in finding the right sponsor and mentor, and in deciding whether and how to put research above all other goals during a time when patient care and child rearing are also likely to be priorities.

The Future for Women in Medicine

In viewing the increase of women medical students over the last two decades, one arrives at an inevitable question: Will women ever comprise the majority of physicians in the United States? In 1988, women were 20 percent of all physicians, nearly triple the seven percent figure for 1967. Furthermore, over 42 percent of women physicians were under age 35, compared to only about 25 percent of men (American Medical Association, 1987), which suggests that as the physician population ages, it will become increasingly female. On the other hand, males still outnumber female medical students by a good margin, so the answer to the question may depend on such factors as retirement patterns and whether the proportion of women in the medical school applicant pool continues to climb.

Perhaps a question more pertinent than whether women will ever become a majority of the nation's doctors is what an increase in their numbers means to the quality of medical practice. Past comparisons indicate that women physicians work fewer hours per week, see fewer patients per hour, and are more likely to be in part-time practice than men. These differences are beginning to narrow, a fact that may be related more to male physicians working less than to females working more (Bowman and Gross, 1986).

But one possibility is that women see fewer patients because they spend more time with each patient. Moreover, in rating physicians, trained observers say that female physicians are more respectful and egalitarian in their relationships with patients; they interrupt patients less, and they are more likely to engage in therapeutic listening and counseling than male physicians (Arnold, Martin, and Parker, 1988). If women keep bringing these qualities into the practice of medicine, their increasing numbers are clearly good news for patients.

Women in Business

FAITH H. ANDO

WOMEN HAVE BEEN STARTING BUSINESSES in such record numbers in recent years that the proportion of businesses owned by women—which was 25 percent of the 12 million U.S. firms in 1982—may reach 50 percent by the year 2000 (U.S. Congress, 1988). It is therefore time for the American business sector to pay more attention to women business owners and their firms. Who are these women? Why are so many of them opting to become their own bosses? How are their businesses faring? What determines success or failure?

The 1982 Characteristics of Business Owners (CBO), an important data base that is rich in information on more than 100,000 business owners and their firms, provides an answer to some of these and other questions about women business owners. (The CBO is further described in Ando, 1988b and U.S. Bureau of the Census, August 1987.)

According to the Census Bureau, there were 2.9 million women-owned businesses in the United States in 1982, the latest year for which Census data are available. The vast majority—93 percent (or 2.7 million)—were sole proprietorships; nearly five percent (134,000) were women-owned partnerships, and another three percent (89,000) were women-owned subchapter S corporations. The Census Bureau did not collect information on the number of non-subchapter S corporations in 1982. (A subchapter S corporation is a special Internal Revenue Service designation that enables corporations with 25 or fewer shareholders to elect to be taxed as individuals rather than as corporations. This results in certain tax advantages.)[1]

Overall, minority women—who were approximately 20 percent of the total female population in the United States in 1982, but who owned only seven percent of the women-owned firms—are clearly underrepresented among women business owners. Underrepresentation is characteristic of black women, who were 12 percent of the female population in 1982 but only 3.5 percent of women business owners, and Hispanic women, more than six percent of the female population and two percent of the female owners. In contrast, Asian women were 1.7 percent of both the total female population and the female owner population (Ando, 1988b; U.S. Bureau of the Census, December 1983b and January 1988).

Unfortunately, the 1982 CBO provides few insights into the reasons *why* these women decided to go into business for themselves; in fact, scholarly research on this important issue is relatively rare. Nonetheless, it is generally assumed that women who start businesses are motivated by some of the same factors that encourage men to go into business, as well as by some that distinguish them from men.

On the one hand, women—like men—may relish the risks and thrills of starting and managing businesses of their own, of being their own bosses. On the other hand, particular workforce patterns and experiences more common to women (see Barrett, 1987) may also influence women's entrepreneurial decisions. First, women's employment opportunities may be less promising or rewarding than those of men with comparable skills, abilities, and training. Entrepreneurship may be regarded as a means to overcome occupational segregation and/or wage and benefit discrepancies, enabling women to put their talents to better use.

Second, women with primary responsibility for young

children may have problems finding acceptable and/or affordable child care. Although there are many disadvantages to working with small children around, entrepreneurship may enable women to adjust the timing or number of work hours per week while meeting child care responsibilities.

Third, many women who reenter the labor force after years of performing unpaid work in the home may find that previous employment skills have atrophied and/or that employers dismiss or diminish the relevance to paid work of homemaking skills. Job opportunities may be limited, so for some of these women, entrepreneurship is a way to capitalize on organizational skills acquired or polished during the years of caring for and managing a home.

The 1982 Characteristics of Business Owners data base is an especially fruitful source of information on the characteristics of women (and men) who have become owners. Analysts can turn to the data base to examine two important issues, namely (1) whether women business owners, regardless of race or ethnicity, resemble one another more than they do men owners of the same race or ethnicity or (2) whether women business owners of a particular racial or ethnic group are more similar to their male counterparts than they are to other women business owners. In other words, when it comes to factors that may have an impact on business success or failure, does sex dominate ethnicity or does ethnicity dominate sex? The answer is by no means clear-cut: in some instances, gender appears to be more important than race or ethnicity (referred to simply as ethnicity in the rest of this chapter), while in others, ethnicity appears to "explain more" than gender.

This chapter looks at Asian, black, Hispanic, and nonminority female business owners. These women are compared

to one another and to their male counterparts along a number of dimensions selected because of their prominence in
research on minority entrepreneurship (Ando, 1988a).[2] Demographic, socioeconomic, and entrepreneurial characteristics of the owner, as well as access to capital, all play a role in
business start-up and performance.

For example, because there are substantial human and
financial capital transfers within a marriage (Benham, 1974;
Mincer and Polachek, 1974), a married business owner has
potential access to a source of human and financial capital for
investment that is unavailable to a never-married owner.
Thus, other things being equal, a firm belonging to a married
owner will do better or outperform a firm owned by someone
who has never married.

Most business owners are married, but differences—especially by sex—are apparent. About 72 percent of nonminority female owners—but 85 percent of nonminority male
owners—in the CBO survey were married. Regardless of ethnicity, female owners were considerably less likely than their
male counterparts to be married (74 percent of Asian women
and almost 88 percent of Asian men, nearly 55 percent of
black women and 82 percent of black men, 72 percent of
Hispanic women and 86 percent of Hispanic men). Thus,
when it comes to marital status, sex dominates ethnicity. To
the extent that human and financial capital transfers within a
marriage have an impact on a firm's performance, these statistics suggest that—all other things being equal—firms owned
by women will be outperformed by those owned by men.

Whether a business owner has completed at least one year
of college and whether he or she has had any managerial
experience in paid employment have been identified as the
most important components of an owner's "human capital"

determining a minority firm's performance (Ando, 1988a).
Each factor also has an effect on an owner's financial capital. In evaluating credit risk, banks may consider a loan applicant's educational attainment and consider someone with more education the more promising risk. In addition, the higher salaries typically associated with managerial positions may enable potential business owners with that experience to accumulate more net worth than those without it to apply toward the start-up of a firm. (Of course, education and managerial experience are likely to be correlated: employers use education as a device to identify potential managers [Riley, 1979; Spence, 1974; Stiglitz, 1975].)

As for the years of formal education, the CBO survey found that 53 percent of nonminority female *and* male business owners had completed one or more years of college. Gender differences among the three ethnic groups studied were as follows: one or more years of college had been completed by 71 percent of the female Asian business owners and 74 percent of the Asian men, 51 percent of the black women and 44 percent of black men, and 39 percent of both the female and male Hispanic owners. Thus, when analyzing education, ethnicity seems to dominate sex, i.e., each group of women business owners is closer to its comparable group of men business owners than to each other. Insofar as this measure of educational attainment has an impact on business performance, one would expect the businesses of Asians to fare best, followed by those owned by nonminorities, blacks, and then Hispanics.

The picture is different when it comes to previous managerial experience in paid employment, which is less common among women. Forty percent of nonminority female business owners, but 56 percent of their male counterparts, had been employed in a managerial capacity before going into business for themselves. This was true of only 38 percent of Asian women but 51 percent of Asian men, 37 percent of black women and 44 percent of black men, and 32 percent of Hispanic women and 46 percent of Hispanic men.

Thus, when it comes to managerial experience, sex appears to dominate ethnicity. Each group of women business owners is more similar to the other groups of women than to their male counterparts. Again, other things being equal, to the extent that prior managerial experience affects a firm's performance, women-owned firms will be outperformed by those owned by men.

A key question that evolves from the above discussion is, of course, how women-owned businesses actually perform. The CBO contains four measures of a firm's performance, two of which—sales or receipts and firm survival—were analyzed for this chapter.[3]

If receipts are the sole measure of performance, women-owned firms, regardless of the ethnicity of the owner, do not perform as well as those owned by men. For example, 54 percent of the firms owned by nonminority women—but only 37 percent of those owned by nonminority men—had receipts or sales of less than $5,000 in 1982. Sales of less than $5,000 were reported by 47 percent of the Asian female owners and 34 percent of the Asian males owners, 57 percent of black female owners and 43 percent of black males, and 48 percent of Hispanic females and 31 percent of Hispanic males.

While there are many reasons, both voluntary and involuntary, why a firm may go out of business, (and while an apparently successful business may actually be foundering), firm continuity is—at least on the surface—one measure of positive performance. The CBO survey has data on whether a firm survived until 1986, the year the survey was mailed to respondents. Among CBO respondents, male-owned firms were more likely to survive than those owned by females, a difference that held for minority and nonminority respondents. The percentages of firms surviving to 1986 were as follows: nonminority women, 58 percent, nonminority men 65 percent; Asian women, 58 percent, Asian men, 66 percent; black women, 51 percent, black men 62 percent; Hispanic women, 55 percent, Hispanic men, 64 percent.

Sales and survival are probably highly correlated, that is, if a firm had receipts of under $5,000, its owner was more likely to end operations by 1986, other factors being equal. However, other things may not always be equal, and there are be several reasons why an owner might tolerate low receipts for a relatively long period of time.

One reason that low receipts might be tolerated is that they might be temporary, especially in a start-up firm. Although receipts in a new business are often modest, owners expect earnings to improve. A second reason for low receipts is that business ownership may be a side activity or a secondary source of income. For example, a college teacher might be a consultant on the side, relying on his/her academic salary as the main source of income.

Third, it has been suggested that some married women who can afford to tolerate low receipts choose to do so when their paid employment alternatives include only part-time, low-income jobs. This possibility raises the issue of the "opportunity costs of doing business," which is simply a comparison of actual self-employment income with the wages or salary that might have been earned in paid employment. Because women typically earn less than men, their business opportunity costs are lower. That lower opportunity costs may have had implications for the entrepreneurship of women in the CBO survey is evident in the finding that although women-owned firms had smaller profits than those owned by men, women were less likely than men to cite insufficient profits as the primary reason for discontinuing their businesses.

However, the CBO survey also reveals that married women, perhaps because of the human and financial capital transfers discussed above, had financial returns from their businesses that were substantially above those of never-married women. Firms owned by married nonminority women in 1982, for example, averaged $18,863 in 1982 receipts, compared to an average of $10,010 for never-married nonminority women.

Studies of minority entrepreneurship reveal that the most critical component of a firm's start-up capital is the amount of noninstitutional equity seed capital available, that is, the amount of informal equity (non-borrowed money) contributed by the owner and the owner's spouse, other family members, and friends (Ando, 1988a; Chen et al., 1982). Access to commercial bank credit is viewed as a second-best, albeit important, financing choice for minorities.

However, women business owners have identified commercial bank loans as the prime financial ingredient in determining a firm's performance (Castro, 1988; U.S. Congress, 1988). The CBO survey considered only two factors on access to bank credit: whether an owner (1) borrowed money from a bank to acquire a business and/or (2) cited insufficient financing as the chief reason the business did not survive. Unfortunately, the survey does not indicate whether an owner applied for a bank loan but was rejected. Nor can risk of default be evaluated from the available data. Nonetheless, according to the CBO survey, bank loans were generally less common among female owners; they had been taken out by 61 percent of nonminority female owners and 66 percent of nonminority males, 46 percent of Asian female and male owners, 50 percent of black female and 57 percent of black male owners, and 51 percent of Hispanic female and male owners.

On the whole, very few owners blamed insufficient financing as the chief cause of firm nonsurvival. Each group of female owners was slightly less likely than its corresponding group of male owners to cite inadequate funding. Among women, the percentages ranged from one percent in the case of nonminorities to five percent for blacks; the figures for men were about twice as high, ranging from two percent among nonminorities to nine percent among blacks.

The 1982 Characteristics of Business Owners survey leaves many questions about business owners unanswered. Nonetheless, while information on women business owners is still sketchy, it is improving in scope and quality, and the CBO survey adds greatly to our knowledge base of this growing group of entrepreneurs. Given some of the projections about women business owners, even more attention needs to be paid to who these women are, why they see ownership as an attractive alternative, and the methods they are using to make their American dream come true.

Behind the Scenes:
Women in Television

SALLY STEENLAND

ALTHOUGH MORE WOMEN than ever before are employed in the television entertainment industry, many of them in decision-making positions, it is still much more difficult for women than for men to get jobs and promotions in that business. Despite almost two decades of rising female employment in television networks and production studios, the top jobs remain largely male-dominated. Furthermore, like women in many other fields, women in the television industry too often end up in occupational ghettoes rather than in those industry jobs considered nontraditional for females, e.g., writing for action-adventure shows or producing. As is true in other industries, females employed in television generally earn less than their male counterparts, even when controlling for such variables as type of job and job tenure, among other factors.

An examination of the most recent data available on women working in three key television job slots—as producers, directors, and writers—shows the extent of women's progress and how far they still have to go.

Producers

Women are employed as producers, supervising producers, and coproducers on a number of programs, although they have yet to make substantial inroads among executive producers, who are at the top of the producer pecking order. (In general, producers oversee the budget and logistics of program episodes.) Women worked as producers of some type on half of the 20 top Nielson-rated shows of the 1986-87 television season. On nine of them, the women shared producer credits with men. However, women were executive producers of only four of the 20 top-rated shows. On three of these, they shared executive producer credits with men. Only one program—"My Sister Sam"—was produced solely by a woman.

When one shifts the analysis and examines the total number of producers who are female, rather than the number of shows with one or more female producers, the picture is even less rosy. The total number of producers is quite high, since each program employs several. However, although the 20 top-rated shows of the 1986-87 season employed a total of 101 producers, only 21 were female.

The trend in the following year was not encouraging. The 26 new TV shows of the 1987-88 fall season employed a total of 113 producers, of whom only 16—or 14 percent—were female. Only nine of the new shows (35 percent) employed women as producers of any type, and on only three (12 percent) were women part of the executive producer team.

By some accounts, the 1988-89 television season seemed to have been a step forward for women. Two premiering shows, "Roseanne" and "Murphy Brown," contained strong female leads as well as women producers behind the scenes. Furthermore, both programs enjoyed critical and ratings success. However, the high visibility of these shows should not obscure the overall employment figures for women. A selection of 20 programs airing during the 1988-89 season reveals that out of 107 producers, 15 were women. Moreover, women were part of the executive producing team on only three of the 20 shows.

Directors

The job of director is a nontraditional one for women in the television entertainment industry. The director holds a position of visible authority, not only over a cast but also over a crew that may be largely or entirely male, and over the handling of technical equipment. It is the position in which the fewest women can be found.

Of the 20 top-rated programs of the 1986-87 season, only six (30 percent) employed any women directors at all during the entire year. On only two of these shows ("Amen" and "My Sister Sam") did women direct over half of the season's episodes. In fact, on average, women directed only 12 percent of all the episodes of the season's 20 top-rated programs.

Writers

More women are employed as television writers than as producers or directors, but women writers are more likely to be freelancers than to be employed on the staff of a show.

Freelancers have less steady employment than staff writers, less influence over the final versions of their own scripts, and virtually no influence over the developing story lines of a show. Moreover, freelancers are denied opportunities open to staff writers, who—after a few seasons with a show—often move up to producer level, which means more money and more creative control.

Of the top 20 shows of the 1986-87 season, 17 (85 percent) hired women writers at some point during the year.

Only "Amen," "Murder, She Wrote," and "Falcon Crest" had no scripts written by women during the entire season. However, on only two programs ("Who's the Boss" and "My Sister Sam") were more than half of the writers women. On average, women accounted for 21 percent of the writers employed over the season on the 17 shows that had hired women writers.

Salaries are another measure of workplace equality or inequality in the television industry. In May 1989, the Writers Guild released a major study of television and film industry employment patterns relating to employees' gender, race and ethnicity, and age (Bielby and Bielby, 1989). The study, which covered the period from 1982 to 1987, included the following major findings concerning women writers:

- In 1987, women writers for television and film earned only 63 cents for every dollar earned by white male writers, a drop from 73 cents in 1982.

- From 1982 to 1987, over three-quarters of all the writers employed in television and film were white males.

- Although the earnings gap between men and women who began their writing careers in 1982 was not large in the early years (less than $1,000 in 1983), women did not sustain their career momentum.

- For minority female writers, the numbers are worse. From 1982 to 1987, minority writers (both women and men) accounted for only two percent of all writers employed in television and film.

Overall, the statistics about women in the television industry show that women have yet to achieve a critical mass in any of the three occupations discussed in this chapter. (Critical mass, thought to be achieved when a minority holds about 30 percent of the jobs, seems to be necessary before the minority can exert real influence and make change.) In addition, the data show employment patterns in television that at best only parallel overall employment patterns for women—and in some cases appear to be worse.

And the numbers do not tell the behind-the-scenes stories. Anecdotes abound of talented women unable to find work while mediocre men find themselves in great demand; of a double standard whereby female failure carries a personal stigma, while male failure is seen as valuable experience; of sexual harassment that must be dealt with, yet not reported lest a woman become known as a "troublemaker."

However, the reasons for women's lack of equality are difficult to document in an industry with a high failure rate for both sexes and an idiosyncratic operating style. Persons working in this tough, intensely competitive, and risky industry offer varying views of women's employment prospects.

Some insiders claim that the barriers impeding women's rise in the industry rest with women themselves, i.e., women need to become more competitive, more assertive, and more willing to take risks. Women, so this argument goes, need to learn the rules of working in a male-dominated business and to play by them. When women learn to adapt their behavior and attitudes to the industry culture, their employment problems will be solved.

Not all insiders agree with this perspective, however. Those who disagree argue that sex discrimination and bias run strongly throughout the television entertainment industry. In fact, some see it as a closed, backward industry where personal compatibility and the "right chemistry" rank unusu-

Barbara Corday, executive vice president of prime time programs for CBS, one of the highest ranking positions in entertainment television. *Courtesy CBS*

ally high in hiring and promotion decisions. In a business that relies heavily on informal social groupings, women lack access to opportunities that advance their careers; thus, they remain stuck at lower levels—if they are hired in the first place. Their male colleagues, on the other hand, readily find mentors who help them to move up. According to this view, real progress for women in the television industry will not occur until industry practices of sex discrimination begin to change.

Increasing women's opportunities for employment and advancement in the television industry is an issue of simple fairness, but most Hollywood insiders agree that increased numbers of women would bring about noticeable changes in both the process and the product of television.

Many believe that with more women in key jobs, outmoded industry practices based on "macho" concepts would be questioned and replaced by more commonsense methods of work, and that there would be greater sensitivity to the demands of balancing job and family. Further, with more women in creative control behind the camera, the image of women in front of the camera would be more authentic and multidimensional. Subjects that are of particular interest to women—but perceived as unimportant or taboo to men—might find their way onto the screen.

These hypotheses have yet to be proven. But although women's progress is slower than it should be, more women are employed in the television industry than ever before, and they are primed for power. Many women are working their way up through the network and production studio ranks, and others are independent producers and entrepreneurs.

Whether or not the television industry is moved by appeals for simple workplace equity, it is in the industry's self-interest to move women up. By their sheer numbers and ability, women can expand the talent pool, increase the diversity of television programming, and improve the industry's long-range strategic planning.

Women in Art

ELSA HONIG FINE

IN 1905, W. S. SPARROW, in *Women Painters of the World*, sought to prove that although male and female "genius" may differ, "there is room in the garden of art for flowers of every kind," and only those who do not think would ask: "Where is there a woman artist equal to any man among the great masters?" In 1971, Linda Nochlin posed a similar question in "Why Have There Been No Great Women Artists?" One of her conclusions was that it was not genetics but society itself that prevented "greatness" in women from developing. "Art is not a free, autonomous activity of a super-endowed individual . . . but rather . . . occur[s] in a social situation, [is an] integral element of this social structure, and [is] mediated and determined by specific and definable social institutions . . ." (Nochlin, 1971: 32). Thus, she refuted the "golden nugget of genius" and other myths developed around male artists.

Dabbling in the arts has always been an acceptable female pastime. Indeed, in the nineteenth century, when, because of demographic changes, there emerged in the United States and Europe significant numbers of "redundant" women (unmarried middle-class women needing to support themselves), many turned their feminine artistic "accomplishments" into fee-paying work with little loss of status. They worked as china and pottery painters and illustrated children's books and stories in ladies magazines. They were colorists in graphics studios, copyists at the Louvre, and plan tracers in architectural offices. They began taking private students.

Women's colleges were the first to develop comprehensive art history programs and art museums to prepare their graduates to be consumers, connoisseurs, and volunteers; only recently, however, have they prepared women to be professionals. Many of the women who have become professionals—on art faculties and in museums—still are underpaid and outranked. (It is only in this decade that women have been appointed art department chairs or museum directors.)

While historically a majority of gallery owners have been women—a phenomenon that can be viewed as an extension of women's traditional role of nurturer—most galleries are reluctant to house too many women in their stables. Women's art does not sell well, states the myth, and is a bad investment. (None of the works auctioned for high prices during the 1988 auction mania in New York City and London were done by women.)

Fearful that their criticism would not be taken seriously, many women critics were reluctant in their advocacy of women artists. Higher ranked art historians hesitated in their support of dissertations on women artists and courses on women in art. In recent years, both situations have changed. Respected critics such as Lucy Lippard and Arlene Raven publish feminist criticism in mainstream journals; dissertations on Mary Cassatt, Berthe Morisot, Cecilia Beaux, Suzanne Valdon, Miriam Schapiro, and Irene Rice Pereira, among others, have been completed or are in process; courses on women artists, once consigned to interim sessions or off-peak hours, are oversubscribed and continue to proliferate in institutions throughout the United States.

Research and Writing

When I went to the card catalogs in the mid-1970s to begin research on *Women and Art: A History of Women Painters and Sculptors from the Renaissance to the 20th Century* (Fine, 1978), most of the books I found were variations on "how to paint beautiful women" or the "100 most beautiful women in art." Aside from some artists' memoirs and a few monographs and exhibition catalogs, the bulk of material for *Women and Art* came from biographies of famous male artists, many of whom were married to or the fathers of talented women.

The new wave of feminism had stimulated many feminist art historians, and the mid-1970s saw the publication of several surveys: Eleanor Tufts's *Our Hidden Heritage* (1974), Cindy Nemser's *Art Talk* (1975) (interviews with contemporary women), Karen Petersen's and J. J. Wilson's *Women Artists: Recognition and Reappraisal* (1976), and Hugo Munsterberg's *A History of Women Artists* (1975). These books were "additive," designed for the most part to supplement the predominantly male-dominated texts used in introductory art history courses. Responding to pressure from (and threats of boycotts by) feminists, the mid-1980s revisions of these introductory texts included token representations of women. Although American feminists pioneered in the extrication of women artists hidden in the history of other countries, it was not until 1982 that a survey of American women artists was published: Charlotte S. Rubinstein's *American Women Artists: From Early Indian Times to the Present*. (Her survey of American women sculptors is forthcoming.)

The first periodical devoted to women in the arts, *The Feminist Art Journal*, was founded in 1972 and ended with Volume 6, Number 2 in the summer of 1977. New York-based, it had as its goals to be the woman artist's voice in the art world, to improve the status of women artists, and to expose sexist exploitation and discrimination. Perhaps its most important legacy was articles on women's traditional art (see Rom, 1981/82: 19-24). This serious consideration of "crafts" by feminist art historians is also part of current art historical revisionism—the recognition that artists other than the "masters" can contribute to our understanding of the art of a period; that "bad" art can be as instructive in understanding a period as "good" art, and, indeed, that there is no such thing as "bad" art; and that artisans as well as fine artists are worthy of study.

The *Feminist Art Journal* also published original research on historical and contemporary women artists, as did *Womanart*, whose eight issues were published in New York in the late 1970s.

Feminist researchers in the 1970s took several directions. Some celebrated vaginal imagery; others looked for commonalities in women's art. Judy Chicago celebrated 39 great women in history with *The Dinner Party*, which focused on a series of plates and place settings on elaborately embroidered runners that carried her female-form language. Lucy Lippard, in her catalog essay for the 1975 Paris Biennale, "The Women Artists' Movement—What Next?," suggested that art by women had "a central focus (often 'empty,' often circular or oval), parabolic bag-like forms, obsessive line and detail, veiled strata, tactile or sensuous surfaces and forms, associative fragmentation, autobiographical emphasis" (Lippard, quoted in Alloway, 1976: 68). These ideas were eventually refuted, however, as close examination of art by men found that they used similar forms.

There were attempts to define feminist art and feminist

contributions to the art of the period. Besides redefining the category "fine" art, feminists began to introduce content and emotion into a Modernism that many viewed as sterile; they contributed to the idea of pluralism in art. Art became political again. Feminism sought to "change the character of art," and was viewed as an "ideology, a value system, a revolutionary strategy, a way of life" (Lippard, 1980: 362).

The consensus today is that art by women can sometimes be distinguished from art by men in a given period only by its interpretation of a theme—the female experience of rape, birth, and domesticity does indeed differ from that of the male. But even those attitudes evolve. For example, Carolyn Seifert (1980/81) traced how art reflected the changing attitudes toward household objects and the chores of American women during the last 100 years: the image of the housewife changed from the "epicenter of the home charged with the sacred task of maintaining domestic order," to "frustrated housewife sex-object," to "a feminine power that can transform the reality of the world through fantasy."

Still, the search for a commonality in women's art continues. In a review of the 1985 Reflections: Women in Their Own Image exhibit at Ceres (the feminist cooperative in New York City), where the curators were looking for a mid-1980s feminist art statement, Judith Chiti (1986) did find a commonality—a preoccupation with group and self-exploration.

Another direction taken by researchers in the mid-1970s was the examination of art historical "givens," for example, Norma Broude's 1977 essay "Degas's Misogyny." Because Degas painted women as individualized, sensitive human beings rather than as generalized, voluptuous sex objects with firm, ripe breasts, male art historians have presumed he disdained women. There was also an examination of received

images, as in Carol Duncan's 1973 "Happy Mothers and
Other New Ideas in French Art." Paintings were used to pro-
mulgate the new Rousseauian concept that family life was
blissful and a woman's role was to stay at home, raise the
children, and run an ordered house. These ideas were promoted with a vengeance in the art of Victorian England and
elsewhere, and their messages continue to be decoded by contemporary feminists (see Shefer, 1986).

The archaeological and extrication processes begun by
American feminist art historians in the 1970s continue.
While a few surveys, such as Nancy Heller's *Women Artists: An
Illustrated History* (1987), have been published in the 1980s,
they are for the general reader. Scholarly studies on individual artists abound. Frido Kahlo, Remedios Varo, Berthe
Morisot, Artemisia Gentileschi, Rosa Bonheur, Joan Mitchell, Nancy Graves, Elizabeth Murray, Sofonisba Anguissola,
Julia Morgen, and the doyennes Helen Frankenthaler,
Georgia O'Keeffe, Lee Krasner, and Mary Cassatt have been
the subjects of newly published monographs or book-length
catalogs published in conjunction with full-scale retrospec-
tives. Women who were ignored in historical movements are
finally getting their due (see, for example, Behr, 1988; Chadwick, 1985; and Katz, 1986/87).

The lives and works of many women artists are now being
extricated from those of their more famous mates. Recently
brought to light in the pages of *Woman's Art Journal* have
been the important oeuvres of Mary Nimmo Moran (wife of
Thomas), Mary Fairchild MacMonnies (Frederick), Josephine
Nivison Hopper (Edward), Sally Michel Avery (Milton), Dorothy Dehner (David Smith), Elsie Driggs (Lee Gatch), to
name just a few of the Americans. Robert Hobbs called the
Avery relationship a collaboration—at times she would fol-

low him, but just as often "their ideas evolved simultaneously" (Hobbs, 1987/88: 6). Such could be said of many
artist couples. While their mates sought renown in the art
world, the women often painted in the privacy of their homes
while they managed children, households, and their husbands' careers.

Most of the books and articles cited above are concerned
with instating women into the traditional framework. This
approach has been attacked in recent years by some feminist
art historians. According to Thalia Gouma-Peterson and Patricia Mathews in "Feminist Critique of Art History" (1987),
an essay as critical to the late 1980s as Nochlin's was to the
1970s:

Such an approach is ultimately self-defeating, for it fixes women
within preexisting structures without questioning the validity of
these structures. Furthermore, since many of the same women artists have been repeatedly discussed, feminist art history has come
dangerously close to creating its own cannon of white female artists
(primarily painters), a canon that is almost as restrictive as its male
counterpart (p. 327).

Two New York-based feminist art periodicals founded in
the late 1970s—*Women Artists News* and *Heresies*—continue
to publish. *Women Artists News* lists art exhibits and other
events of interest, sponsors and reviews symposia, and presents short reviews of books and exhibitions. *Heresies*, de-
scribing itself as "an idea-oriented journal devoted to the examination of art and politics from a feminist perspective," is
run by a collective.

Reflecting the spirit of the 1980s, *Woman's Art Journal*
began publishing in Knoxville, Tennessee in the first year of
the decade. Whereas previously, women's work and books
about women artists were welcomed uncritically by feminist

and feminist journals, the editor offered *Woman's Art Journal* as a vehicle for honest criticism: "Without a critical voice, women's work will again be perceived with lesser value." *Woman's Art Journal* "has maintained a reputation for publishing scholarly articles on women artists from all historical periods, with a variety of viewpoints" (ibid.: 331).

The *Journal's* articles represent the various "feminisms." They are still concerned with rescuing women's work from the basement of art history and with extricating the work of women artists from that of their famous spouses. The articles in *Woman's Art Journal* also deconstruct received images of women, offer discourses on the ways women negotiate power for themselves, deal with issues of class, race, and sexual preference, psychoanalytic theory, and goddess imagery. That books about women in the arts have become big business is evident in the *Journal's* review section. Up to 16 books are reviewed in each issue. Men as well as women serve on the editorial board and are published regularly in the periodical.

Institutions and Organizations

Feminist pressure for institutional change begun in the mid-1970s has had some effect, but not as much as one would have expected. In 1975, women comprised about 75 percent of the art school undergraduate population and about half the graduate population; at the instructional level, women were gathered in the lower ranks. According to a 1988 Women's Caucus for Art survey, those figures have changed little. But government affirmative action hiring programs have had some effect: whereas in 1975, 21 percent of the art schools surveyed reported no women on their studio faculties, in 1988, none had fewer than 10 percent and 19 percent had female chairs.

In 1972, a national survey showed that only 18 percent of the commercial galleries had women artists in their stables, and of those museums that collected contemporary art, only six to 10 percent of their purchases were from women artists. By 1988, "women artists [were] 38% of all artists . . . but only about 10% of [gallery] exhibitions [were] of women artists' work. For prestigious museums, the percentage [was] even lower" (Downie, 1988: 16). In 1985, about 16 percent of the one-person shows in New York City were of women's work.

Tired of exclusion and tokenism, women organized alternative programs and exhibition spaces—in New York at the Women's Interart Center and Soho 20, in Chicago at Artemisia Gallery, and in California in Judy Chicago's and Miriam Schapiro's feminist art programs at Fresno State College and the California Institute of the Arts, respectively.

Beginning as an arm of the politically active Art Worker's Coalition, Women Artists in Revolution (WAR) sought funds in 1969 to open a center from which to direct their activities. WAR's Women's Interart Center opened in 1971 and two years later organized Women Choose Women, the first of a series of all-women shows that culminated in Women Artists: 1550-1950, which opened at the Los Angeles County Museum in 1976.

A women's ad hoc committee was formed in 1970 to protest the low representation of women artists in the Whitney Museum of American Art's Annuals. From a low of five percent representation in 1969, women artists were 23 percent of the total in 1973, and 29 percent in 1985. New York's Museum of Modern Art was picketed in 1973; it was picketed again in 1984 to protest the low percentage of women in its reopening show—15 out of 166. It was in 1984 that the anonymous activist group, the Guerrilla Girls, emerged. They have become the conscience of the art world, publishing advertisements and posters to show the percentage of women represented in various museums, galleries, and art reviews (Loughery, 1987).

The most effective women artists organization is perhaps the Women's Caucus for Art, founded in 1972 as an arm of the College Art Association (CAA). Now also a grassroots organization with chapters throughout the country, the caucus sponsors feminist panels at the annual CAA meetings and sees that the larger professional organization is responsive to women's needs.

As if in response to the lack of visibility of women artists, the National Museum of Women in the Arts (NMWA) was founded in Washington, D.C. in 1981 and opened its doors to the public in 1987. With an astonishing 90,000-plus membership, it has as its objectives acquisition, research, and exhibition, but its agenda is not feminist. In counterpoise to the new museum's opening exhibition of mostly genteel paintings by American women artists of 1830 to 1930, Washington's Project for the Arts mounted Too Hot to Handle, an exhibit that was "intentionally confrontational, the works display[ing] a consciousness of political, sexual, and social issues conspicuously absent in NMWA" (Fahlman, 1987/88: 58).

Whether conservative or radical, the National Museum of Women in the Arts and Too Hot to Handle both represent separatist visions—art segregated for no other reason save gender. Some believe that the existence of the National Museum of Women in the Arts leaves establishment museums "off the hook," since now that there is a museum to showcase women's art, they will no longer feel the responsibility to purchase and feature it. But that is not necessarily the case. During NMWA's opening year, Washington's National Gallery of Art featured one-woman shows of works by Georgia O'Keeffe and Berthe Morisot.

The National Museum of Women in the Arts building before its recent renovation and conversion to a museum.
Courtesy National Museum of Women in the Arts

The same criticism might be made about *Woman's Art Journal*, i.e., the existence of a publication devoted exclusively to women's art relieves other arts journals from the responsibility of publishing articles about women. Richard Martin, former editor of *Arts Magazine*, would disagree. He claims that *Woman's Art Journal* is a constant reminder—an irritant, if you will—for everyone in the art world. Separatist operations need to exist because there is still so much catching up to do; they are also a reminder that full integration is the ultimate goal.

A Portrait of Hispanic Women in the United States

GLORIA BONILLA-SANTIAGO

HISPANIC WOMEN ARE PART of a very fast growing segment of the U.S. population. Between 1980 and 1988, the number of Hispanics in this country increased by 34 percent, a rate more than four times that (eight percent) of the U.S. population as a whole. This rapid growth, produced in about equal parts by immigration and natural increase (births minus deaths), brought the Hispanic proportion of the U.S. population up from 6.5 percent in 1980 to eight percent in 1988 (U.S. Bureau of the Census, August 1988b). These and other statistics about the U.S. Hispanic population in general furnish the context for a discussion of the situation of Hispanic females, who in 1988 accounted for 51 percent of the 19.4 million persons of Hispanic origin in the United States.

There have, of course, been significant numbers of Hispanic women and men in North America for hundreds of years—since long before the United States became a republic—and Hispanics, from Mexico in particular, have been migrating to the United States in substantial numbers since the early 1900s. People of Mexican origin constitute the oldest and still by far the largest Hispanic subgroup in the United States—62 percent of the total Hispanic population.

Since World War II, however, the other major Hispanic subgroups have increased appreciably. People of Puerto

Rican origin now account for 13 percent of all Hispanics, those of Central and South American origin for 12 percent, and those of Cuban origin for five percent. (The remaining eight percent are people of "other" Hispanic origin, who range from recent immigrants from Spain to people whose families have been in this country for centuries and who no longer claim a specific Hispanic country of origin.)

Decennial census data about Hispanics' places of birth suggest the role that immigration plays in the growth of the major Hispanic subgroups, especially those of other than Mexican origin. Only about a quarter of people of Mexican origin living in the United States in 1980 were foreign born. But about half of the Puerto Ricans were born in Puerto Rico, and three-quarters of the Cubans and four-fifths of Central and South Americans were born outside the United States (Valdivieso and Davis, 1988).

Indeed, approximately three million Latin Americans immigrated to the United States between 1960 and 1970, and more than two million immigrated between 1980 and 1988. (Because Puerto Ricans are U.S. citizens, these numbers do not include the Puerto Ricans who moved to the mainland.) High immigration rates from Latin American countries seem likely to continue because of unstable economic and political conditions in many of those countries (ibid.).

Historically, immigrants to the United States have tended to locate where other immigrants (or the descendants of recent immigrants) from their country of origin live, and this pattern prevails among Hispanic-origin immigrants. Nine states contain nearly 90 percent of this country's Hispanic population; California and Texas alone account for 55 percent. The geographical location of Hispanic subgroups is determined largely by their "point of entry" into the United

States (ibid.). Most Hispanics of Mexican origin live in California or Texas, while almost all Cubans live in Florida—about half of them in Dade County. Central and South Americans are concentrated in California, but sizable communities also exist in eastern cities. Puerto Ricans are most likely to be along the East Coast, a large number of them in New York City.

The migration to the United States of Mexicans, Puerto Ricans, Cubans, and other Hispanic groups earlier in this century resulted in the eventual movement of whole families. The male head of household or a younger male member might come first, followed later by the rest of the family, but two-parent families often migrated together as well. In the last 10 years, however, a growing proportion of Hispanic immigrants have been families consisting of women with children. This development may relate to the fact that although the majority (70 percent) of Hispanic families in the United States today are married-couple families, the proportion comprising families headed by women has been growing (from 21.5 percent to 23.4 percent between 1982 and 1988).

Hispanic families in general are considerably less well off than non-Hispanic families; median income for Hispanic families overall was $20,306 in 1987, one-third less than that of non-Hispanic families. The median for Hispanic families headed by women was only $9,805 (U.S. Bureau of the Census, August 1988c).

As these figures suggest, poverty is a serious problem among Hispanic families and is particularly acute among those headed by women; more than half of the latter were poor in 1987. Even among Hispanic families overall, the poverty level proportion was 2.5 times that of non-Hispanic families (26 percent vs. under 10 percent). However, poverty rates differ greatly, depending on the Hispanic subgroup: families of Puerto Rican origin had the highest poverty rate (38 percent), followed by those of Mexican origin and "other" Hispanics (26 percent each), and families of Central and South American origin (19 percent). Families of Cuban origin were the least likely of Hispanic families to be poor (14 percent).

A number of factors contribute to the socioeconomic status of Hispanic women (and men) in the United States. Many of them confront a language barrier, which may create problems for them in school and in the workforce. On the whole, Hispanics have had less schooling than the rest of the U.S. population. Indeed, as of 1987, only half of all Hispanic adult females had completed high school, compared to over three-fourths of their non-Hispanic counterparts. Twelve percent of Hispanic women had completed less than five years of schooling; the comparable proportion among non-Hispanic women was less than two percent. And, at the other end of the educational continuum, Hispanic women were about half as likely as non-Hispanic women to have completed college— eight vs. 17 percent. However, the educational attainment of Hispanic women has been rising; as of 1987, Hispanic adult females had completed an average (median) of 12 years of schooling, up from 10.5 in 1981 (U.S. Bureau of the Census, August 1984 and August 1988a).

Educational attainment is, of course, extremely important, especially to success in the labor market—to good, steady jobs, to higher earnings, and to reducing the probability and duration of unemployment. The comparative lack of education among Hispanic women tends to depress the earnings of those who work and may discourage others from entering the labor force.

In any case, Hispanic women in general are somewhat less likely than non-Hispanic women to be in the labor force (51 percent vs. 56 percent in 1987), and Hispanic women in the labor force are more likely than other women to be unemployed (9.5 percent vs. 6.4 percent). However, overall labor force statistics conceal wide variations among Hispanic subgroups. Women of Cuban and Central and South American origin have labor force participation rates (55 and 59 percent, respectively) that are close to or above the rate of non-Hispanic women. On the other hand, the rate among women of Mexican origin is 51 percent, and among those of Puerto Rican origin, it is only 40 percent. Unemployment rates also vary, with Cuban-origin women historically experiencing less unemployment than other Hispanic women.

Recent research by the National Council of La Raza (1988) highlights the marginal position that Hispanic women occupy in the U.S. labor market. Their relatively low level of educational attainment compared to that of other women in the United States, coupled with language problems and employment discrimination on account of sex (as well as national origin and sometimes race), contributes to the segregation of many Hispanic women in low-skilled, low-paid occupations and jobs that are vulnerable to layoff, often in declining industries.

The proportion of Hispanic women in clerical occupations is fairly similar to that of all U.S. women, but Hispanic women are far more heavily concentrated than other women in operative jobs, such as dressmakers, assemblers, machine operators, and the like. Conversely, they are less likely than other women to be in managerial and professional specialties. (Even in these occupations, Hispanic women are likely to hold highly visible positions in such areas as public affairs, rather than decisionmaking positions in upper management [Bonilla-Santiago, 1988].)

The occupational distribution of Hispanic women has a

strong effect on their median earnings, since earnings vary greatly by occupation. (In 1987, for example, female operatives had median weekly earnings of $231, barely half of the $458 median earnings of female professionals [U.S. Bureau of Labor Statistics, 1988].) Median annual earnings for Hispanic women workers overall were $8,554 in 1987. Again, however, generalizations about Hispanic women workers conceal differences among the various subgroups. Women of Mexican origin, who are more likely to be operatives than other Hispanic women, had median earnings in 1987 of $7,912—the lowest of all Hispanic female subgroups. The highest earners ($11,327) were women of Cuban origin, who were more likely than either Hispanic women workers in general *or* non-Hispanic women workers to be professionals or managers (27 percent of the Cuban-origin women workers were in such occupations, compared to 16 percent of Hispanic women workers overall, and 26 percent of non-Hispanic women workers).

On average, however, Hispanic women workers earn substantially less than other workers in the United States. Hispanic women who usually work full time earn about 82 percent of what all comparably employed white women earn, about 85 percent of what their Hispanic male counterparts earn, and only 56 percent of what white men earn.

Even though their labor force participation is currently lower, and their labor market difficulties are greater, than those of their non-Hispanic counterparts, Hispanic women will comprise a growing proportion of the U.S. workforce in the future (National Council of La Raza, 1988). A key reason is that Hispanic women (and indeed, Hispanics in general) are a youthful population compared to the U.S. female population as a whole. Forty-eight percent (compared to 36 percent

Gilda Oliveros, first Cuban-born female mayor in the United States.
Paul Rubiera/Miami Herald

of U.S. females overall) had not yet reached their prime employment years—they were under 21 years old. The median age of Hispanic females was just under 26 in 1988, compared to almost 33 for the total female population. Conversely, less than six percent of Hispanic women were 65 or over, compared to 13 percent of U.S. females overall (see Table 1 in the statistical appendix).

The high fertility rate (number of births per 1,000 women 18 to 44) among Hispanic women is another indicator that Hispanics of both sexes will constitute a growing proportion of America's workforce. Although the fertility rate among Hispanic women has declined during the 1980s, it is still considerably higher than that of non-Hispanic women in the

U.S.: 96 compared to 69 in 1987 (U.S. Bureau of the Census, May 1988). Eleven percent of all births in the United States in that year were to Hispanic women.

Even this brief statistical profile of Hispanic women suggests the diversity among and within the various Hispanic subgroups, and the common sociocultural elements that bind them as "Hispanas," "Latinas," or "Hermanas." Hispanic women typically share the cultural heritage of Spain, the Spanish language, and the Catholic religion, but Indo-Hispanic traits and heritage characterize some, and African-Indo-Hispanic traits and heritage characterize others. However, all tend to share certain values and cultural attributes, such as an orientation toward persons rather than abstractions; commitment to individual autonomy within a context of familial and traditional Hispanic values; emphasis on the central importance of the family; and emphasis on the father or husband as the main authority figure (Dieppa and Montiel, 1978).

Female (and male) Hispanic immigrants may bring with them traditional Latin American notions about gender roles—women are expected to be "gentle, mild, sentimental, emotional, intuitive, impulsive, fragile, submissive, docile, dependent, and timid" and men to be "hard, rough, cold, intellectual, rational, far-sighted, profound, strong, authoritarian, independent, and brave" (Natera, 1988).

Immigrant women from Latin America confront the "culture shock" that awaits Hispanic immigrants of both sexes—the language barrier; different cultural traditions; different values, beliefs, and lifestyles; different institutional systems; racial and/or ethnic discrimination; and, for many, adaptation from an agrarian or rural environment to an urban one. In addition, Hispanic women may find that the dominant (non-Hispanic) U.S. culture has expectations about the appropriate female role that, while ambiguous, are quite different from those to which they are accustomed. Their generally low level of education, inability or limited ability to speak English, and discrimination in employment relegate many Hispanic women to poverty (Bonilla-Santiago, 1988).

Nevertheless, the typical Hispanic woman appears to be trying to bridge two cultures—struggling to achieve greater economic success and more personal and vocational opportunities within both the dominant society and the Hispanic community. Hispanic women have been described as, among other things, strong minded, hard working, and self-assured (Bonilla-Santiago, 1988). Recent research has found that the typical Hispanic woman promotes her children's educational achievement, has strong ties with extended family, closely identifies with the Hispanic community, and has a strong sense of identity and self-esteem (Natera, 1988).

These are important strengths. But improvements in the occupational and socioeconomic condition of Hispanic women require measures to provide more educational and vocational opportunities as well as more effective enforcement of laws barring discrimination in employment. These key steps will not only improve the situation of Hispanic women in this country; they will help ensure a better qualified U.S. workforce in the years to come.

A Portrait of Asian and Pacific American Women

JUANITA TAMAYO LOTT

THE PREVAILING FRAMEWORK for examining and explaining the status of women and people of color in the United States has been that of a minority population whose members are commonly seen as second-class citizens and/or marginal producers and consumers. This framework can be found in research, the mass media, and the public policy arena. However, over the last two decades, demographic changes in the United States and economic changes at a global level have contributed to a growing recognition that the framework is outdated and incomplete. Asian and Pacific American (APA) women are a part of those changes.

Until recently, the history of Asian and Pacific American women in the United States has been little known and of relatively little interest to most Americans. The reasons for this are deeply rooted in history. For decades, Asians and Pacific Islanders were actively discouraged from immigrating to the United States and becoming citizens. An exception was the limited immigration permitted in order to develop the West Coast and Hawaii. The early pioneers were Chinese women (Mark and Chih, 1982) and Japanese women (Glenn, 1986) who came in the late nineteenth and early twentieth centuries to provide domestic services to, respectively, Chinese men and Japanese men.

Japanese women, in particular, came as wives to labor alongside their husbands in the fields of Hawaii and California (Young and Parish, 1977). They were followed in the early decades of the twentieth century by Filipino and Korean women, whose male counterparts encountered the restrictive immigration and labor patterns of earlier APA immigrants.

Then, during World War II, immigration restrictions began to be relaxed for Asian brides of U.S. servicemen returning from the war in the Pacific and later, the Korean War (B. Kim et al., 1981), though the APA population continued to be minimal until the repeal of the national origins quota system in 1965.

With relaxed immigration policies and the growth of second and succeeding generations of Asian and Pacific Americans, the APA population began to increase substantially. The 1980 census, the latest year for which detailed data are available, counted a total of 3.7 million Asian and Pacific Americans, and for the first time the majority were women— 1.9 million, or 52 percent (U.S. Bureau of the Census, 1983a). Women are now dominant among APA immigrants.

The 1980 census also documented the diversity of APA women by ethnicity, nativity, age, fertility rate, educational attainment, English-language ability, place of residence, labor force participation, income, and occupation. The diversity of these women complicates attempts to develop generalizations about Asian Pacific Americans.

As society in general tries to understand APA women, it must be understood that they do not define themselves in relationship to white men, white women, or other women of color. Their identities are rooted in civilizations that are thousands of years old. The APA populations (interchangeably referred to here as Pan Asian or Asian and Pacific Islander

populations) come from cultures and countries containing
the majority of the world's population. Those countries vary
by language, religion, economic system, and government.
Some, such as Japan and China, have been independent nations for centuries, and some, such as India and Guam, bear a
colonial legacy from Western and other Asian countries.

Despite these historical diversities, Asian and Pacific
Americans tend to be treated as one entity, in part because of
their similar treatment and experiences in the United States.
For example, Pan Asian women often get stereotyped as docile, subservient, alternately erotic or sexless, and limited in
their English-language ability. Likewise, the U.S. soldiers of
Japanese, Chinese, and Filipino ethnicity who fought in
Southeast Asia were identified, at peril of their lives, as Vietnamese, Laotian, and Cambodian soldiers.

Although there is notable variation among ethnic groups,
the educational attainment of APA women in general is un-
usually high compared to other American population groups.
This is due in large part to restrictive U.S. immigration policies that favor college-educated professionals. In 1980, 27 percent of Asian and Pacific Islander women who were at least 25
years old had four or more years of college. In comparison,
the figure was 21 percent for white men, 13 percent for white
women, eight percent for black women, and six percent for
Hispanic, American Indian, Eskimo, and Aleut women. But
low educational levels are also found among some groups of
APA women. For example, about one-third of Vietnamese
women, one-fourth of Chinese women, and about one-fifth of
Guamanian, Korean, Filipino, and Samoan women had completed eight or fewer years of education.

Historically, APA women have had higher rates of labor
force participation than other women, and that remained

true at least through 1980 (Glenn, 1986; Lott, 1985). According to the 1980 census, labor force participation rates varied from a high of 68 percent for Filipino women to a low of 47 percent for Asian Indian and Samoan women. These figures compared to 50 percent for all American women and 58 percent for all Asian Pacific Islander women.

While for most women a high education level often means increased participation in the labor force, for APA women additional factors are involved. These factors include traditional APA values of a strong work ethic, self-reliance, and disapproval of welfare (E. Kim, 1983).

Also significant is the fact that, for Pan Asian families, life in the United States almost dictates multiple wage earners and long work hours. That these families have more multiple wage earners than families of other backgrounds suggests that APA women must work to support their families.

For selected groups, such as Korean and Asian Indian communities, small family businesses are a major source of income. Pan Asian wives and daughters often work as primary, and unpaid, help. This small business atmosphere is reminiscent of the small businesses found in Chinese and Japanese communities before World War II, with the distinction that those businesses were usually confined to serving their own ethnic groups in Chinatowns and Japantowns.

The vast majority of APA women are found in traditionally female occupations, and their income is not commensurate with their education (Lott and Pian, 1979). And, while the median income of Pan Asian women is slightly above that of the U.S. female population in general, it is less than the median income of any group of males. (For example, in 1980, Pan Asian women had a median annual income of $6,685. White men had a median annual income of $12,881, APA men of $11,718, and black men of $8,296.) Furthermore, that income is more readily consumed because APAs had, at least as of 1980, the second largest number of persons per family— 3.75—among all families in the United States. That contrasts to 3.83 for American Indian families, 3.69 for black families, and 3.19 for white families. Among all APA families with children under the age of 18 in 1980, 10 percent were headed by single females. That represented a rise of one percentage point over the figure for 1970.

Another characteristic of Pan Asian women is a high interracial marriage rate. In some groups it is between one-fourth and one-third. The rate of "out-marriages" that began among APA women who married U.S. servicemen during World War II, the Korean War, and the Vietnam War has increased among the subsequent generations of U.S.-born Asian and Pacific American women, as has marriage with other Pan Asian groups. Within a group, for second and subsequent generations, the interracial marriage rate can be as high as one-half.

While there is still considerable ignorance about APA women, there are signs that both society in general and APA women themselves are beginning to realize that their numbers and diverse backgrounds are valuable assets to the future of this country.

A cursory review of the popular media indicates a growing visibility that was not evident even 10 years ago. Catalogs and advertisements regularly include APA female models. In 1986, such nationally visible magazines as *Time*, *Ms.*, *Savvy*, and *Mother Jones* featured Asian women on their covers, including Philippine President Corazon Aquino, who was educated in American schools. Personalities such as television reporter Connie Chung are presented for both their American and Asian identities.

"Personalities such as television reporter Connie Chung are presented for both their American and Asian identities." *Courtesy CBS News/Joe McNally*

Among APA women themselves, the recognition is growing that their diverse background is an asset, not a handicap. This is manifested by regular communication and travel across the Pacific by both immigrants and U.S.-born Pan Asians. Although APA women for the most part continue to retain their Asian and Pacific culture, language, food, and religion, they are adapting them to an American setting and available resources.

At the national level, the growing presence of APA women is reflected by such groups as the Organization of Pan Asian American Women, which focuses on public policy issues, and the Organization of Chinese American Women, which provides direct services and education programs. Gradually, Pan Asian women such as Irene Natividad of the National Women's Political Caucus and Elaine Caho and Wendy Lee Gramm, who held high-ranking posts in the Reagan administration, are becoming known nationally. U.S. Representative Patsy Saiki of Hawaii and international financial consultant Lilia Clemente have extended the scope of APA women beyond a national focus to global concerns as they address such issues as immigration, population growth, scarcity of resources, world trade, and greater understanding of Asia and the Pacific regions.

As the number of Asian and Pacific American women begins to reach a critical mass, their talents and contributions are beginning to be acknowledged. These women possess bilingual and bicultural skills that are beneficial to a global economy and a pluralistic society.

A Portrait of American Indian
Women and Their
Labor Force Experiences

C. MATTHEW SNIPP

AMID THE CONCERN about job opportunities for women in general, and women of color in particular, the experiences of American Indian women in the labor force have received little notice. There are many reasons for this neglect.

Although American Indian women have the distinction of being among America's "first" citizens, they belong to one of the smallest and least visible sectors of American society. (For the sake of convenience, the term "American Indians" includes American Indians and Alaska natives throughout this chapter.) In 1980, the latest year for which data are available, American Indians numbered just 1.4 million, or about one-half of one percent of the total U.S. population. American Indians and Alaska natives lack the numbers to attract public notice by swinging elections, influencing the gross national product, or affecting unemployment rates. Contributing to their very low visibility is the fact that over half of all American Indians reside outside of large metropolitan areas, often in remote and virtually unknown places.

Yet, for a number of reasons, American Indian and Alaska native women deserve much more attention than they get. A major reason is that poverty rates, though dismayingly high among American Indians as a whole, are especially high among Indian women. Their 1979 poverty rate of 27.6 percent was nearly three times as high as that of white women. Almost one-fourth of all American Indian families had incomes below the poverty level, and, as is the case with poor American families in general, a disproportionate share of these poor families (45 percent) was headed by single women. It is impossible to comprehend fully the wealth of a society without also understanding the dimensions of its poverty. Information about America's poorest groups, and this certainly includes American Indian women, has provided a bench mark for understanding statistics about "average" Americans.

Second, because of treaties, legal agreements, judicial settlements, and other policies, American Indians hold a unique relationship with the federal government that distinguishes them from other groups in the United States. Unfortunately, many of these federal actions and policies, which date back to the country's founding, have had adverse consequences. Recently, federal authorities have tried to deal with the severe economic hardships facing American Indians, but with little success.

Third, the labor market experiences of American Indian women are particularly interesting because these women are relative newcomers to the paid workforce. Compared to other women, American Indian women have historically had low rates of participation in the labor force, although, as discussed below, this has been changing in recent years.

Though they possess a special cultural and political status in the United States, American Indian women must confront the same problems that confront other groups of women in

American society. Gender discrimination, occupational segregation, and wage differentials are no less common among these women than they are among all women in the United States. And the economic disadvantages faced by American Indian men are compounded for American Indian women simply because of their gender.

Before turning to the limited data available about American Indian women, it should be noted that this population is extremely diverse. The tribes that constitute America's Indian population vary greatly in size, culture, and economic problems. Unfortunately, a lack of statistical data makes it impossible to explore completely this diversity.

In fact, reliable data as a whole—much less extensive data—about American Indians are difficult to obtain. The usual sources of labor information, such as the Census Bureau's Current Population Survey, do not contain enough Indian respondents to be useful. As a result, as of 1989 the only large-scale source of data about American Indians in the workforce was the 1980 census.

In 1970, according to Census Bureau data, only 35 percent of American Indian women age 16 and over were in the labor force, compared to 48 percent of black women and 41 percent of white women. Just 10 years later, that proportion of slightly over one-third had jumped to nearly one-half—48 percent. The increase during the 1970s was notably greater for American Indian women than for black women, 53 percent of whom were in the labor force in 1980, or for white women, whose labor force participation rate stood at 49 percent (U.S. Bureau of the Census, 1983a).

This increase in labor force participation would seem to be good news; however, while the increase is certainly encouraging, it masks some deep-seated problems that American Indian women face as their presence in the mainstream workforce grows.

Census data, for example, indicate that unemployment is a serious problem for American Indian women, especially when they are compared to white women. The unemployment rate of American Indian women was double that of white women in both 1970 and 1980. During the 1970s, the unemployment rate for white women rose from five percent to six percent, while it increased from 10 percent to 12 percent among American Indian women. American Indian women also experience greater joblessness than do black women, whose 1970 and 1980 unemployment rates were eight percent and 11 percent, respectively. However, because the unemployment rate of black women increased more rapidly during the 1970s than it did for American Indian women, the unemployment gap between these two groups narrowed somewhat over the decade.

Many factors, some of them common to most women, shape the labor force experiences of American Indian women. There are certain stages of life, for example, that are more conducive to labor force participation than others. As teenagers, American Indian women are most likely to be out of the labor force, but their participation and work experience sharply increase as they complete their schooling. Young American Indian women who have recently completed their education are less likely to have child care responsibilities than relatively older women and are more likely to be working. For instance, 31 percent of American Indian women under the age of 21 were employed in 1980, compared to 49 percent of Indian women between the ages of 21 and 25. Interestingly, American Indian women in their peak childbearing years (20 to 35) do not have workforce participation rates significantly lower than those of older women. In fact, Indian women in their 30s are the most likely to be working outside the home, followed by women in their 20s. Employment is least common among older women, which may well be a reflection of the barriers that prevent older, inexperienced American Indian women from entering the job market.

The impact of age on labor force participation is particularly important in connection with the childbearing and child care responsibilities of Indian women. The fact that lower fertility is related to higher labor force participation is well known, though not well understood. At issue is whether women curtail their childbearing to take advantage of opportunities in the labor market, or whether childbearing necessarily limits the ability of women to be active in the workforce (Bianchi and Spain, 1986).

American Indian women have higher rates of fertility than either blacks or whites. However, they generally resemble black and white women in how their fertility is related to their labor force role. Regardless of age, 1980 data indicate that employed American Indian women had substantially fewer children than women not in the labor force—2.6 vs. 3.4 for ever-married women between the ages of 15 and 54.

Child care responsibilities pose a major obstacle to American Indian women's labor force participation. Among American Indian women with children ranging in age from infancy to 18, only 47 percent were in the labor force in 1980. In contrast, 69 percent of all American Indian women without children were either working or looking for work. These statistics are significant, as they suggest that the extensive kin networks prevalent in many American Indian communities do not necessarily facilitate female labor force participation.

But there are considerations other than age and family obligations that have a strong bearing on whether American Indian women participate in the labor force. American Indians are heavily concentrated in rural areas where economic opportunities are limited (51 percent of the Indian population reside outside of metropolitan areas). Nonmetropolitan labor markets are not only usually more sluggish than metropolitan markets, but they typically have fewer of the types of jobs—such as in clerical or service work—traditionally open to women. In addition, most Indian reservations are located in nonmetropolitan areas and generally have depressed local economies.

Because of their geographic isolation, along with the race and gender barriers they may encounter, only 37 percent of all rural American Indian women held jobs in 1980. In contrast, 46 percent of urban American Indian women were working at that time. Likewise, rural Indian women had a higher unemployment rate than their urban counterparts—13 percent versus 11 percent.

Another reason for the higher employment rates among urban American Indian women is that they are better educated than those in rural areas. Indeed, the employment opportunities in metropolitan economies are powerful influences for relatively well-educated American Indian women to relocate to, or remain in, urban settings.

As expected, the higher the education level, the greater the rate of employment. Sixty-six percent of American Indian women with a college education were employed in 1980, but this was the case for barely 20 percent of those who had finished less than nine years of schooling.

On the other hand, high school dropouts (nine to 11 years of completed schooling) had the highest unemployment rate (17 percent) among Indian women. American Indian women with some college had unemployment rates in the 10-percent range, which was still higher than the six-percent rate for all white women. Only the unemployment rate of American Indian women who were college graduates (five percent) was below that of the white female population as a whole.

In deciding whether to enter the job market, married American Indian women—just as women of any background—make their decisions within the framework of the family unit. As a consequence, the job situation of their husbands is a major factor in this decision. Given their disadvantaged position in the labor market, it might be assumed that American Indian women who work do so purely out of economic necessity. For example, having an employed husband might lessen the pressure to work or to take a job that would be both unrewarding and also interfere with family responsibilities. But this view of the economic compatibility of husbands and wives does not match reality.

Very simply, husbands and wives tend to resemble one another in a number of respects. Men with few skills and little education tend to have wives who also lack skills and education. Of American Indian women married to unemployed men, nearly one-half were not in the labor force; of the women in the labor force, nearly 21 percent were unemployed in 1980. Like their husbands, the wives of unemployed men are also frequently unemployed. This means that while American Indian women may seek work because their husbands are unemployed, they are not necessarily going to find it.

The situation is similar regarding the income of husbands. In view of the fact that American Indian men tend not to have high-paying jobs, the assumption would be that this would present the motive for the wives to augment the family income. However, there is little evidence that American Indian wives seek employment to supplement the low incomes of their husbands, whether those husbands are American Indians or not.

Rather, the data suggest the opposite. The better off the husband is, the more likely it is that his wife is working. Among men with personal incomes of $20,000 or more, nearly six out of 10 (58 percent) had employed American Indian wives in 1980. In contrast, only three in 10 of the wives of the poorest men—those with incomes under $5,000—were working. And even when American Indian wives of the poorest men seek to augment the family income, they are relatively unsuccessful, as over 15 percent of them were unemployed.

This sketch of statistical information about American Indian women indicates the problems and obstacles they face. The bleakest figures come from the official statistics on poverty in the United States mentioned earlier. Compared to black women, American Indian women are somewhat more likely to reside in homes with intact families whose poverty rates tend to be lower (Sandefur and Sakamoto, 1988). Even so, sizable numbers of Indian women, both single and married, have incomes below official poverty levels.

These figures are unlikely to improve unless American Indian women can participate more fully and equitably in the U.S. labor force. Indeed, reflecting the effect of federal cutbacks since 1981, data from the Bureau of Indian Affairs suggest that unemployment among American Indians—and the accompanying poverty and economic hardship—is actually on the rise.

Unless more effective steps are taken to provide American Indian women better access to the labor force and employment opportunities, the "first" among American women will be the last to gain their share of this country's wealth.

Flourishing in the Mainstream: The U.S. Women's Movement Today

SARAH HARDER

ASSESSING THE HEALTH and effectiveness of the women's movement in America offers pundits endless opportunities. Books like Nicholas Davidson's *The Failure of Feminism* (1988) appear with a trumpet of publicity, providing talk show hosts and local columnists with yet another chance to ponder what it is that women want and whether women will ever get their act together. The accepted approach for friend or foe is to minimize the accomplishments of the women's movement, to dissect its shortcomings, and then to proclaim or predict its demise.

Quite a different view of the effectiveness of U.S. women's organizations was delivered on behalf of the Reagan administration in 1988 to the United Nations Commission on the Status of Women. The commission was assessing the "national machinery" that governments worldwide had put in place to oversee implementation of the Nairobi *Forward-Looking Strategies*, the 1985 blueprint for equality adopted at the World Conference of the United Nations Decade for Women.

The U.S. delegate reported that "women's NGOs" (nongovernmental organizations) now maintain that responsibility in the absence of national machinery:

American women have become adept at using our system to work for the advancement of women in every field of endeavor. American women have repeatedly demonstrated the effectiveness of using NGOs to further their objectives. . . .

In the United States, nearly all NGOs give information and training to their members *and* to decisionmakers. NGOs can tap public opinion quickly and, frequently, beat the official bureaucracy in identifying the socioeconomic changes affecting women's status. . . . NGOs form part of our effort for monitoring and improving the status of women. Unlike many other countries the United States has no single "national machinery" to promote the advancement of women. I hope that this intervention, however, helps show that such machinery is not the only way to promote advancement (Grefe, 1988).

It is true that the Reagan administration's praise of women's voluntary organizations served in part to justify its dismantling in 1981 of the national machinery, the federal commissions that had existed through five previous administrations to monitor and improve the status of U.S. women.

However, it is also true that voluntary women's organizations in America have moved into the breach. They have created their own national machinery—increasingly effective delivery systems operating at the local, state, and national levels. And more and more intentionally, those separate systems are being linked in a sophisticated design that will speed the rate of progress, so that women's needs and perspectives inform sound public policy.

This is the point where critics always say, "Progress toward what? What is it that women want, and how can you pretend to speak for all women?" The fact is that remarkable consensus exists among women on the issues to be addressed. While women have been without federal leadership on those issues since 1981, they have not been without a plan.

For many U.S. women, 1977 was the point of entry into the organized women's movement. That year, 130,000 women participated in state and territorial meetings defining a "National Plan of Action for Women" and electing delegates to a national convention of the kind first envisioned in 1848 in Seneca Falls by Elizabeth Cady Stanton. Seven thousand women participated in the National Women's Conference held in Houston, Texas, where a 25-point Plan of Action, distilled from recommendations from every state and territory, was amended and ratified by 2,000 delegates. Apart from gender, these delegates were the most diverse elected group ever assembled, representing all ages, races, ethnic and religious backgrounds, and economic statuses. They committed to paper a comprehensive policy agenda for the future, a national blueprint for equality ranging from art and humanities to welfare and poverty.

The National Women's Conference proved an extraordinary catalyst in bringing U.S. women and their issues into the political process, and the issues set forth in the Plan of Action have continued to be rallying points for thousands of U.S. women coming together in organizations, coalitions, and networks.

Many of the specific issues in the plan have been further defined; in working with them, women have both developed new leadership skills and fostered public understanding of their needs. The international meetings held in connection with the U.N. Decade for Women drew American women to Copenhagen and Nairobi. There U.S. women learned the survival aspect of equity issues worldwide. They returned knowing that water is a women's issue, that most refugees are women and children, and that many cultures sanction violence against women. These understandings and a commitment to progress are incorporated into the *Forward-Looking Strategies* and the U.N. Convention on the Elimination of All Forms of Discrimination Against Women. (See Arvonne Fraser, "Women and International Development," elsewhere in this volume.)

In 1987, an assessment of the U.S. Plan of Action was completed, not by the government, but by the voluntary "machinery" which has been maintained by women. *Decade of Achievement: 1977-1987*, a report based on a survey of thousands of local, state, and national women's groups, was commissioned and published by the National Women's Conference Committee (NWCC). This is the all-volunteer continuing committee from the International Women's Year, appointed in 1978 under Public Law 94-167, which established U.S. initiatives for the U.N. Decade for Women. Its purpose is to "stimulate the formation and growth of networks at all levels, mobilize public support for the National Plan of Action, and act as a network among networks."

Susanna Downie, editor of *Decade of Achievement*, asserted in a news release on the report that "the American women's movement is alive and well and bigger and more diverse than ever." She stated:

The study shows phenomenal growth of a wide variety of women's and feminist groups in every part of the United States over the last 15 years, with no sign of slowing down. This phenomenon is not only national, it is "grassroots." It has not been coordinated by any one group or even a coalition of groups, though the participants are clearly in agreement on long-range purposes and underlying principles.

Decade of Achievement documented the establishment of new community institutions, new centers for information, and service delivery. Writing in 1988, Downie illuminated the contrasts:

- In 1970, no one even knew what a "battered women's shelter" was. Now there are at least 1,200 such centers or shelters.

- In 1970, no one had ever heard of a "women's center." A recent compilation by the National Association of Women's Centers has discovered that there are at least 4,000 women's centers.

- In 1970, the idea of a Rape Crisis Center was germinating in perhaps three minds in the United States. There are now 600 Rape Crisis Centers.

- Displaced Homemakers were first recognized in the early 1970s. Now there are over 1,000 displaced homemaker groups, programs, or services in the U.S. (Downie, 1988: 1-2).

The decade Downie described was one of expansion and regrouping. There were frustrations and disappointments as women's priorities confronted intractable budget constraints or institutional resistance to equity for women, but the reaction in the women's movement was a strengthening of resolve. In 1980, the "New Federalism" of the Reagan administration turned attention to the states at the same time that a new conservatism stalled action at the federal level. Failure to ratify the Equal Rights Amendment in 1982 led to a temporary vacuum as women's organizations at the national level regrouped and refocused. Nevertheless, the late 1970s and early 1980s generated what has become the prototype for action in the U.S. women's movement—permanent, flexible alliances among organizations to address issue priorities on the basis of opportunity and need.

The first multi-issue interorganizational advocacy networks were developed in states where the women's movement faced reversal or crisis. Typically, that crisis related to the elimination of a state commission on women. In the 1960s and 1970s, most states had established commissions on women paralleling the federal model. Usually appointed by the governor, the commission was generally the only state agency responsible for looking out for women's needs when economic and social policy was being formulated at the state level. But in the conservative shift at the end of the 1970s, a number of governors defunded or redirected the commissions, leaving no single agency on which women could depend to be their advocate with state policymakers.

In 1979, the elimination of commissions in the states of Washington and Wisconsin led to creation of the networking model on which others have built. Crisis showed organizations in both states the need to create an outside-of-government vehicle to draw women in the state together on broader fronts for common advocacy.

These networks, which grew out of connections made in coordinating state meetings before the 1977 National Women's Conference, were built upon support for principles in the Plan of Action and upon the premise that although participating groups were not required to subscribe to every recommendation in the plan, no participating group would work actively against plan issues.

This strategy made it possible for network task forces representing special constituencies to broaden their base of support.

For example, the Wisconsin Women's Network got be-hind proposed ground-breaking legislation that not only ad-dressed sex law reform (Wisconsin had an antiquated law making intercourse between unmarried adults a punishable offense) but also prohibited discrimination based on sexual orientation. (Inclusion of the plank on sexual preference in the National Plan of Action had established the premise that groups advocating for lesbians were full participants in the women's movement.) Not every organization in the Wiscon-sin Women's Network took a position on the measure, but public education by means of statewide network and organi-zational newsletters generated widespread support for the leg-islation, which was enacted into law.

Unlike other coalitions in which the umbrella pretends to more importance than the organizations it represents, these new alliances were developed with the understanding that their role was primarily to support and reinforce the organiza-tions whose efforts they orchestrated. Their purpose was to target achievable objectives, to build momentum on success. In selecting priority issues, they used the criteria of viability (readiness for results), critical need (issues most vital to large numbers), and strong member support (priorities most deeply shared).

In 1982, the National Women's Conference Committee, following its mandate to "stimulate the formation and growth of networks," orchestrated media events across the country to coincide with the July 1 deadline for ERA ratification. In 300 communities large and small, local and state groups an-nounced the birth of new organizational networks as partici-pants in "A New Day Beyond ERA." Organizing kits for the event included media and advocacy tips for local activists, as well as suggestions on how they could link with national ef-forts on eight Plan of Action issues: child care, education, elective/appointive office, employment, health, homemakers and family law, international issues, and violence. While the announced "National Task Forces" on these issues were largely mythical, they provided the model and the incentive to coordinate policy advocacy on the state and local level.

The NWCC then turned to large national organizations with local and state constituencies. The American Association of University Women (AAUW) responded in 1983 with a major two-year initiative, "Empowering Women: Achieving Change Through Advocacy Networks," directing its state divisions and 1,900 branches toward the network-building process. The National Council of Negro Women advocated Plan of Action networks. Leagues of Women Voters and NOW groups provided leadership in many states.

As network management models and strategies proved successful, the NWCC and AAUW undertook the process of conscious transplant by targeting states ripe for new networks and support and providing consultation to state leaders. Bylaws and operating policies were shared as prototypes to help diverse groups pull together in new sites.

In most states, resource sharing enabled networks to hire staff for organizational coordination and lobbying in state capitals. Sophisticated systems of outreach into legislative districts proved that networks could make the difference in mobilizing constituents and moving issues. Permanent linkages among organizations had been established in more than 30 states by 1988 and were underway in at least 10 more states in 1989. Only 10 states had done nothing as of 1989. Some states were also reviving moribund commissions on women, structured to involve greater legislative participation and thus less subject to gubernatorial whim than their predecessors.

During the 1980s, model laws have been passed in most

states to address the policy gaps named in the National Plan of Action. Laws dealing with marital property reform, domestic abuse and sexual assault, pay equity, gender discrimination in insurance, child support enforcement, welfare reform, and family/medical leave have been grafted from state to state; some have been translated into federal statute. That process, too, has become more intentional and sophisticated.

National organizations have played an increasing role in both transplant and translation strategies in order to build public policy gains for women. New institutions have been created to help the process. For example, the Women's Economic Justice Center of the National Center for Policy Alternatives in Washington, D.C. disseminates information about model laws developed by state women's agenda projects. The Center's March 1989 leadership brief, *Policy Choices in Family and Medical Leave*, for example, analyzes laws now evolving in 20 states.

Since 1985 a growing number of national women's organizations have allied as a "Council of Presidents" in Washington, D.C. The council was formed initially for the exchange of information among a small group of leaders of the largest organizations. In over-organized Washington, there was no shortage of groups coalescing, often temporarily, to lobby on specific issues, but there was no forum where leaders responsible to diverse nationwide constituencies could shape larger strategies that would build momentum and impact. There was also a need to extend connections beyond largely white middle-class feminist organizations to include leaders from an increasingly diverse women's movement. (The media continues to describe a "white, middle-class" women's movement. However, Downie's survey reported that 56 percent of white and 65 percent of black women called themselves feminists, and that of 1,000 women-of-color groups nationwide, many organized around Plan of Action issues [Downie, 1988].)

In 1986, the Council of Presidents first focused priority action on the federal Civil Rights Restoration Act, legislation to restore the broad reach of antidiscrimination laws that had prevailed before the Supreme Court's 1984 decision in *Grove City v. Bell*. Seventeen groups committed themselves to public education and lobbying in order to breathe life into an issue congressional leaders and the media called dead. Efforts to move the legislation through Congress had been repeatedly derailed by conservatives' tactics linking it to the inflammatory issue of abortion. In 1986, organized media efforts and grassroots advocacy spearheaded by council organizations brought the issue back to life in Congress, even though the Civil Rights Restoration Act was not passed that year.

For the opening of the 100th Congress in 1987, council organizations agreed to concentrate on seven additional legislative priorities: family and medical leave, welfare reform, child care, pay equity, raising the minimum wage, protection of reproductive health care, and reintroduction of the Equal Rights Amendment. This focus provided the allied organizations with access to congressional leadership and to the press that they had not achieved separately.

Just as important, it spurred the orchestration of new national outreach strategies which allowed varying membership constituencies to be utilized for greatest impact. Collaboration with the Congressional Caucus for Women's Issues offered new opportunities to assess support and timing in an effort to move legislation. While the 100th Congress dealt more disappointments than successes, the Civil Rights Restoration Act was enacted in 1988, and important momentum was built for child care, family leave, pay equity, and raising the minimum wage.

For the 1988 elections a nonpartisan issues strategy was launched by the Council of Presidents under the banner of the "Women's Agenda." The strategy was built on the experience of Women's Vote Project coalitions reaching back to 1982, which had been primarily voter registration drives. The Women's Agenda served as a new means to produce a set of issue priorities, a kind of chorus on a shared song sheet, which invited organizations to add their verses. It was the first time since 1977 that so many groups had signed onto a multiple issue document. More than 40 organizations representing 10 million grassroots citizen-activists pledged to press the agenda "with candidates for national, state, and local office whatever their party."

The 1988 Women's Agenda included: (1) family policies assuring access to housing, child and elder care, family and medical leave, and equitable education; (2) economic opportunity, including occupational preparation, pay equity, raising the minimum wage, and welfare reform; (3) comprehensive health care and safety, including long-term care, minimum health coverage, and reproductive health care; (4) a federal budget balancing adequate defense with global economic and human development; and (5) equality under the law including the Equal Rights Amendment, and protection of civil rights and reproductive choice.

These 40 groups cosponsored the first Women's Agenda Conference, which was coordinated by BPW/USA (National Federation of Business and Professional Women's Clubs, Inc.) and held in Des Moines, Iowa, in January 1988. Over 2,000 women from around the country gathered in Des Moines to decide strategy for forwarding the Women's

Agenda during the election campaigns. Discussions centered on crucial policy issues such as education, health care, reproductive choice, and child care and on how these issues could be addressed in different electoral contexts. In 1989, the Women's Agenda became the legislative agenda for the women's movement in many states as networks organized state Women's Agenda conferences.

What the 1988 elections showed is that women are and will be an increasing factor in election outcomes. Analysts attribute the Bush election to his success in narrowing an early disadvantage among women by emphasizing such issues as child care. Women's groups are learning, as are political parties, how to assess and mobilize the women's vote and how to present the issues. Analysts working with Council of Presidents organizations have assisted in identifying what spurs women to act upon the issues in which they believe. Media consultants are assisting these groups in publicizing issues that disproportionately affect women.

Organizational leaders are consciously addressing the political realities in both parties that will shape policy strategies for women. The Coalition for Women's Appointments, coordinated by the National Women's Political Caucus, was formed well before the 1988 election for the purpose of getting more women appointed to high-level positions in whatever administration should be elected. Having worked methodically to identify qualified women in many fields who would be acceptable to one or the other (or both) political parties, the coalition was well-positioned to promote female appointments by the Bush administration.

Even before President Bush took office, Council of Presidents representatives met with him as well as with Senate Majority Leader George Mitchell. Strategy sessions with the

Congressional Caucus for Women's Issues further help orchestrate legislative activities inside the Capitol with constituent outreach and advocacy.

The Council of Presidents has recognized that women's issues become marginalized if they are perceived as partisan—if only Democratic or only Republican solutions are promoted. It was a 100th Congress controlled by Democrats that stalled pay equity, child care, family medical leave, and a number of other priorities. However, while hoping to avoid impasses like those it reached with the Reagan administration's social agenda, many groups carry grave concerns about Bush administration challenges to reproductive choice. The Council of Presidents' priorities for the 101st Congress include family and medical leave, child care, and health care—particularly reproductive and long-term health care. Acceptable components for bills in each area have been agreed upon as a basis for the long process of negotiation in Congress.

Nationally in the Council of Presidents, and in more than 30 statewide networks, organizations as diverse as the AAUW, the Mexican American Women's National Association, the Older Women's League, and the YWCA play crucial roles. Deeply rooted in their community bases, such organizations can measure the public temper and test key women's agenda issues in terms of both readiness and approach. Each organization contributes its special strengths and expertise. As the cutting edge of public policy change shifts to the states, statewide alliances across organizations will also continue to grow in number, strength, and sophistication.

Primed by hard-won experience in the past decade, the U.S. women's movement has the will and the capacity to lead a public change from self-interest to common concern. It has built strength, sensitivity, sophistication, and sisterhood across the diverse mainstream of American women. It has established an expanding effective delivery system, in essence creating its own national machinery at the federal level and in many states.

Now may be the time to ask the U.S. government to renew its official participation in the effort to achieve equity for women, as the governments of so many other countries do. Discussions of a new federal council for women are proceeding in the Council of Presidents and in Congress. Models employed by nations such as Canada are being examined, as is the experience of U.S. councils and commissions charged with assuring that public policy addresses women's needs.

The converging of experience, individual and national, has made this movement strong enough to take us where we need to go. Time and economic trends are on our side, even though the costs now borne by individuals remain too high. But proclamations of failure, whether from friend or foe, are clearly premature. The women's movement in America has proven its resiliency and staying power. Although the challenges of the National Plan of Action are not yet fulfilled, women's organizations have surely carried forth the plan's promise of American women on the move.

Women and International Development: The Road to Nairobi and Back

ARVONNE S. FRASER

IN TERMS OF WOMEN, the whole world is developing. There is no "developed" world when women's economic and political status is the measure and inequality impedes their progress. That was the consensus among the 15,000 women—including 2,000 Americans—who attended the historic world conference on women held in Nairobi, Kenya in 1985. Indeed, a recent study of the status of women in 99 countries documented that in no country are women the equals of men in health, education, employment, social security, or marriage. Only seven countries were rated "very good" in this study; 18 were "extremely poor" (Camp, 1988). The United States ranked third, behind Sweden and Finland. Interestingly, countries rated extremely poor in women's status were also extremely poor countries. Poverty and inequality go hand in hand.

Sixty percent of the conference participants came from the so-called developing world, and the conference report, *Forward-Looking Strategies* (United Nations, 1985), was adopted by 150 governments. No longer can it be asserted that the women's movement is a white, middle-class, U.S.-dominated phenomenon.

This achievement, however, was the result of over a century of coalition and consensus building, much of it led, organized, or modeled by American women. In 1840, Elizabeth Cady Stanton and Lucretia Mott strolled the streets of London together after being denied participation in the World Anti-Slavery Congress because they were female. Like many women before and after them—including the women active in the U.S. civil rights movement in the 1960s—Stanton and Mott had learned that those who opposed abrogating the rights of men could nevertheless be discriminators against women.

As they walked and talked, Mott and Stanton decided to hold a women's rights meeting after returning to the United States. The result was the famous Seneca Falls meeting in 1848, which could be said to be the beginning of an international women's movement.

Only a small number of U.S. women have been deeply involved internationally at any one time. However, by exercising four basic U.S. freedoms that citizens of many other nations do not have—freedom of speech, of association, of publication, and of travel—American women have been major contributors to international development. Americans assume these freedoms; others assume constraints. American women's ability to express new ideas, to call meetings to discuss those ideas, and to create new organizations to promote or implement ideas is widely known and often silently admired; it has also served as an impetus for change.

Public opinion is a strong force in the shaping of world events. Changing international public opinion depends on communication. International communication in Stanton's and Mott's day was by letter and through books, meetings, and travel. Historically, the printed word and meetings have been the primary vehicles for the development of an international women's movement and for women's individual development. With twentieth century technology, especially through radio and television, the whole world is linked almost instantaneously. As a result of the Nairobi conference, the world knows there is an international concern among women about their situation and a desire to do something to improve it.

It is not a coincidence that International Women's Year, the United Nations Decade for Women (1976-85), and women-in-development programs were all established shortly after a new wave of feminism swept the United States in the late 1960s and early 1970s. Because postage and printing have always been relatively cheap in the United States, reports and printed materials about women's activities produced by U.S. women's groups (or produced by others and reproduced by U.S.-based groups) have been circulated among active and interested women all over the world. Travel, meetings, and conferences have also been important elements of this communications network.

Stanton, Mott, and their contemporaries carried on massive letter writing and petition campaigns and organized international conferences to promote women's right to vote, to hold property in their own name, to be guardians of their children, and to have access to education, health services, and employment outside the home.

The recent contributions of American women to the newly revitalized international women's movement have been similar. They have defined and discussed new issues and given them publicity, including issues that may not affect U.S. women directly, such as female circumcision and bride burning. They have created new domestic and international networks or organizations around a wide variety of specific issues, including domestic violence, women's access to education and health services, and nondiscrimination in employment. They have conducted research, published, organized conferences, and raised money for their issues and for women's projects in developing countries. All this activity by American women has helped develop a new consciousness about the situation of women worldwide and to give women in other countries the courage and determination to speak out and organize on their own behalf. The U.N. Decade for Women made concern about women's status an international concern.

Networking among women internationally is not a new phenomenon, but since Nairobi, the process has been named and become more visible. U.S. women have not, by any means, been responsible for all the international networking, nor today are they even a major part of it. American women are not aware of, nor are they welcome at, every international women's meeting. Because of their geographic and language limitations, American women may not even be, proportionately, as internationally experienced or aware as many of their non-American counterparts. However, they have often been the model builders and idea generators because they have had the freedom, energy, and means to become so involved.

American pioneers in the international women's movement have been constantly, although often quietly, communicating with non-American women since the exclusion of women from the World Anti-Slavery Congress in 1840.

In 1888, in Washington, D.C., Stanton and Susan B. Anthony hosted the first International Congress of Women. Its goal was to recognize "universal sisterhood," to address questions of women, and deal with equality and justice (Bell and

Offen, 1983). This congress led to the organization of the International Council of Women, which held its centennial celebration in Washington in 1988.

The council was, however, too timid for Stanton and Anthony. In 1902, they, along with Carrie Chapman Catt, later founder of the League of Women Voters, organized what became the International Alliance for Women (IAW). The alliance, with headquarters in Europe, campaigned for women's suffrage, equal pay for equal work, improvements in women's education, health, and legal status, and women's equal participation in international affairs. In 1926, at its tenth congress in Paris, the IAW president stated that the goals of the international women's movement were equality, international understanding, and peace (Whittick, 1979; Fraser, 1987). That phrase, with one modification, became the theme of the U.N. Decade for Women: equality, development, and peace.

In San Francisco in 1945, Alice Paul of the U.S. National Woman's Party and Latin American feminists succeeded in having an equal rights provision included in the new U.N. Charter. (Paul also led the early effort to have an Equal Rights Amendment added to the U.S. Constitution.)

In 1947, the U.N. Commission on the Status of Women was established to "prepare recommendations and reports . . . on promoting women's rights in political, economic, civic, social, and educational fields . . . and to develop proposals to give effect to such recommendations" (Galey, 1979: 275). An intergovernmental body currently comprising representatives of over 30 nations, the commission has always included an American delegate. Four of the commission's early recommendations dealt with women's political rights, the legal rights of married women, education, and employment, including equal pay. International Women's Year (IWY) and the Decade for Women were commission initiatives, although the idea for IWY originated with nongovernmental women's groups having U.N. consultative status.

Thirty years of commission recommendations were combined into a new international bill of rights for women called the "Convention on the Elimination of All Forms of Discrimination Against Women," which passed the U.N. General Assembly in 1979. Essentially, the convention is the equivalent of the U.S. Equal Rights Amendment spelled out in 16 substantive articles. (In international terminology, a convention is a document.) In 1980, Sarah Weddington of Texas, as the U.S. representative at the Copenhagen mid-decade world conference on women, signed that new convention on behalf of President Carter.

Now an international treaty ratified by 97 nations, the convention is the most concise and usable document to come out of the U.N. Decade for Women and a framework for equitable development. So many ratifications in so short a time are evidence of the increasing political efficacy of women. Billie Heller of California B'nai B'rith Women and others are leading the drive to have the United States ratify this convention. (Signing of a convention by governments only obligates governments to do nothing that contravenes the principles set forth in the convention. Ratification or accession obligates governments to pursue a policy of eliminating discrimination and to report on progress in that effort to the Committee on the Elimination of Discrimination every four years.) A new global consortium, the International Women's Rights Action Watch (IWRAW), with headquarters in Minnesota and New York, is monitoring worldwide implementation of this convention.

Mexico City in 1975 was an important but somewhat

traumatic stop on the road to Nairobi for U.S. women. The first world women's conference ever held under government auspices, the U.N. Conference of International Women's Year, and the parallel nongovernmental conference drew 6,000 women. About half came from North America and Mexico. For most American women it was a first personal experience with international conflict over ideology.

Expecting sisterhood and a discussion of feminism and equality issues, they often got strong doses of international politics laced with anti-American rhetoric. Some very vocal Southern Hemisphere women argued that better economic conditions for their countries should take precedence over equality for women; others argued that children and family should come before women's rights.

Controversy got the media's attention at the Mexico City conference. However, many U.S. women worked quietly and accomplished much. Irene Tinker brought together scholars from around the world in a women-in-development seminar that resulted in the book, *Women and World Development*, edited by Irene Tinker and Michele Bo Bramsen (1976). Michaela Walsh of New York created the now thriving Women's World Banking, a group that offers women entrepreneurs financial credit and experience. Margaret Snyder lobbied through the official conference the idea of a Women's Voluntary Fund, now called UNIFEM, to support Third World women's projects. The American organizers of the nongovernmental tribune, Rosalind Harris and Mildred Persinger, later set up the International Women's Tribune Center in New York, which played important roles at the Copenhagen and Nairobi conferences.

New publications also emerged: *WIN News*, published by Fran Hosken of Massachusetts to cover women's activities and organizations around the world, brought the issue of female circumcision before the public. Hosken was criticized strongly for interfering with traditional cultural practices, but by 1985, indigenous women's groups in the countries practicing female circumcision had taken up the issue. *ISIS*, the journal of a resource and documentation center for the international women's liberation movement, was organized by a European collective which included two expatriate Americans. The first issue of *ISIS* was a report on an international tribunal on crimes against women and described the activities of local women's liberation groups around the world—sometimes anonymously in order to protect the groups.

Another issue to gain prominence after Mexico City was the role women play or could play in the economies of developing countries—a factor generally overlooked in the programs mounted by the industrialized countries after World War II to assist the newly independent nations. The goal of these foreign assistance programs was to bolster the economies of the new nations and help meet the basic human needs of the people in those countries. The emphasis was on economic improvement and increases in the gross national product. The economic model was Western and the effort was often called "modernization."

The economic contributions of women were seldom considered in this new development effort. Relations between men and women were assumed to be part of the culture with which the modernization process would not tamper. The importance of agriculture was recognized but, again, the Western model was assumed; i.e., men farmed, women were housewives. In 1969, a Danish woman, Ester Boserup, wrote *Women's Roles in Economic Development*, challenging this theory by documenting women's importance in agricultural pro-

duction in developing countries and their exclusion from the
formal economic sector. Her book, published in English in
1970, profoundly influenced U.S., European, and Third
World women with international interests (Tinker, 1983).
The phrase "women in development" (WID) was coined in
the early 1970s to describe and give focus to efforts to ensure
that women's roles would no longer be ignored.

    In 1973, one year after the U.N. General Assembly had
approved the recommendation of the Commission on the
Status of Women for International Women's Year, U.S. Senator Charles Percy, an Illinois Republican, offered a women-
in-development amendment to the U.S. Foreign Assistance
Act. The amendment called for U.S. assistance to "give particular attention to those programs, projects, and activities
which tend to integrate women into the national economies
of foreign countries, thus improving their status and assisting
the total development effort" (Section 113 of the Foreign
Assistance Act of 1961, as amended). The phrase "thus improving their status" was significant. It set out the relationship between women's status and the development effort. The
amendment had been drafted by Mildred Marcy, former head
of the Overseas Education Fund of the League of Women
Voters. It was guided through Congress by Irene Tinker and a
coalition of leaders of traditional women's organizations and
new feminist groups. Tinker, a political scientist who had
lived and worked overseas, was one of those influenced by
Boserup's book.

    By the time of the 1980 world conference on women in
Copenhagen, virtually all nations giving foreign aid, including the United States, had women-in-development offices. An
active WID donor network funded the participation of hundreds of women from developing countries, as well as numer-

ous workshops, at the Copenhagen conference. About 1,000 U.S. women attended that conference. Again, international political issues—specifically the Israel-Palestine question—dominated the official conference and media coverage of the nongovernmental forum.

By this time, however, the International Center for Research on Women, the Equity Policy Center, the Overseas Education Fund, the International Division of the National Council of Negro Women, and a consortium of WID research scholars in U.S. universities had been established and were gaining overseas development experience working on WID field projects. A body of literature on women in developing countries was being created. Women leaders in those countries were being identified and smaller conferences were being held, which included U.S., European, and Third World women.

In the early 1980s, American women with international interests could be divided into three groups: those with women-in-development interests, those working in population and family planning organizations, and those concerned with women's status and rights issues. These women were inside government, in nonprofit organizations, and at universities; a few were in major foundations—Ford, Carnegie, and Rockefeller. Each group was part of an international network of peers, and their identification with feminism ranged from cool to ardent. Preparations for and follow-up to the Nairobi conference brought these various groups together.

The Wingspread Foundation in Racine, Wisconsin and the Rockefeller Foundation conference center in Bellagio, Italy hosted several international preparatory meetings organized by U.S. women, with the support of Jill Sheffield, a program officer at the Carnegie Corporation, and a private female donor. Attending these meetings were women leaders with international experience from every region of the world, including American black and white women. African women were prominent in these preparatory conferences, for they had lobbied hard to have the 1985 conference held in Africa. The Ford Foundation helped fund the DAWN (Development Alternatives with Women for a New Era) group of Third World feminist intellectuals, some of whom also participated in the Wingspread and Bellagio meetings. Among the leadership network preparing for Nairobi, there was agreement that the conference would not be an occasion merely to mark the end of the U.N. Decade for Women, but rather an occasion to assess and celebrate women's progress and to develop specific strategies for the future.

The Bellagio conference preceding Nairobi saw a subtle shift in focus away from dealing with women's projects per se to examining how women could better use the political systems of their own countries to establish policies and programs to improve women's situations. This resulted in numerous legal and political sessions at the Nairobi Nongovernmental Organizations' Forum and the highlighting at the official U.N. conference of the U.N. Convention as an important international mechanism for achieving equality for women and as a framework for women's equitable participation in the development process. Because there was also concern that Nairobi could not physically accommodate all the women who wanted to attend, a U.S. initiative was a paper circulated worldwide on how to participate in the international women's conference without leaving home. It urged women to host local meetings to develop strategies for equality by the year 2000.

The 2,000 U.S. women who went to Nairobi ranged from

those taking their first trip overseas to experienced professionals leading workshops or attending as U.S. delegates. Maureen Reagan, the lead U.S. delegate to the official conference, deserves much credit for getting the inflammatory political references removed from the conference document, thus obtaining consensus on adoption of the *Forward-Looking Strategies*, the U.N. conference document.

The forward-looking emphasis proved effective. Fifteen thousand people traveled to Nairobi. Their actions were covered by 1,500 journalists, and millions of women were avid participants at home—reading about the conference, watching it on TV, listening to radio programs about it, and developing their own strategies for the future. The Nairobi experience generated new momentum, especially at the state and local levels in the United States, and new American efforts to collaborate internationally. Since Nairobi, new groups have formed and new activities have been organized; examples include the Global Fund for Women, Family Care International, the World Bank's Safe Motherhood Initiative, the Eleanor Roosevelt International Caucus of Political Women, and the Mt. Holyoke College International Conference on Women's Education. These, along with the Association for Women in Development, the Trickle-Up program, and the groups growing out of the Mexico City conference mentioned above, are only a few of the U.S. women's groups working internationally.

The interrelationships between women's status and their integration into the economic development process have been a source of intellectual and programmatic tension in the United States and worldwide. This parallels the confusion generated when improving a country's economy through growth in its gross national product and meeting basic human

"15,000 women attended the historic world conference on women held in Nairobi, Kenya, in 1985." *Deborah Ziska, photographer*

needs are assumed to be mutually compatible and easily attainable goals. The inclusion of women in the development discussion has illustrated the complexities of the development process. The question of whether economic concerns are of primary importance in determining political and social status, or whether political and social status largely determines an individual's or group's economic status is a chicken and egg question.

In the short interval of human history encompassed by the period between Seneca Falls and Nairobi, increasing numbers of women in the United States and around the world have been educated, entered paid employment, become voters, been elected or appointed to decisionmaking positions, become healthier, had fewer children, and lived longer.

Women have established new fields of endeavor—women in development is but one example. Women have initiated or helped pass numerous pieces of legislation, including antidiscrimination laws.

There is now a new generation of women leaders and women-in-development experts in the so-called developing world. These women are not only literate; many are well educated, proficient in more than one language, and experienced at international meetings. Many hold important posts in their own governments, at universities, or in international organizations. They resent any implication that all women in developing countries are barefoot, pregnant, and working in the fields, even though some of them were rural girls who became educated, and many of them have mothers and grandmothers who are village women. Their work on behalf of women, like that of their American counterparts, is not always visible, but it is effective. Instead of defining equality as parity with men, they are asserting that until men become more responsible for families, true equality cannot be achieved. That issue is not one American women have effectively addressed. In terms of women the whole world *is* still developing.

Women and the Peace Movement

KATE MCGUINNESS

AMERICAN WOMEN ARE A FORCE to be reckoned with in the organized peace movement. Not only are there a number of national women's peace organizations with hundreds of local affiliates—and many independent local women's peace groups—but women are leaders in peace organizations whose membership is open to men as well as women.

Women are motivated to work for peace for a variety of reasons, ranging from traditional concerns about the safety and security of their children and grandchildren to concerns more theoretically feminist in nature. The approaches and ideologies of the various women's peace organizations tend to reflect this diversity. Some focus their efforts largely on seeking changes in national defense and foreign policies and international relations; others, believing that patriarchal social institutions are inimical to the creation of conditions for a peaceful world, seek fundamental changes in personal and social attitudes and behavior. Nevertheless, groups across the spectrum of the peace movement are increasingly incorporating the concerns of women for equality and social justice into their agendas.

Women owe their present influence in the peace movement not only to their own hard work and commitment, but also to the efforts of women who labored for peace before them. Historically, the most active periods of women's participation in the peace movement have been the periods when women have claimed increased roles and rights for themselves in society as a whole. In this regard, it is no coincidence that women are among those who have brought to the peace movement a vision of peace that incorporates issues of social justice.

For the most part, women were excluded from the formal ranks of the early and mid-nineteenth century peace movement. Women were not permitted to join the American Peace Society until 1877, more than 50 years after its founding (Curti, 1936). The attitude prevailing through much of the century was articulated by such male peace leaders as William Ladd and Noah Worcester, who told women that their maternal instincts should compel them to work for peace, but that they should do so within the framework of their own charitable organizations—not within the peace movement (Curti, 1936).

There were notable exceptions, however. By 1826, nearly half of the members of the Portsmouth branch of the Massachusetts Peace Society were women. In the North East Resistance Society, formed in 1838, women were entitled to the same privileges as men, including voting rights, decisionmaking, and committee membership (Curti, 1929).

During the latter part of the nineteenth century, women not only exerted greater influence in the general peace movement but took more independent initiatives for peace. In the Universal Peace Union, founded in 1866, women constituted one-third of the membership, holding office and participating in decisionmaking at all levels (DeBenedetti, 1980). In 1873, Julia Ward Howe organized women's peace festivals in several cities; these festivals continued to be held for a number of years (Swerdlow, 1984). The peace department of the Women's Christian Temperance Union, headed by Hannah

Bailey, worked extensively to promote the cause of peace in the late 1880s.

The growth of women's clubs and women's participation in social reform movements (notably suffrage, settlement houses, and women's union groups) provided a precedent for separate women's action for peace and produced organizers and leaders who were enlisted to work for peace. Jane Addams, Carrie Chapman Catt, Emily Green Balch, and Lillian Wald were among these leaders. The traditional appeal to women's "maternal instincts" also served successfully to unite women the world over on behalf of peace.

It was in the twentieth century that the first clearly defined women's peace movement emerged. Women mobilized rapidly to fill the void left by traditional peace groups that failed to respond to the outbreak of World War I. Answering a specific call to action from European women—Rosika Schwimmer of Hungary and Emmeline Pethick-Lawrence of England, in particular—women in the United States offered some of the strongest opposition to the war in Europe.

In 1914, 1,500 women marched in a New York City peace parade to protest the war. Several months later, the Woman's Peace Party was formed at a January 1915 conference in Washington, D.C. that drew over 3,000 women (Steinson, 1982). The Woman's Peace Party offered tangible solutions to the European conflict, including mediation by neutral nations and international nonmilitary sanctions. The group's other goals included women's suffrage and the elimination of the economic causes of war. Within months the Woman's Peace Party claimed 40,000 members and 165 chapters throughout the United States (Elshtain, 1980).

American women made significant contributions to the development of an international women's peace movement.

Jane Addams, president of the Woman's Peace Party, chaired a 1915 international congress of women at The Hague that was attended by over 1,000 women from 12 countries. The Woman's Peace Party platform was endorsed by this congress, which also adopted a resolution to send envoys to world leaders requesting that a conference of neutrals be convened to begin the process of mediation. The passage of this resolution relied heavily on American leadership (International Congress of Women, 1915).

In 1918, American women attended a second international meeting held at the same time as the peace talks at Versailles. The three-year-old international women's peace network born at the Hague congress adopted a formal structure and became the Women's International League for Peace and Freedom (WILPF). American leadership was again key: Jane Addams was elected president and Emily Green Balch secretary-treasurer. The Woman's Peace Party became the United States branch of WILPF (International Congress of Women, 1918).

WILPF condemned the Treaty of Versailles, saying it established a peace that granted too many privileges to the victors and required reparations that would mean poverty for many Europeans, conditions that WILPF members believed would lead to future wars (ibid.). In addition to working for peace, the group addressed issues related to economic injustice and to ensuring an equal place for women in society (Degen, 1939).

This was an important period for the development of women's role in the peace movement. American women created a network that enabled them to establish a solid presence in the peace movement, both in the United States and abroad. By addressing issues of women's rights and economic inequality, they incorporated an idea of social justice into the

The Washington State branch of the Women's International League for Peace and Freedom, 1922.
© *The WILPF Collection, Swarthmore College Peace Collection*

peace movement, a significant development at the time (DeBenedetti, 1980).

In recent years, there has been an increase in the number of women's peace organizations. Seven of the nine national women's groups (which are listed at the end of this chapter) have been formed since 1980. In addition, there are more independent local women's peace groups than ever before. The 1988-89 edition of the *Peace Resource Book*, a guide to peace organizations, issues, and literature, lists 7,000 peace groups in the United States. Nearly 550 of these are women's organizations, including national groups, their local affiliates, and independent local groups. Just four years earlier, this directory listed fewer than 200 women's peace organizations (Institute for Defense and Disarmament Studies, 1984 and 1988).

Women's peace organizations have evolved and matured.

For a long time entirely dependent on volunteers, many are now professionally staffed. For example, the Women's Action for Nuclear Disarmament (WAND) and WILPF had professional staffs of 10 to 15 and budgets of approximately half a million dollars each in 1988. While foundations provide some support, most organizations rely primarily on membership dues, fees from special events, contributions, and literature sales for their income.

The growing number of women's peace organizations represents a concerted effort on the part of women to respond to increasing conventional and nuclear militarization. These organizations address issues ranging from military and foreign policy (nuclear and conventional disarmament, comprehensive test ban treaties, U.S. global intervention, and military spending) to social justice (economic inequity, racism, and women's rights). A more radically feminist segment of the peace movement sees patriarchy as the underlying cause of violence, advocating extensive social change aimed at dismantling male-dominated social structures. Women's peace groups implement many strategies to attain their goals, among them political pressure and lobbying, grassroots organizing and education, extensive networking, and occasionally civil disobedience.

Women have also had an impact on other organizations in the peace movement. Over half of the individuals identified as contacts for the groups listed in the *Peace Resource Book* are women. Groups such as the Mobilization for Survival, SANE/FREEZE, Fellowship of Reconciliation, and the War Resisters League report that women and men are fairly equally represented in staff positions and on their boards. Each has a feminist or women's task force at the national level and some, such as SANE/FREEZE and the Mobilization for Survival, encourage their local staffs or affiliates to establish similar task forces. Task Force activities range from including women's concerns, such as safety while canvassing and access to leadership roles in training sessions for canvassers at SANE/FREEZE to incorporating a feminist analysis of militarism into all of the work at the War Resisters League.

Many of the recently founded national women's peace organizations seek a greater voice for women in military and foreign policy formation—areas where they have been traditionally excluded—in order to create a safer, more peaceful world. For example, WAND develops strategies that effectively involve women in the political process at all levels by providing written materials and coordinating training sessions on electoral and lobbying processes. The WAND political action committee (WAND PAC) provides campaign support, endorsements, and financial contributions to candidates with disarmament agendas. (In 1986, 32 of the 46 candidates endorsed by WAND PAC were elected.) Another group, Peace Links, has developed a network of 170 prominent women, among them elected officials, who are committed to finding alternatives to the arms race. WAND, WILPF, and Women Strike for Peace have active legislative offices in Washington, D.C. with staffs that lobby Congress on foreign policy, the military budget, and disarmament issues.

The relationship between growing military budgets and decreased spending for social services and the trend toward the "feminization of poverty" has become an increasingly important issue for women's peace groups. This connection provides one basis for the continued integration of social justice issues into the peace movement.

The Women's Budget, first published by WILPF in 1985, illustrates how redirecting 50 percent of the military budget into social programs would benefit women and their families and create a national security defined by a more equitable

economic system, rather than by military strength. The
Women's Peace Initiative is working to unite an already
strong women's movement behind peace issues, especially reducing military spending; WPI members see this as a necessity
for the further success of a women's agenda. In fact, nearly
every major national peace organization includes among its
priorities some reference to the need for funding social programs instead of the arms race.

Social justice issues provide common ground for networking with organizations and people traditionally outside of the
peace movement. WILPF's 1988-89 program includes a racial
justice campaign designed to train members to recognize and
take action against, and establish networks with groups working against, racial violence. The Jobs With Peace Campaign,
which calls for a complete change in national budget priorities, has been somewhat successful in enlisting the support of
working-class women of color for the peace movement (Rizzo-
Harvi, 1987).

Although the radical feminist perspective in the peace
movement has been limited, one of its significant contributions has been to provide an analysis of violence that is structural in nature; that is, identifying patriarchy as a root cause
of violence. The Women's Pentagon Action of the early
1980s, which drew over 1,000 women to protest at the Pentagon, regarded patriarchy as a source of political, economic,
and personal violence, and sought to activate women in re-
structuring society. WILPF intends to study the connections
between international violence (economic, military and cultural domination) and personal violence against women
(rape, battering, and abuse). The feminist task force of the
War Resisters League has published a number of articles and
pamphlets on the relationship between militarism and vio-

lence against women; the resource handbook of the Women's Encampment contains similar information.

The empowerment of women is a key function of every national women's peace organization. Groups work to educate women about military issues, but at the same time assure them they need not be experts to express their concerns about the arms race. Women Strike for Peace, WAND, and Peace Links, for example, train women as speakers, enabling them to educate and mobilize other in their own communities. WILPF offers three leadership development programs for women designed to familiarize them with global peace efforts and feminist political analysis, to build skills in group process, and to develop lobbying, public relations, fundraising, and membership outreach skills.

Consensus and nonhierarchical organizational models, designed to facilitate broad participation in decisionmaking, are important processes that the women's peace groups have learned from the women's movement. Some national women's peace groups, such as Women Strike for Peace and the Women's Encampment, have made a conscious choice to use consensus as their form of decisionmaking and are committed to decentralized organizational structures. Local groups, because of their smaller size, may be more inclined than larger national groups to use these models.

Women continue their history of international networking. WILPF is part of the largest international network, with sister organizations in 28 countries and nongovernmental organization ("NGO") status at the United Nations. Women for a Meaningful Summit has organized an international women's presence at summit meetings since 1985. The Women's Encampment was begun in solidarity with European women's peace camps to organize American protests against the deployment of Pershing II and Cruise missiles in Europe. Peace Links and Grandmothers for Peace coordinate exchanges between U.S. and Soviet women. Local women's peace groups support international networking as well, by hosting speakers from abroad and attending international conferences.

It is widely believed in the peace movement that women are its mainstay; while no statistics exist to document this perception, the substantial proportion of women among activists in peace organizations—whether women's organizations or not—is suggestive. Certainly, organizations are reaching out and mobilizing large numbers of women to work creatively and effectively for peace. Many of them do so with a commitment to empower women by using grassroots organizing techniques.

Any true assessment of the last several decades of work toward greater equality between women and men must include the activities of women's peace organizations to increase U.S. women's voice in the formation of their country's foreign and military policy. History proved the wisdom of the International Congress of Women's objections to the terms of the Versailles Treaty 70 years ago. Today, as then, women bring to the peace movement a multi-issue perspective that is valuable for understanding more fully the nature and causes of violence, and hence how it can best be eradicated.

National Women's Peace Organizations

Grandmothers for Peace, 909 12th Street, Suite 118, Sacramento, California 95814, (916) 444-5080

This group, founded in 1982, believes that the possession of nuclear weapons and the intent to use them is morally wrong. The fear that their grandchildren may be the last generation has motivated its members to work for peace. As of 1988, there were 3,000 people on its mailing list, 500 dues-paying members, and contacts with women in 27 countries.

Mothers Embracing Nuclear Disarmament (MEND), P.O. Box 2309, La Jolla, California 92038, (619) 454-3343

Using the universal appeal of motherhood and education about the dangers of nuclear weapons, MEND seeks to inspire a mutual commitment among all nations to eliminate nuclear weapons. Founded in 1985, it had grown to over 1,600 members in 1988.

Peace Links, 747 8th Street, S.E., Washington, D.C. 20003, (202) 544-0805

Peace Links, a nonpartisan organization begun in 1982 by Betty Bumpers, currently has a network of 30,000 women throughout the United States. The group works to increase a mainstream constituency of women behind peace issues. The 1988 program areas included mobilizing a peace vote, improving U.S.-Soviet relations through "citizen diplomacy," and educating high school students about nuclear weapons issues.

Women for a Meaningful Summit (WMS), 2401 Virginia Avenue, N.W., Washington, D.C. 20037, (202) 785-8497

WMS was founded as an ad hoc coalition, comprised primarily of women's peace groups, in order to create a voice for women at the 1985 summit meeting. Key activities include meetings with Soviet leader Gorbachev and U.S. State Department officers, and an assembly hosted by Margarita

Papandreou in Greece. The board of directors represents a worldwide grassroots network, with four million members in the United States. Congresswomen Claudine Schneider and Barbara Boxer cochair the group.

Women's Action for Nuclear Disarmament (WAND), P.O. Box 153, New Town Branch, Boston, Massachusetts 02258, (617) 643-6740

WAND seeks to empower women politically to shape U.S. policies toward a world free from the threat of nuclear war. Founded in 1980 by Helen Caldicott, WAND now has over 11,000 members and 80 affiliates in 35 states. It has focused on election issues, developing a grassroots legislative lobbying network, and political skills building. WAND has also established a separate education fund and a political action committee.

Women's Encampment for a Future of Peace and Justice, 5440 Route 96, Romulus, New York 14511, (607) 869-5825

The women's peace camp was organized in 1983 by the Upstate Feminist Peace Alliance (which had been a part of the Women's Pentagon Action), and the Women's International League for Peace and Freedom as an American response to the deployment of Cruise and Pershing II missiles in Europe. In 1983, over 12,000 women visited the camp for actions at the U.S. Army depot at Seneca, New York. Women continue to live at the camp as an ongoing presence against militarism, though their numbers are much reduced from the camp's earlier days. Currently, Women's Encampment has a mailing list of 8,000 people.

*Women's International League for Peace and Freedom (WILPF),
1213 Race Street, Philadelphia, Pennsylvania 19107, (215)
563-7110*

WILPF is one of the oldest peace organizations in the
United States, and, with affiliates in 28 countries, the most
internationally oriented women's group. There are 120
branches in the United States, with approximately 15,000
members. WILPF has worked extensively on peace and justice
issues since its beginning. Its 1988 goals include organizing a
racial justice campaign, promoting activism against U.S. global intervention, and working toward disarmament by the
year 2000.

*Women's Peace Initiative, 2 Lamson Place, Cambridge,
Massachusetts 02139, (617) 868-8421*

Begun in 1987, the Women's Peace Initiative is a national
network that seeks to unite an already organized women's
constituency behind its five-point peace platform. The platform calls for achieving nuclear disarmament, reducing the
threat of conventional war, ending military intervention, re-
ordering federal spending priorities, and promoting equality
for women. The group is working to build both its political
and grassroots constituency.

*Women Strike for Peace (WSP), 145 South 13th Street,
Philadelphia, Pennsylvania 19107, (215) 923-0861*

Women Strike for Peace began in 1961 when over
100,000 women gathered to protest nuclear testing in the
atmosphere. Their current network numbers 10,000; there

are 11 local chapters. The group focuses on grassroots education and organizing and recently distributed 50,000 copies of a primer on the Strategic Defense Initiative ("Star Wars"). WSP is also organizing a lobby-by-proxy project in which signatories authorize the group to lobby for peace issues on their behalf. Over 20,000 proxies had been collected by 1988.

The Emergence and Growth of Women's Studies Programs[1]

ONE OF THE MAJOR achievements of women in higher education over the last two decades is the evolution of women's
studies as a formal area of teaching and research. The idea of
women's studies emerged on college and university campuses
in the late 1960s as feminist scholars, influenced by the
women's movement, began to question the content of the
academic curriculum. The progress of women's studies since
then has been phenomenal. Against all odds—financial, political, and intellectual—a cadre of committed women scholars, joined by a few men, succeeded in gaining recognition for
the legitimacy of the field and led the way to the establishment of courses and degree programs throughout the country.

According to a recent survey of campus trends conducted
by the American Council on Education, over two-thirds of all
universities, nearly half of all four-year colleges, and about
one-fourth of all two-year institutions now offer women's
studies courses. Moreover, the world of feminist scholarship
today includes over 50 centers or institutes for research on
women, numerous professional journals for the publication
of the new knowledge, and more than a hundred feminist
bookstores across the country.

How did all this come about? Although women's studies

as such did not come into being until the late 1960s, courses on women were not entirely unknown prior to that time. They were, however, few and far between. One of the earliest that we know of was a course on the "Status of Women in the United States," offered by the department of sociology at the University of Kansas in 1892. There were also some examples in the early decades of the twentieth century, such as the course given in the Economics Department at the University of Washington in 1912 by Professor Theresa McMahon. The subject was "Women and Economic Evolution, or the Effects of Industrial Change on the Status of Women," a topic that is even more relevant at the present time than it was then. Courses in women's history began to appear in the 1960s, and more systematic studies of women across the disciplines followed.

Women's studies appears to have originated on the East and West Coasts more or less simultaneously. In 1969, a group of feminists at Cornell University organized a conference that was concerned with issues raised by the women's movement. One of the results of the conference was the formation of a faculty seminar to examine the portrayal of women in the curriculum of the social and behavioral sciences. The seminar led in turn to the establishment at Cornell of an interdisciplinary course on women, followed in 1970 by a coordinated female studies program consisting of six courses from different departments of the university. At about the same time, a similar effort was under way in California, where a women's studies program was started at San Diego State University. It included courses such as "Women in Literature," "Women in Comparative Cultures," and "Contemporary Issues in the Liberation of Women."

From then on, women's studies courses and programs spread rapidly, both in the United States and abroad. At the same time, women's studies, which started as a marginal and not quite respectable area of academic endeavor, has become increasingly institutionalized and integrated into the liberal arts curriculum as a whole. The first step was to move from individual courses to the organization of coordinated degree programs. Today there are interdisciplinary degree programs and minors or joint majors with specific fields.

The next step in the institutionalization process was the development of fellowship programs in women's studies. That came in 1972 when the Ford Foundation initiated faculty and dissertation awards for research on the role of women in society. At the time, some feminists felt that the recognition that such a national fellowship program bestowed on the field was at least as important as the funding it provided. In any event, it was soon followed by fellowships in women's studies from other foundations and from government agencies such as the National Endowment for the Humanities and the Women's Educational Equity Act program.

The third step was the formation of women's studies research centers, beginning in 1974 at Stanford and Wellesley. Of the 50 or so centers in existence today, the majority are campus-based. The others are independent centers with research programs that tend to be policy oriented rather than curriculum oriented. All of the centers provide resources for research about women, strengthening the efforts of individual scholars. The centers offer such facilities as libraries, staff support, forums for the exchange of ideas, assistance in project development, and financial aid. Collectively, they have made an essential contribution to the advancement of women's studies, its capacities, and its recognition in the academic community. The National Council for Research on Women is a consortium of these centers that was formed in 1982 to facilitate collaborative work.

A fourth and essential element in the evolution and institutionalization of women's studies was the development of scholarly journals and textbooks. Journals such as *Women's Studies* and *Feminist Studies* first appeared in 1972, and the leading journal, *SIGNS: Journal of Women in Culture and Society*, made its debut in 1975. Textbooks, while not abundant even today, also began to appear around this time. Some of the earliest texts came in courses about women in the law. Comprehensive introductory textbooks were generally not available until the 1980s.

Next came the establishment of the National Women's Studies Association (NWSA) in 1977. The purpose of the association, as stated in the preamble to its constitution, is "to further the social, political, and professional development of women's studies throughout the country and the world, at every educational level and in every educational setting." NWSA now has about 3,000 members, including scholars, administrators, community activists, and other women's studies practitioners as well as school teachers. NWSA serves an important function, then, in spreading women's studies beyond higher education and into schools and the community.

A further milestone in the evolution of women's studies was the establishment during the 1980s of professorships or chairs in women's studies on various campuses. At the present time, there are upwards of about a dozen such chairs in colleges and universities across the country, for example, at Brown, Rutgers, and the University of Southern California.

There were two other notable developments during the 1980s. In 1983, the Center for Education Statistics of the U.S. Department of Education began to include data on degrees earned in women's studies in its annual reports of earned degrees conferred; for purposes of official data collection, women's studies is now classified as an interdisciplinary field. This is surely a major sign of recognition and institutionalization. And finally, University Microfilms International, which maintains a unique information service on doctoral dissertations and master's theses, now publishes catalogues of dissertations in women's studies. It reported over 2,000 dissertations in women's studies in the period 1981-84.

Clearly, women's studies, once considered a fad, is now firmly established in higher education. Moreover, its influence on the curriculum extends beyond women's studies courses as new knowledge has been brought to bear on the mainstream liberal arts disciplines. One of the circumstances facilitating this process of integration is the fact that women's studies programs are rarely organized as separate departments. In nearly all institutions, women's studies is an interdepartmental program, headed by a director or coordinator rather than a department chair. The curriculum usually consists of an introductory interdisciplinary core course, followed by a selection of courses offered by various departments. These might include, for example, courses such as the "Psychology of Women," "Women in Colonial America," "Images of Women in Literature," or "Women in the Economy." A recent study of women in higher education, carried out under the aegis of the Russell Sage Foundation, shows a steady growth in the number and size of these interdisciplinary programs.

How women's studies has affected the rest of the curriculum is more difficult to determine. One of the main objectives of women's studies from the beginning was not only to compensate for the absence of a women's perspective in the traditional curriculum by adding new courses, but also to bring the new perspectives into the so-called "mainstream" liberal arts

"Women's studies, once considered a fad, is now firmly established in higher education." Here Phyllis Palmer (center) teaches a class in the fifteen-year-old women's studies department at The George Washington University.
Courtesy Department of Women's Studies, The George Washington University

curriculum that is taken by all students, men as well as women. This is not easily done since the new perspectives often challenge the basic assumptions of the methodologies of the disciplines. As women's studies scholars have pointed out, you can't simply add the idea that the world is round to the idea that it is flat and go on as before. You need to rethink the whole universe.

The first formal effort to assess the impact of women's studies on the liberal arts curriculum was undertaken by a group of women faculty members at Princeton in 1976. The project was limited to an examination of the introductory courses in four disciplines that have been among the most active in women's studies—history, sociology, psychology, and English. Some 355 course syllabi from 172 departments in a variety of institutions were collected and analyzed, and supplementary information was gathered through question- naires sent to department heads, directors of women's studies programs, and publishers of textbooks. It was found that, with few exceptions, the study of women was being given little or no attention. Department chairs reported that the pres- ence of women in their departments, and to a lesser extent the existence of women's studies programs on campus, were important in determining whether individual faculty mem- bers were taking heed of the new scholarship on women and incorporating it into the basic courses. Based on these find- ings, it was concluded that special efforts were needed to in- form faculty members more broadly of the nature and rele- vance of the new material on women to their respective fields.

Since that time various kinds of curriculum integration or mainstreaming activities have been undertaken. One was the preparation of a monograph on *Teaching Women's History*, written by Gerda Lerner (1981), a leading women's studies scholar and historian. Lerner's monograph, which was pub- lished and widely distributed by the American Historical As- sociation, provides a guide to relevant topics and source mate- rial, including material from other disciplines, making it easier for faculty members to incorporate women's history into existing courses. Other curriculum integration projects have taken the form of faculty workshops, summer institutes, conferences, and faculty development or curriculum revision programs. Many of these have been funded by government agencies or private foundations.

By 1981, a directory of curriculum integration programs prepared by the Center for Research on Women at Wellesley listed nearly 50 projects. One of the more ambitious during this period was an institution-wide effort at Wheaton College in Norton, Massachusetts, to integrate the study of women into the entire liberal arts curriculum. The Wheaton project culminated in a national conference in 1983 that was attended by 250 women and men who were involved in curriculum integration projects or were interested in initiating them. According to the conference report, published in 1984, the project was intended as "both a spur to the process of gender balance in the curriculum of American higher education and a means of expanding the network of those undertaking this effort."

Summer institutes in women's studies for faculty members have been held by the Great Lakes Colleges Association and at Memphis State University. Duke University has conducted summer institutes in women's studies for high school as well as college teachers, with a particular focus on intersections of race, sex, and class. Recently, the New Jersey Department of Higher Education gave Rutgers University $362,500 for a statewide project entitled "Integrating the Scholarship on Gender." The project will involve all of the state's 56 public and private colleges and is expected to provide a model for other states.

Today there are, all told, over 100 curriculum integration projects in process in colleges and universities. Many of these have been funded by the Ford Foundation. For example, one program initiated in 1985 with Ford support is designed to introduce new perspectives on women into the curriculum of 10 formerly all-male colleges. As part of the program, Columbia University has restructured its well-known "Contemporary Civilization" curriculum. Similarly, at Stanford University, the course on "Western Civilization" required of all undergraduates was revised to include material by and about women and minorities as well as studies of non-Western cultures. In 1988, this course was replaced by a new course entitled "Cultures, Ideas and Values."

What is the nature of the changes that are being made? In what ways and to what extent has the new scholarship on women affected the disciplines since the exploratory Princeton study of 1976? In recent years several volumes of essays on this subject have appeared. One of the foremost is *The Prism of Sex* (Sherman and Beck, 1981), which shows how feminist research has challenged the premises and content of six disciplines—history, literature, psychology, sociology, philosophy, and political science. Another volume, entitled *Men's Studies Modified*, edited by Dale Spender (1981), looks at the impact of feminism on a number of other academic disciplines including anthropology, economics, and biology, as well as professional fields such as education and law.

The new scholarship has challenged the traditional assumptions of the academic disciplines as well. For example, in history we are familiar with periods labeled as "the Dark Ages" and "the Renaissance," but feminist scholars have shown that the way we have identified historical periods such as these is based primarily on a male perspective. The female experience in those eras was sharply different, indeed, the opposite from that of men. The Dark Ages were a period of ascendancy for women and the Renaissance a period of contraction in women's roles in society. In other words, according to feminist historians, there was no renaissance for women in the Renaissance.

Another example can be found in the field of economics, where it used to be common practice in studies of labor force participation to examine a combined sample of men and women, or even to limit the sample to men and assume that the conclusions applied to women as well. The labor force participation of women as distinct from that of men has been studied exhaustively by feminist scholars, male and female, over the last 20 years. As a result, it is now known that the response to wage changes is considerably more complex than the textbooks had assumed, and that the labor force participation of women depends not only on wages, but on decisions regarding the allocation of time between work inside and outside the home, the income needs of the family, the stage in the life cycle, the availability of part-time or flex-time work, the value placed on leisure, and possibly other considerations. In the process of studying all these elements, we have learned a great deal more than we knew before about labor force participation as such—of men as well as of women.

History and economics are only two of the fields in which feminist scholars have made an impact. In psychology they have questioned the long-accepted Freudian theories of female behavior and in literature they have uncovered lost writers, minorities as well as women, whose work has much to contribute to our literary heritage and to the richness of the liberal arts curriculum. Course materials in these fields now include works such as Jean Baker Miller's *Toward a New Psychology of Women* (1976) and Paul Lauter's *Reconstructing American Literature* (1983).

The changes chronicled here are ongoing. Women's studies as a field of scholarship continues to grow, and the new knowledge is gradually being integrated into the liberal arts curriculum. The dramatic increase in college enrollment by women over the last 20 years has given added impetus to the acceptance of women's studies on campus. In the long run, however, the objective of women's studies is to bring new perspectives and understanding to bear on the education of all students, men as well as women.

The Congressional Caucus for Women's Issues in the 101st Congress

THE MEMBERS OF CONGRESS WHO BELONG to the bipartisan Congressional Caucus for Women's Issues are involved individually, as well as collectively, in efforts on behalf of women and families. The 21 women who constitute the caucus's executive committee in the 101st Congress hail from 15 states. Fourteen are Democrats, seven are Republicans.

This section, which was prepared in the spring of 1989, begins with a report from Representatives Patricia Schroeder (D-CO) and Olympia Snowe (R-ME), in their capacity as its cochairs, on the caucus's collective activities and concerns, particularly in the first session of the 101st Congress. Following the cochairs' report, 19 of the Congresswomen who belong to the caucus report briefly on their particular activities and perspectives on matters of concern to women. All of the women and men who are members of the caucus as of mid-June 1989 are listed alphabetically at the end of the section.

The Cochairs Report . . .

The Honorable Patricia Schroeder and the Honorable Olympia J. Snowe: As we celebrate the bicentennial of the first Congress, the Congressional Caucus for Women's Issues is looking forward to more victories for women and their families. The 101st Congress promises to be a busy one, and we will be working to enact legislation to increase women's access to opportunities in the workplace and to protect them from violence and abuse in the home.

Many of the issues on the caucus agenda have received early attention from Congress this session. Child care and family and medical leave legislation has already been acted on by committees in both the House and Senate. Other issues of concern to the caucus, such as the problems of domestic violence, displaced homemakers, and infant mortality, are also slated for action this year.

The Congressional Caucus for Women's Issues was founded in 1977 as a bipartisan organization dedicated to improving the status of women. Today, there are well over 100 members. Twenty-one Congresswomen compose the executive committee, which sets the caucus's priorities and goals.

A major focus of the caucus is the Economic Equity Act (EEA), a package of bills that constitute the heart of the caucus's legislative agenda. The caucus has introduced the EEA in each Congress since 1981 and has had notable success with many of its components. The EEA is designed to promote economic equity for women.

Through the EEA and other legislation, the caucus attempts to help women balance their work and family roles. One of the most important bills in this area is the Family and

Medical Leave Act (FMLA), legislation that is long overdue. The United States is the only industrialized country, except for South Africa, that does not provide its workers with any type of job-guaranteed maternity leave. Most other countries also provide disability insurance for employees who become temporarily unable to work for nonoccupational reasons. American workers are not even guaranteed job protection in the event of a short-term illness or provided leave to care for a newborn child. The caucus is working to enact the FMLA to give American families the flexibility needed to fulfill their responsibilities as employees, spouses, parents, and children of aging parents.

Child care is another critical problem facing American families as more and more women enter the workforce. The need for affordable, quality child care has become a fact of life for millions of families. Today, approximately 10 million preschool children require some form of child care and the supply falls far short of the need; there are only 2.8 million licensed day care slots across the country. The caucus believes the federal government can play a vital role in increasing the supply and improving the quality of child care services for all American families.

In an effort to involve more of our nation's public policy leaders in the child care debate, the caucus issued the Child Care Challenge to members of the 100th Congress. The challenge illuminated the steps taken by the business community to respond to the inadequate supply of quality, affordable child care services. Members of Congress were encouraged to identify the most innovative examples of employer-sponsored child care programs in their congressional districts and states. The response was tremendous. Seventy members of Congress nominated over 160 employers. While much of the responsibility for child care lies with the parents, federal and state governments and the private sector can play an important role in easing the burdens of today's families.

Reducing infant mortality is another item on the caucus agenda in the 101st Congress. The United States is in the embarrassing position of being ranked 19th in the world in the prevention of infant mortality, behind countries ranging from Japan to Sweden to Hong Kong and Singapore. In the United States in 1988, nearly 40,000 infants—a majority of them black infants—died before their first birthday. These are inexcusable statistics, and they are largely preventable. Prenatal care would save many infants' lives, and the caucus is working on legislation to provide women with prenatal care and prenatal education in an effort to decrease the incidence of infant mortality.

Not long ago, during the trial of Joel Steinberg, we learned in graphic detail of the horrors of family violence. We were reminded that domestic violence affects families of every economic, social, and religious segment of our country. The problem of domestic violence is neither new nor insolvable. The caucus has been working on the issue of domestic violence and services for its victims for many years. We must ensure that women and their children are protected from batterers and that they have the support necessary to begin new lives.

Much work lies ahead of us for the 101st Congress. However, we look forward to these challenges and take pride in what the caucus has achieved thus far. The victories we have achieved over the last twelve years demonstrate the effectiveness of the Congressional Caucus for Women's Issues. When members of Congress work together in a bipartisan spirit, American women and families win. The caucus will continue its fight this year, and we look forward to expanding our record of achievement.

The Congresswomen Report . . .

Representative Lindy (Mrs. Hale) Boggs (Democrat; Louisiana, 2nd District): The interests of women receive consideration in all of my congressional work. A particular focus is in the area of economic equality, which broadly encompasses such issues as equality of opportunity and access, preventing spousal impoverishment, the availability of quality child care, parental leave, the problems of displaced homemakers, pay equity, access to equal credit, and employment practices that encourage the advancement of women.

As a member of the executive committee of the Congressional Caucus for Women's Issues, I strongly support the Economic Equity Act and its component parts. A significant achievement for women in 1900 was the enactment into law of the Women's Business Ownership Act that included the major elements of a bill I had coauthored with Chairman LaFalce of the House Small Business Committee to ensure equality of access to business credit for women and minorities. Our bill was a component of the EEA. I am also pleased to report that I have again been successful in securing funding for an important demonstration program establishing child care centers in public housing developments. Additionally, I continue to require reports from public officials on their progress in hiring women *for*, and promoting them *to*, middle- and upper-level positions, as well as progress reports on federal agencies' contracts with women-owned businesses.

I have the privilege of serving on the House Select Committee on Children, Youth and Families and of chairing its

Crisis Intervention Task Force, investigating such areas as child abuse, teen pregnancy, infant mortality, domestic violence, and alcohol and drug abuse and their effect upon families. I have also continued my involvement in representing American elected women through the International Interparliamentary Union. I expect to actively pursue and develop all of these areas and others of concern to women during the 101st Congress.

Representative Barbara Boxer (Democrat; California, 6th District): The Select Committee on Children, Youth and Families, of which I am a member, held a number of hearings of interest to women and families in 1988. As chair of the House Budget Committee's Task Force on Human Resources, I held hearings that focused on the issues of maternal and child health, high school dropouts, infant mortality and children with AIDS.

Economic equity for women continues to be a major priority. I am hopeful that we will finally pass the Family and Medical Leave Act in 1989 and that we will also be able to move on the Economic Equity Act.

I am the author of new legislation to attack the high school dropout problem by having model students create exciting programs for grade school students.

Representative Cardiss Collins (Democrat; Illinois, 7th District): 1989 marks the convening of the 101st Congress. During this critical juncture in the history of our great nation, I will continue to push for legislative initiatives that directly address the health and education needs of, and provide equal opportunity for, women and our nation's families.

I have again introduced legislation that comprehensively addresses the need for affordable, quality child care services. Furthermore, in my capacity as chair of the House Government Activities and Transportation subcommittee, I held follow-up hearings this year to press the General Services Administration (GSA) to provide additional on-site day-care facilities in federal buildings.

Since entering Congress, I have been a strong advocate of reproductive rights. It is necessary that we address a full range of issues related to reproductive health, such as the right to choose or not to choose abortion, access to family planning and all methods of birth control, teen pregnancy, prenatal care, child care, and medical abuses against women.

Because of my concern about a significant increase in the number of women afflicted with uterine cancer, on the first day of the 101st Congress I introduced legislation to require Medicare Part B coverage for routine Pap smear tests. The catastrophic health care insurance bill that was signed into law in 1988 included my amendment requiring Medicare to cover mammography/breast cancer screenings for women over age 65.

Representative Nancy Johnson (Republican; Connecticut, 6th District): In my view, the most important mission of the Congressional Caucus for Women's Issues is to strive for the empowerment of American women. Today's working women do not simply need more day care for their children, they also need the freedom to structure their lives to be with their children. That's empowerment.

Today's parents need to know that they can take time off, not only in family emergencies, but also for the school play, the parent-teacher conference, or the chicken pox—the important events in a child's life.

Empowerment is the bottom line in women's issues. So many of the issues that American women grapple with involve a tradeoff between a desperately needed job and the welfare of one's family. My goal in the 101st Congress is to integrate these tradeoffs so that American women can meet both their responsibilities at work and their obligations at home. We must empower women to make the best decisions for themselves and the future of their families.

Representative Marcy Kaptur (Democrat; Ohio, 9th District): I am pleased to see the ambitious agenda for the 101st Congress set out by the Congressional Caucus for Women's Issues. Child care continues to attract a great deal of attention, and the debate on how to provide it and how to finance it promises to be lively. In the last Congress, I was able to include in the omnibus housing bill a provision authorizing funds to help nonprofit organizations establish child care programs in public housing. I believe we must continue to widen access to child care, and I am sponsoring a measure to encourage day care centers in private homes. This bill, a companion to one sponsored by Senator David Durenberger (R-MN), would permit the federally chartered corporations that buy mortgages in the secondary market to purchase mortgages for homes with family day care centers. Such purchases are not allowed under present law; as a result, local lenders that expect to sell their mortgages to Fannie Mae, Ginnie Mae, or Freddie Mac are reluctant to approve mortgage-loans for homes where family day care centers will be operated.

I am also interested in improving working conditions and enhancing career potential for long-term care nursing aides, 90 percent of whom are women. Virtually all of them work for very low wages and often have few or no fringe benefits. To bring attention to the very important work that they perform, I plan to introduce a resolution highlighting basic facts about chronic care workers and calling for better pay and employment conditions. I will also introduce a bill to address the

shortage of chronic care workers by encouraging the involvement of volunteers in providing some chronic care services
under the Older Americans Act's Demonstration Grants Program.

Senator Nancy Landon Kassebaum (Republican; Kansas):
During the 101st Congress, my primary focus on issues of
concern to women and families will be in the area of education. In my new position as ranking Republican member of
the Senate Education Subcommittee, I will be a strong voice
for efforts to assure that our educational system meets the
standards we need and expect.

Assuring that our children receive a good education ranks
among the most prominent concerns of American families. I
think it is particularly important that we focus on the early
years and that we recognize that schools alone are far from
the only factors with an impact on learning. In this connection, maintaining a strong Head Start program is a priority.

In addition, I intend to continue my efforts on behalf of
our international family planning programs. Unfortunately,
policies that weaken our efforts in this area remain in effect.

Representative Barbara B. Kennelly (Democrat; Connecticut, 1st District): Although women have been a large part of
the American work force for many years, only now are the
inequities they face—and the work we still have to do—
becoming clear, partly through the work of the Congressional
Caucus for Women's Issues and the legislative initiatives in
which I have been involved.

In the last Congress, we passed the welfare reform bill,
now signed into law. As the only woman then on the Ways
and Means Committee and as a member of its Human Resources Subcommittee, I worked hard on this bill through
very difficult times. The bill promotes jobs, education, and

child care in order to help free women from the welfare dependency cycle that saps them of their confidence and dignity.

In 1989, the House and Senate passed the long-anticipated increase in the minimum wage. Because 60 percent of minimum-wage workers are women, many of whom are their families' sole support, I have long believed that the adequacy of the minimum wage is the single most important economic issue facing women today.

I hope this year to succeed in expanding the Maternal and Child Health Services Block Grant, which provides prenatal care for low-income women. The adequacy of funding for prenatal care is critically important to millions of women who otherwise will not or cannot get medical attention during their pregnancies. We must turn around this country's high infant mortality rate, now higher than the rates in 21 other industrialized countries.

This year, I am also serving on the Speaker's Special Task Force on Children's Issues, which will identify and work on legislation concerning child care, foster care, and parental leave. I am a cosponsor of the Act for Better Child Care and hope to see more day care services for families as well as minimal health and safety standards for the children in day care.

Representative Nita M. Lowey (Democrat; New York, 20th District): As one of only two women elected to Congress in November 1988, I am enthusiastic about my new role and delighted to participate in the Congressional Caucus for Women's Issues.

The 101st Congress will face a number of exceedingly important issues related to the future of women and families and to the quality of life in our nation. I have already been active, as a member of the House Committee on Education and Labor, in pushing for enactment of parental leave and minimum-wage legislation. A job-protected period of leave following childbirth or during the illness of a family member is critical in a society where busy careers and family responsibilities compete for limited time. Similarly, a raise in the minimum wage is long overdue and will help millions of American families that are struggling to make ends meet. The Education and Labor Committee will also act this year on legislation to help increase the supply of quality, affordable child care. This is crucial to the demands of our society and to the consciences of millions of American parents.

An equally pressing goal is the preservation of the *Roe v. Wade* decision, which affirms the constitutional right of women to choose a safe, legal abortion. The Supreme Court will rule this year on a case that could weaken or overturn this landmark decision. I joined hundreds of thousands of Americans on the Mall in Washington, D.C. in demonstrating our support for this fundamental right. As a member of Congress, I believe we must be vigilant in protecting this precious right.

Representative Jan Meyers (Republican; Kansas, 3rd District): The U.S. Department of Labor not only documents the extent to which women have increasingly joined the ranks of the American work force but projects that this trend will continue into the 21st century. In fact, the majority—over two-thirds—of new entrants to the labor force between now and the year 2000 will be women and minorities.

The changing demographics of the labor market require Congress to keep a finger on the pulse of the concerns of working families. One of the more pressing of these is child care. There is not any one solution to our nation's child care problems; child care needs vary among families, communities, and states. Congressional action on child care should adopt a multi-dimensional approach. I support legislation that allows each state to determine its child care needs. Block grant funds allow states to choose from a list of priorities to provide affordable and quality child care to families.

Latchkey children are in dire need of after-school child care. States should be given funds to encourage schools to establish after-school programs for these children.

The business community also has a role in meeting child care needs. Many large employers already provide on-site or near-site care. To encourage small and medium-size businesses to get involved in child care, tax credits for start-up costs should be authorized.

I will be working throughout the 101st Congress with the Congressional Caucus for Women's Issues on child care legislation and other issues of primary concern to women and families.

Representative Constance A. Morella (Republican; Maryland, 8th District): As a member of the Committee on Post Office and Civil Service and the Select Committee on Aging, I have devoted substantial efforts to issues affecting federally employed women and older women. My legislative priorities emphasize family and medical leave, pay equity, the need for protection against the costs of long-term and home health-care services, and the expansion of quality health care.

I am an original cosponsor of the Act for Better Child Care Services and the Economic Equity Act. These comprehensive packages address the need for affordable and accessible high-quality child care and issues of equity for women in such areas as pay, business, and pension benefits.

In the international arena, I have worked with women "refuseniks," and divided spouses and families, and I traveled to the Soviet Union to meet with government officials in this effort.

Representative Mary Rose Oakar (Democrat; Ohio, 20th District): The 101st Congress holds real promise for addressing many issues that are of the utmost importance to women.

Along with parental leave and child care, pay equity continues to move forward. A study of the federal government's pay and classification scales is presently being pursued through an investigative arm of Congress, and I have introduced new legislation regarding pay equity in the 101st Congress. The goal of the Pay Equity Technical Assistance Act is to make resources and assistance available to those employers who have decided to address wage inequities in their workplaces.

In addition, we have a real opportunity to make a difference in health care. I am currently serving on the Bipartisan Commission on Comprehensive Health Care. This commission has two primary goals: first, to examine the shortcomings in current health care policies that limit individuals' access to comprehensive health care, and second, to make specific recommendations about improving long-term care services and comprehensive health care services for all Americans. I am strongly committed to ensuring that the commission issues just and sound recommendations and equally committed to securing substantial improvements in the U.S. health care system based on those recommendations.

Representative Elizabeth J. Patterson (Democrat; South Carolina, 4th District): As a member of the Congressional Caucus for Women's Issues, I have become increasingly concerned about matters that affect children, women, and families. During my first term in Congress, I introduced a bill to establish child care centers at veterans' medical centers for the employees' children. It is my hope that during the 101st Congress, I can continue my efforts on behalf of our children by introducing legislation to establish a "Children's Trust Fund" for the purpose of providing grants and low-interest loans to innovative programs that provide social services for children, including child nutrition, child health care, foster care, and services for neglected or abused children. The trust fund would be funded by contributions donated by taxpayers from their federal income tax refund. It is my hope that this legislation will help expand and improve services for our children.

Representative Nancy Pelosi (Democrat; California, 5th District): As a member of the House Banking, Finance and Urban Affairs Committee, I have had the opportunity to work on affordable housing for families. Our country should provide the basic necessities, food, clothing, and shelter for everyone, and it is not doing this. Of particular importance to me is the plight of homeless children. They are forgotten, frightened youngsters who have lost not only their homes, but also their self-esteem and their sense of belonging to a community. They are a generation growing up uneducated, neglected, and endangered by a society that has turned its back on this most poignant aspect of homelessness. As a nation we need to outline our priorities. It is imperative that we invest in our future—in our children, who will grow up to be the leaders of our country.

Representative Patricia Saiki (Republican; Hawaii, 1st District): Women increasingly are entering untraditional fields of professional activity and their interests and requirements are reflected in many major legislative areas.

As a member of the Banking Committee, I have been involved in finding solutions to the crisis within the nation's savings and loan industry. Restoring stability to America's financial institutions will strengthen the general economy, a benefit to everyone.

I am particularly interested in seeing our nation's young people become the beneficiaries of an improved educational system. As a former teacher, I understand the value of quality education. Our nation's effort to improve educational opportunities must be refined to allow our young people to remain competitive in our increasingly sophisticated technological environment.

Health issues confront women directly. Not only are women the majority of our nation's elderly, but an overwhelming number of health care workers are women. Therefore, I consider long-term health care legislation a high priority before this Congress.

Additional priorities for me in this Congress are child care and family and medical leave policies. I am pleased that these measures have already received committee attention. Considering the new demands placed upon families, it is obvious that the availability of quality child care and personal leave must be addressed.

Most of these issues are among those promoted by the Congressional Caucus for Women's Issues. The caucus is a vital force behind initiatives aimed to assist women and a focal point for the social and economic concerns of women. I am pleased to be an executive committee member of the caucus and I applaud its efforts.

Representative Claudine Schneider (Republican; Rhode Island, 2nd District): I look forward to the challenges we face in the 101st Congress and I am confident that progress will be made on a number of fronts that are critical to moving us toward greater equality.

Full access to quality education for women and girls has never been more important to our nation. If we are to compete successfully in the global economy, we must enter the 21st century with adequate numbers of well-educated workers. As women become an ever increasing percentage of the workforce, providing adequate opportunities for women goes beyond a concern for equity; all entrants into the labor market must receive training that is second to none.

One of my major concerns in this area is that women and girls not be denied equal access to quality vocational education that will prepare them for good jobs with good pay. The choice to enroll in nontraditional courses and exposure to opportunities in nontraditional occupations are essential components for reducing women's poverty and dependence. Early in the 101st Congress I introduced legislation to ensure that federally funded vocational education programs continue to provide women and girls with these opportunities. I am happy to report that the vocational education reauthorization bill recently approved by the House responds to these concerns by preserving funds explicitly for the purpose of ensuring sex equity in vocational education and also specifying that displaced homemakers will continue to be eligible for vocational education programs.

We must also do much more to encourage the participation of women and girls in math, science, and engineering. As a ranking member of the Science, Space and Technology Committee, I am concerned about the future of the scientific workforce and the need to ensure that more women enter and remain in the science education pipeline. Science education has often been described as a leaky pipeline—this is especially true where women are concerned. At each stage, women leak out in greater numbers than do men. At the various endpoints of the pipeline—baccalaureate degrees, Masters' degrees, Ph.D. programs, and science faculty positions—the percentage of women declines.

To ensure a sufficient number of science, math, and engineering professionals, we must increase the number of women entering these specialties and prevent their falling by the wayside. I have introduced legislation in the 101st Congress to expand the opportunities for women by increasing the availability of innovative programs to bring women into the scientific professions and providing scholarships to encourage women to continue their education in scientific specialties.

Representative Patricia Schroeder (Democrat; Colorado, 1st District): Developing fair, cost-effective policies that enhance the lives of American families is a high priority on my agenda for the 101st Congress. Three of my bills go to the heart of family policy. First, I have introduced the Family and Medical Leave Act that establishes a right for working parents to a job-guaranteed leave when they have or adopt a baby, when their children or parents are seriously ill, or when they experience a serious medical condition. The Family and Medical Leave Act coalition, which includes groups from the labor, women's, religious, health, family, and disability community, has done a fantastic job of fine-tuning this legislation so that it represents a fair, carefully crafted, response to the increasing and competing demands of work and family.

Second, I have introduced the Part-Time and Temporary Workers Protection Act that amends the Employee Retirement Income Security Act of 1974 (ERISA) to include part-time employees in pension and health insurance plans on a "pro-rata" basis. In many two-earner families, one spouse— usually the woman—works part-time, sometimes in order to accommodate child care needs, but in many cases because only part-time work is available. My bill recognizes that these part-time workers and their families have a right to benefits.

Third, I have introduced the Family Building Act, which requires that all federal employee health insurance plans cover family building activities, including medical procedures necessary to overcome infertility and necessary expenses related to adoption. While the bill will only apply to federal workers, it will serve as a model for all employees.

Representative Louise M. Slaughter (Democrat; New York, 30th District): My commitment to the issues affecting women remains strong as I begin my second term in the House of Representatives. I intend to actively represent my upstate New York district in debating and shaping women's and family legislation in the 101st Congress.

As the numbers of children living at or near the poverty level reach frightening levels and families struggle to meet more competing responsibilities than ever before, Congress and the president must respond with workable solutions for families. Though our nation must make difficult spending decisions in the face of a sizable federal budget deficit, families must remain a priority. It is essential that we commit to effective programs for our children in the form of family and medical leave, child care, and preventive programs such as health care and nutritional assistance.

I am currently working on child care legislation that involves a cooperative effort between business and the federal government. We all have a stake in ensuring the availability of quality, affordable child care: parents, business, and society as a whole. In addition, I am an original cosponsor of the Family and Medical Leave Act. I will work with my colleagues to pass these and other family legislative initiatives this Congress.

Representative Olympia Snowe (Republican; Maine, 2d District): The care provided to America's children has been of particular importance to me for many years; I first held child care hearings back in 1983. Evidence abounds that many working parents have great difficulty in making affordable, suitable arrangements for the care of their children. I am deeply concerned, for example, that an estimated 1.5 million preschool children are left unattended for at least part of the time their parents are working.

Because I believe we have a responsibility to help make sure that working parents have access to good child care, I have been a principal cosponsor of the Act for Better Child Care Services in both the 100th and 101st Congresses. The intent of this legislation is to assist families with child care expenses and improve the availability of quality child care services. As part of a dual strategy to address the crisis in child care, I have also reintroduced my Dependent Care Tax Credit legislation, H.R. 994, to expand the current tax credit for child care expenses and make it refundable to families whose incomes are below current tax liability levels. This legislation also allows credit for respite care expenses for elderly dependents.

As a member of the House Select Committee on Aging, I have been a leader in caregiver issues, introducing the Alzheimer's Disease Tax Credit Act which would provide a tax credit for family caregivers of victims of Alzheimer's. This is the fourth year that I have introduced the National Osteoporosis Prevention Week legislation, bringing attention to the growing problem of osteoporosis in older women. The Intergenerational Library Literacy Act, which I have introduced, is designed to encourage the use of older adult volunteers to provide library literacy programs to latchkey children.

Representative Jolene Unsoeld (Democrat; Washington, 3rd District): My top priority in Congress is to help strengthen America's families, which are foundations of healthy communities and a vibrant society.

To promote strong families we must ensure that workers are able to find good jobs with decent wages. Parents must be able to buy a home. They should have access to safe and affordable child care. Our neighborhoods must be free of drugs and toxic waste.

America must make a greater investment in its children. Our children are the parents of tomorrow and the building blocks of our economic future. If this country is to remain competitive and adapt to a changing world economy, we must ensure that our education system is second to none. Teachers should be given the salaries, prestige, and working conditions they so richly deserve. Students must be allowed to attend the college of their choice.

Ensuring that we make these commitments today is not merely an option, it is an obligation.

Congressional Caucus for Women's Issues

Gary Ackerman (D-NY)
Michael Andrews (D-TX)
Les Aspin (D-WI)
Chester Atkins (D-MA)
Les AuCoin (D-OR)
Jim Bates (D-CA)
Anthony Beilenson (D-CA)
Howard Berman (D-CA)
*Lindy (Mrs. Hale) Boggs
(D-LA)
Robert Borski (D-PA)

*Barbara Boxer (D-CA)
George Brown, Jr. (D-CA)
Ben Nighthorse Campbell
(D-CO)
Tom Campbell (R-CA)
Benjamin Cardin (D-MD)
Thomas Carper (D-DE)
William Clay (D-MO)
Ronald Coleman (D-TX)
*Cardiss Collins (D-IL)
Silvio Conte (R-MA)

John Conyers (D-MI)
George Crockett (D-MI)
Peter DeFazio (D-OR)
Ronald Dellums (D-CA)
Julian Dixon (D-CA)
Thomas Downey (D-NY)
Richard Durbin (D-IL)
Bernard Dwyer (D-NJ)
Don Edwards (D-CA)
Ben Erdreich (D-AL)
Lane Evans (D-IL)
Dante Fascell (D-FL)
Vic Fazio (D-CA)
Hamilton Fish, Jr. (R-NY)
Thomas Foglietta (D-PA)
Thomas Foley (D-WA)
Barney Frank (D-MA)
Martin Frost (D-TX)
Jaime Fuster (Del-D-PR)
Robert Garcia (D-NY)
Sam Gejdenson (D-CT)
Richard Gephardt (D-MO)
Benjamin Gilman (R-NY)
William Gray, III (D-PA)
Bill Green (R-NY)
Frank Guarini (D-NJ)
Steve Gunderson (R-WI)
Augustus Hawkins (D-CA)
Charles Hayes (D-IL)
Steny Hoyer (D-MD)
*Nancy Johnson (R-CT)
*Marcy Kaptur (D-OH)
*Nancy Kassebaum (Sen-R-KS)
Joseph Kennedy (D-MA)
*Barbara Kennelly (D-CT)
John LaFalce (D-NY)
Tom Lantos (D-CA)

Jim Leach (R-IA)
William Lehman (D-FL)
Mickey Leland (D-TX)
Sander Levin (D-MI)
Mel Levine (D-CA)
John Lewis (D-GA)
*Jill Long (D-IN)
*Nita Lowey (D-NY)
Frank McCloskey (D-IN)
Jim McDermott (D-WA)
Matthew McHugh (D-NY)
Thomas McMillen (D-MD)
Edward Markey (D-MA)
Robert Matsui (D-CA)
*Jan Meyers (R-KS)
Kweisi Mfume (D-MD)
*Barbara Mikulski (Sen-D-MD)
George Miller (D-CA)
John Miller (R-WA)
Joe Moakley (D-MA)
Jim Moody (D-WI)
*Constance Morella (R-MD)
Bruce Morrison (D-CT)
Sid Morrison (R-WA)
Robert Mrazek (D-NY)
Stephen Neal (D-NC)
*Mary Rose Oakar (D-OH)
Wayne Owens (D-UT)
*Elizabeth Patterson (D-SC)
*Nancy Pelosi (D-CA)
Carl Pursell (R-MI)
Charles Rangel (D-NY)
Robert Roe (D-NJ)
Martin Sabo (D-MN)
*Patricia Saiki (R-HI)
Thomas Sawyer (D-OH)
James Scheuer (D-NY)

*Claudine Schneider (R-RI)
*Patricia Schroeder (D-CO)
Christopher Shays (R-CT)
Gerry Sikorski (D-MN)
Jim Slattery (D-KS)
*Louise Slaughter (D-NY)
Lawrence Smith (D-FL)
*Olympia Snowe (R-ME)
Harley Staggers (D-WV)
Gerry Studds (D-MA)
Al Swift (D-WA)
Mike Synar (D-OK)

Edolphus Towns (D-NY)
Morris Udall (D-AZ)
*Jolene Unsoeld (D-WA)
Bruce Vento (D-MN)
Ted Weiss (D-NY)
Alan Wheat (D-MO)
Pat Williams (D-MT)
Howard Wolpe (D-MI)
Ron Wyden (D-OR)
Sidney Yates (D-IL)

*Executive committee member.

Appendices

American Women Today: A Statistical Portrait

Highlights of Tables and Figures

Figure 1.   *Population of the United States by Race and Sex, 1988 and Projected 2000*

As of 1988, females were 51.3 percent of the total U.S. population, a figure that should change little between now and the turn of the century. What is projected to change somewhat is the composition of the population, both male and female. Nonwhites will increase their share of the population slightly—from 15.7 percent to 17.1 percent. Nonwhite women, currently 8.2 percent of the female population, will comprise nine percent of the female population in the year 2000.

Table 1   *Age Distribution of the Total Female Population and the Hispanic Female Population by Type of Origin, 1987*

Hispanics, who may be of any race, are one of the fastest growing subgroups in the population. They are also among the youngest, as is evident in the age distribution and median age figures for females in Table 1. Thirty-eight percent of the Hispanic female population, but only 28 percent of the total female population, are under the age of 20. Fewer than six percent of Hispanic females, but over 13 percent of all females, are at least 65 years old. When measured by the median age, Hispanic females are, on average, over seven years younger than the total female population.

Among Hispanics, marked differences in age by type of origin are readily apparent. Mexican females, the youngest of the five Hispanic groups highlighted in Table 1, are over twice as likely as Cuban females to be under the age of 20 but about one-third as likely to be 65 or older. The median age of Mexican women in the United States is nearly 16 years lower than that of their Cuban counterparts.

Table 2.   *Death Rates for All Causes by Age, Race, and Sex, 1984-87*

Death rates vary widely by sex, race, and, of course, age. Among black females in 1987, for example, there were nearly 580 deaths for every 100,000 black females. In contrast, the 1987 death rate of 387 for white females was one-third lower than that of black females. Regardless of race or age, males—especially black males—have substantially higher death rates than do females.

Table 3.   *Percent of Total Population with a Functional Limitation by Sex, Age, Race, and Hispanic Origin, 1984*

Many Americans, particularly at the upper ages, report some functional limitation, defined as difficulty seeing, hearing, speaking, walking a certain distance, lifting or carrying, getting in and out of bed, or getting around inside or outside of their homes. Age is clearly associated with the presence of limitations, but so are sex and race. Regardless of age (persons 15 to 64 or 65 and over), reports of functional limitations are more common among women, and, especially in the case of women, more common among minorities.

Table 4.   *Persons Age 65 and Over with a Functional Limitation by Sex, Family Relationship, and Severity of Limitation, 1984*

Although women in their later years are more likely than older men to experience functional limitations, they are far less likely than men to be living with a spouse or other relative who might provide caregiving assistance. Of the older men with severe functional limitations, for example, nearly seven out of 10 are married and living with a spouse. Fewer than three out of 10 older women with severe limitations reside with a husband. Almost half of these women live alone or, in some cases, with nonrelatives.

Table 5.   *Marital Status of Persons Age 15 and Over by Sex, Race, and Hispanic Origin, March 1988*

Over half of all persons age 15 and over are married and living with a spouse—54 percent of women and 58 percent of men. Men are more likely than women never to have married, while women are more likely than men to be divorced or widowed.

Figure 2.   *Never-Married Women as a Percent of All Women Age 14 and Over, Selected Years, 1890-1988*

The proportion of never-married women 14 and older dropped sharply over the first half of this century. As of 1960, only one out of every five women had not been married at least once, down from one in three in 1900. After 1960—as the median age at first marriage began to rise—the proportion of never-married women rose, although it still remains well below the figures for the early to mid-1900s.

Table 6.   *Never-Married Women by Age, Selected Years, 1940-88*

Most women eventually marry, a fact that is readily apparent in Table 6. Today's young woman (under 25), however, is far more likely than her 1960 counterpart to be single (never married), which is not surprising given a rise in age at first marriage. As of 1988, for example, women between the ages of 20 and 24 were over twice as likely as women of the same age in 1960 never to have married (61 percent vs. 28 percent). And while the majority of women in their mid- to late twenties have married at least once, as of 1988, they were nearly three times as likely not to have done so as 25- to 29-year-olds a generation ago (29.5 percent vs. 10.5 percent).

Figure 3.   Birth Rates for Women Age 20-24 by Race, Selected Years, 1950-85

After rising sharply during the "baby boom" years, the birth rate among young women began to plummet, starting about 1960. The 1960 birth rate for women between the ages of 20 and 24 was 258, i.e., there were 258 live births for every 1,000 women in that age group. By 1985, the birth rate for 20- to 24-year-old women stood at 109, a decline of 58 percent. Young black and white women both have birth rates that are less than half of what they were 25 years ago.

Table 7.   Women Who Have Had a Child in the Preceding Year by Age and Marital Status, June 1987

The younger the woman giving birth, the greater the probability that she will be single: in 1987, over two-thirds (68 percent) of all 18- to 24-year-old women who had a child in the preceding year had never married. In contrast, over two-thirds (70 percent) of 30- to 44-year-old women who had given birth during the previous year were married and living with their husbands.

Table 8.   Unmarried-Couple Households by Presence of Children Under 15 Years of Age, Selected Years, 1960-88

Between 1960 and 1988, the number of unmarried-couple households increased nearly sixfold—from less than a half million to 2.6 million. Over this period, the number of such households with children also increased, although not as rapidly as the total number of unmarried-couple households. As a result, the proportion of unmarried-couple households with children is lower today than it was in 1960—31 percent vs. 45 percent.

Table 9.   Legal Abortion Ratios by Age, Race, and Marital Status of Woman, Selected Years, 1973-83

The number of abortions per 100 live births—the abortion ratio—rose from just under 20 in 1973 to almost 35 in 1983, an increase of over 75 percent. Abortion ratios vary widely by age, race, and marital status. In 1983, for example, there were only nine abortions for every 100 live births to married women; the comparable figure for unmarried women was 135 per 100 live births.

Table 10.   *Household Type, Selected Years, 1940-88*

Dramatic changes in the distribution of households by type, i.e., households consisting of families, persons living alone, or persons living with nonrelatives, have occurred over the past half century. Married-couple families make up a substantially smaller proportion of all households today than they did in 1940 (57 percent in 1988 vs. 76 percent in 1940), while the proportion of nonfamily households has risen sharply. As of 1988, 16 percent of all U.S. households were nonfamily households "headed" by women, nearly triple the percentage in 1940.

Table 11.   *Family Type by Race and Hispanic Origin, Selected Years, 1970-86*

As of 1986, there were over 65 million *families* in the United States, that is, households in which at least two or more members were related to one another. The large majority (nearly 80 percent) of families are married-couple families. Such families are, however, less common among Hispanics (70 percent of all families) and blacks (51 percent) than among whites (83 percent).

The proportion of female-headed families among Hispanics (23 percent) and blacks (43 percent) was almost two to more than three times as high as it was among whites (13 percent). Regardless of race or Hispanic origin, both the number and the proportion of families headed by women have increased sharply in recent years. The proportion of families headed by men without spouses has also increased, but these families are still relatively few in number.

Table 12.   *Families by Labor Force Status of Husband and Wife and by Presence of Children, 1980, 1985, and 1987*

The so-called "traditional family," consisting of a married couple with a nonworking wife and children, represents an ever smaller proportion of U.S. families. As of 1987, only 13 percent of all families fell into this category, down from just over 14 percent two years earlier and 18 percent in 1980. Today's most common family type is the one in which both the husband and wife are in the labor force; two out of every five families are dual-earner families.

Table 13.   *Living Arrangements of Children Under Age 18 by Race and Hispanic Origin, 1980 and 1988*

Changes in family composition suggest changes in where children are living, and, indeed, the percentage of children living with two parents has been declining. Nonetheless, most white and Hispanic children still reside with both parents; a majority of black children, in contrast, live with a single parent, generally the mother. As of 1988, 16 percent of white children, 27 percent of Hispanic children, and 51 percent of black children were living in one-parent families headed by mothers.

Figure 4.   *Families with Female Householders, by Housing Ownership or Rentership and by Race and Hispanic Origin of Householder, March 1987*

As noted in Chapter 2, homeownership is the great American dream and a majority of householders— mainly married-couples—do own their own homes. Homeownership is far less common among families headed by women, who are about as likely to rent (45 percent in 1987) as they are to own (46 percent). Black and Hispanic householders are considerably less likely than white women to be homeowners. Nearly one in 10 families with a female householder resides in publicly subsidized housing.

Table 14. Civilian Labor Force Participation Rates for Persons Age 16 and Over by Sex, Race, and Hispanic Origin, Selected Years, 1950-88

One of the most pronounced developments of the past 40 years has been the influx of women into the workforce, which continues today. As of 1988, 56.6 percent of all women age 16 or older were in the labor force, a rise of six-tenths of a percentage point over the figure for the previous year and an increase of nearly 23 percentage points since 1950. Among women, blacks had the highest and Hispanics the lowest participation rates, but the participation gap between the two groups in 1988 was less than five percentage points.

Figure 5. Civilian Labor Force Participation Rates for Women by Age, 1950, 1970, and 1988

That labor force attachment has increased among women of almost all ages is most graphically portrayed in Figure 5. For example, the labor force participation rate of women between the ages of 25 and 34 more than doubled between 1950 and 1988, rising from 34 percent to just under 73 percent. The rate nearly doubled among the next oldest group, women between the ages of 35 and 54. In fact, it has only been among women 65 and above that participation rates have not increased since 1950.

Table 15. Labor Force Status by Years of School Completed and Sex, March 1978 and March 1988

The labor force is becoming better educated, if completed years of schooling among its members is any guide. Over the 1978-88 decade, the proportion of labor force participants who were college graduates increased, while the proportion with less than a high school diploma decreased. This has been the case among both sexes, and although female labor force participants are still less likely than males to be college graduates, they are more likely than male participants to have finished high school.

Labor force participation varies by educational attainment, with rates substantially higher among the better educated of both sexes. As of 1988, 81 percent of all female college graduates, but only 45 percent of those with fewer than four years of high school, were in the labor force.

Table 16.   Full- and Part-Time Work Experience of Working Women by Age, 1966 and 1986

If women work outside the home, they tend to work full time, and the percentage of women doing so—75 percent—has undergone surprisingly little change since 1966. There has, however, been a growing tendency, most noticeably among 25- to 35-year-old full-time workers, toward year-round employment.

Table 17.   Labor Force and Employment Experience of Women with Young Children, 1960, 1986, and 1988

Over the past three decades, more and more women with very young children have entered the labor force, and today, a majority of women with children under the age of three are working or looking for work. However, full-time work, though it too has been increasing, is not yet the norm among women with small children. Only about one-third of women with children either under the age of three or under the age of six are employed full time.

Figure 6.   Percent of Children with Mother in the Labor Force by Age of Children, Selected Years, 1970-88

⌡   Today, the majority of children under the age of 18—six out of 10—have mothers in the labor force.

Table 18.   Unemployment Rates for Persons Age 16 and Over by Sex, Race, and Hispanic Origin, Selected Years, 1950-88

Regardless of gender, race, or Hispanic origin, unemployment rates dropped between 1987 and 1988, and as of 1988, fewer than six percent (5.6) of all women were officially "unemployed." The unemployment rates for black and Hispanic women (11.7 percent and 8.3 percent, respectively), though lower than the previous year, remained well above the rate for white women (4.7 percent).

Figure 7.   *Reasons for Not Being in the Labor Force by Sex, 1975 and 1988*

Despite rising rates of labor force participation, 38 million women and 19 million men were not in the labor force in 1988. Men who are not in the labor force are generally retired (54 percent in 1988) or in school (21 percent), while women are typically keeping house (63 percent). Over time, the reasons for not being in the labor force have changed markedly, especially among women, who are substantially less likely to say that keeping house is their reason for being out of the labor force. Relatively few men admit that keeping house explains why they are not in the labor force, although the percentage who give this as the reason rose from 1.5 in 1975 to 2.3 in 1988.

Figure 8.   *Occupational Distribution of Employed Women and Men, 1972 and 1988*

Employed women are far more likely than men to be administrative support workers (a category that includes clerical workers) and service workers; in fact, almost half (46 percent) of all women can be found in jobs in these broad occupational groupings. Nonetheless, the occupational distribution of female workers has been changing. Just under 11 percent of all women are now managerial workers, more than double the percentage for 1972. Women are also slightly more likely to be professionals and less likely to be operatives than they were in 1972.

Table 19.   *Women as a Percent of All Workers in Selected Occupations, 1975 and 1988*

Despite persistent and sometimes increasing gender segregation in some occupations (e.g., social work), women are making inroads in many formerly male preserves. In 1988, women accounted for almost 20 percent of all lawyers and judges, nearly triple the proportion of 1975. They were 13 percent of all police officers, up from less than three percent in 1975; 15 percent of all architects, up from less than five percent in 1975; and over half of all editors and reporters, compared to 45 percent in 1975. And although women remain a distinct minority in many occupations, a slight increase in the proportion of pilots, firefighters, and certain repair workers who are female is also evident.

Figure 9.   *Industry Distribution of Employed Women and Men, 1978 and 1988*

Women are far more concentrated than men in certain industries—particularly in what is known as "other service industries," which employ 42 percent of all working women. Another 19 percent are in retail trade. The overall industry distribution of employed women has changed little over the past 10 years.

Table 20.   *Women as a Percent of Employed Scientists (by Specialty) and Engineers, 1976 and 1986*

Although women remain a distinct minority of scientists and engineers, both the number and proportion of females in these occupations have increased in recent years. In fact, their number more than tripled to 700,000 between 1976 and 1986, and, as of 1986, women were 15 percent of the total population of scientists and engineers. Women are more likely to be found among social scientists and psychologists than they are among physical or environmental scientists, and they are still poorly represented among engineers. Nonetheless, their representation in each of the fields shown in Table 20 improved between 1976 and 1986.

Table 21. *Employment Sector of Female Scientists by Racial/Ethnic Group and of All Male Scientists, 1986*

A majority of scientists, regardless of gender, work in business and industry. However, female scientists—especially Native Americans—are more likely than male scientists to be employed by educational institutions or "other" agencies or organizations, which includes state and local governments, nonprofit organizations, and hospitals or clinics.

Table 22. *Women in Elective Office, Selected Offices, 1975-89*

The number of women getting elected to public office continues to increase, at least at the state level, where there were more than 1,200 elected women in 1989. These women were 17 percent of all state legislators, more than double the figure for 1975. At the national level, progress has been less pronounced, although 29 were serving in the 101st Congress in 1989, an increase of four over the 100th Congress.

Table 23. *Historical Data on the Number of Women Directors on Fortune Boards, Selected Years, 1969-88*

The number of women on Fortune boards of directors has risen more than ninefold over the past 20 years. Still, as of 1988, there were only 426 women serving on corporate boards, and more than half of the boards of Fortune companies still lacked a single female member.

Table 24. *Women in the Armed Services, 1973 and 1987*

Women are a growing presence in the Armed Services, where they now number nearly 221,000 or 10 percent of the total. Although progress has occurred in each branch of the military, it has been most noticeable in the Air Force, over 12 percent of whose members are now women. The Marine Corps is only five percent female.

Table 25. *Women and Men Applying to and Being Accepted by Medical Schools, 1973/74-1988/89*

During the 1988-89 academic year, over 10,000 women applied to medical school, up from just over 7,000 in 1973-74. During this same period, the number of male medical school applicants dropped from somewhat more than 33,000 to 16,500. In 1988, women were 38 percent of the applicants to medical school and 37 percent of the students accepted. Fifteen years earlier, women were only 18 percent of the applicants and 20 percent of the accepted students.

Figure 10. *Median Annual Earnings of Year-Round, Full-Time Workers by Sex, Selected Years, 1960-87*

Between 1960 and 1987, the median annual earnings of women who work year round, full time increased by 35 percent, while those of men increased by only 26 percent. Over this nearly 30-year period, the female-to-male wage ratio, when based on the annual earnings of fully employed workers, rose from 61 to 65 percent.

Figure 11. *Median Usual Weekly Earnings of Full-Time Wage and Salary Workers by Sex, Race, and Hispanic Origin, 1988*

The median weekly earnings of white men continue to exceed, by a wide margin, the earnings of minority men and all women. In 1988, white women who worked full time had median weekly earnings of $318, approximately 68 percent of the $465 median earnings of full-time working white men. Black and Hispanic women fared even worse, earning, respectively, only 62 percent and 56 percent of what white men earned. (A comparison of 1988 median weekly earnings of all full-time working women to the earnings of all full-time working men yields a wage ratio of 70 percent, somewhat higher than the ratio computed from annual earnings.)

Table 26. *Median Weekly Earnings of Full-Time Wage and Salary Workers by Sex and Age, 1988*

For the most part, the earnings of females and males continue to be most comparable at the younger ages

when workers are just starting out: in 1988, full-time
working women between the ages of 16 and 24 earned
90 percent of what men in that age group earned (an
improvement of one percentage point over the previous
year). Among workers 25 to 34, however, the female-
male wage ratio was only 78 percent (although again an
improvement over the figure for 1987), and by middle
age it had dropped to 62 percent. In the 65-plus population, however, the ratio improved somewhat.

Table 27.   *Average (Mean) Earnings of Year-Round, Full-Time Workers by
Sex and Educational Attainment, 1987*

At every education level, women who work year
round, full time continue to earn less than their male
counterparts. Female college graduates who worked full
time for all of 1987 actually earned less, on average, than
fully employed men with no more than a high school
diploma—$25,544 vs. $27,293.

Table 28.   *State Government Pay Equity Activity, 1984, 1986, and 1988*

Implementation of pay equity strategies is one way
of improving women's wages relative to those of men.
The National Committee on Pay Equity, which has
been tracking state pay equity activity, finds that as of
1988, 43 states—twice the number of four years ago—
had begun preliminary research into the issue of pay
equity, and 23—also double the number of four years
ago—had begun to examine their job classification and
compensation systems. The number of states that had
taken no action was down to seven in 1988. Few states,
however, have actually *implemented* broad-based pay equity plans.

Figure 12.   *Median Income of Persons Age 15 and Over by Age, Sex, and
Year-Round, Full-Time Employment Status, 1987*

Not unexpectedly, year-round, full-time workers
continue to report incomes well above the incomes of all
persons of the same age and sex. This is true for both
women and men; however, the median income of year-

round, full-time women workers was only $17,504 in 1987; their male counterparts had a median income of $26,722.

Table 29.   *Median Annual Income of Families by Family Type, Race, and Hispanic Origin, 1987*

Working wives contribute substantially to family financial well-being. In 1987, married-couple families in which the wife was in the paid labor force had a median income of $40,422, some 50 percent higher than the median $26,652 for families in which the wife stayed at home. Among black couples, the median family income of those families with a wife in the paid labor force was nearly double that of families where the wife did not go out to work, and among Hispanics, it was nearly 75 percent higher. Families headed by women had a median income of only $14,620 in 1987, although that figure did represent an increase of 3.4 percent in real terms (income adjusted for inflation) over the figure for the previous year, a greater increase than for any other family type.

Table 30.   *Selected Sources of Income for Persons Age 15 and Over by Sex, Race, and Hispanic Origin, 1986*

Given that the majority of women are now in the labor force, it comes as no surprise that, regardless of race or Hispanic origin, a majority—57 percent in 1986—of all women have income from wages or salaries. Women are only slightly less likely than men to report property and interest income, but here differences by race and Hispanic origin are pronounced. In 1986, white women were over twice as likely as their black or Hispanic counterparts to have received property and interest income, although it should be noted that these figures provide no clues as to the amount that might have been received from either of these two income sources. With the exception of social security, received

by some 20 percent of all women in 1986, receipt of
income from other sources is relatively rare.

Table 31.   *Trends in Poverty Rates of Persons by Family Type, Race, and
Hispanic Origin, Selected Years, 1960-87*

Regardless of race or Hispanic origin, the poverty
rates of persons living in female-headed families are, and
long have been, far above those of persons living in
other family types. In 1987, persons in such families
were four times as likely as persons in other families to
be poor—33.6 percent vs. 8.2 percent. Still, the situation for those families improved slightly between 1986
and 1987, if the slight decline in the poverty rate is any
indication. Nonetheless, this improvement occurred
only among whites; the poverty rate for blacks and Hispanics living in female-headed families—and indeed in
other family types—rose between 1986 and 1987.

Table 32.   *Percent of Children Below Poverty Level Living in Female-Headed
Households by Race and Hispanic Origin, Selected Years, 1960-87*

Living in a female-headed family means living in
poverty for the majority of children in those families,
especially if the children are black. In 1987, 79 percent
of all poor black children lived in families headed by
women, a 50 percentage point increase over the past
quarter century.

Figure 1 • POPULATION OF THE UNITED STATES[1] BY RACE
AND SEX, 1988 AND PROJECTED 2000

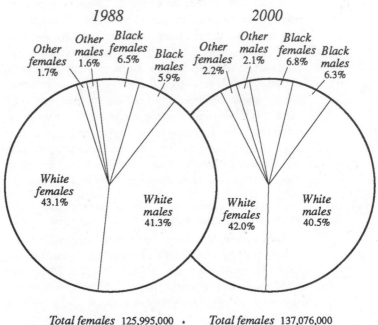

Total females 125,995,000 • Total females 137,076,000

Total males   120,054,000   Total males   131,191,000

[1]Includes Armed Forces overseas.

Source: U.S. Bureau of the Census, January 1989, Table 4.

[1]The statistical appendix was prepared by Barbara Andrew with assistance from Cynthia Doran and Kitty Gretsch. Many of the tables and figures in this section update material presented in earlier volumes of *The American Woman*. Labor force, earnings, income, and poverty data are among the tables and figures that are regularly updated. Other statistics may not be included in every edition of the book because the agencies that collect those data do not do so every year or because year-to-year variations tend to be small. Readers might check earlier volumes of *The American Woman* for statistics not included in this edition.

Table 1 • AGE DISTRIBUTION OF THE TOTAL FEMALE POPULATION AND THE HISPANIC FEMALE POPULATION BY TYPE OF ORIGIN, 1987 (in percentages)

Age	All Females	Hispanic Females[1]					
		Total Hispanic	Mexican	Puerto Rican	Cuban	Central or South American	Other Hispanic
Under 5	7.2	10.5	11.9	10.1	7.0	8.8	6.0
5-13	12.2	10.3	19.6	18.5	8.4	14.8	13.1
14-19	8.7	17.6	11.3	10.1	4.1	8.6	8.3
20-24	8.1	10.0	10.1	10.1	10.5	8.9	10.2
25-34	17.5	18.7	18.0	19.7	15.3	22.1	19.8
35-44	13.9	13.2	11.7	14.9	11.5	19.1	13.5
45-54	9.7	8.1	7.2	7.2	14.6	9.4	10.0
55-64	9.5	6.1	5.3	5.2	14.6	5.1	9.3
65 and over	13.3	5.5	4.9	4.2	13.9	3.2	9.9
Total percent	100.0	100.0	100.0	100.0	100.0	100.0	100.0
Total number (in thousands)	122,756	9,376	5,693	1,225	506	1,133	819
Median age	32.9	25.8	23.5	25.6	39.0	28.6	31.8

[1]Persons of Hispanic origin may be of any race.

Source: U.S. Bureau of the Census, December 1988, Table 4.

Table 2 • DEATH RATES[1] FOR ALL CAUSES BY AGE, RACE,
AND SEX, 1984–87

		Age		
Race, Sex, and Year	All Ages	15-24	25-34	35-44
White females				
1984	391.3	49.6	59.5	123.9
1985	390.6	48.4	58.9	121.2
1986	387.0	51.6	60.6	123.7
1987	386.9	50.0	64.2	115.7
Black females				
1984	585.3	61.6	130.6	285.7
1985	589.1	59.5	136.3	278.4
1986	585.0	59.9	139.7	277.5
1987	579.9	64.0	140.1	295.0
White males				
1984	689.9	138.8	154.3	235.1
1985	688.7	136.3	157.1	241.4
1986	680.7	146.3	167.3	250.8
1987	671.0	145.3	166.7	251.1
Black males				
1984	1,011.7	163.9	335.6	616.0
1985	1,024.0	174.1	347.4	641.8
1986	1,003.4	189.9	379.0	635.9
1987	1,005.4	194.9	370.3	673.5

[1]Rates per 100,000 in specified group.

Source: National Center for Health Statistics, July 1988, Table 5.

Table 3 • PERCENT OF TOTAL POPULATION WITH A
FUNCTIONAL LIMITATION[1] BY SEX, AGE, RACE,
AND HISPANIC ORIGIN, 1984

Sex and Age	All Races	White	Black	Hispanic Origin[2]
Women				
15-64	15.6	14.8	21.7	19.4
65 and over	62.0	60.3	78.9	72.6
Men				
15-64	12.6	12.4	15.3	12.7
65 and over	53.5	52.0	69.0	42.0

[1]Persons who have difficulty seeing, hearing, speaking, walking one-quarter mile or up one flight of stairs, lifting or carrying a full bag of groceries, getting in and out of bed, or getting around inside or outside of a house have a functional limitation.

[2]Persons of Hispanic origin may be of any race.

Source: U.S. Bureau of the Census, December 1986, Table B.

Table 4 • PERSONS AGE 65 AND OVER WITH A
FUNCTIONAL LIMITATION[1] BY SEX, FAMILY
RELATIONSHIP, AND SEVERITY OF LIMITATION,
1984 (in percentages)

	Women		Men	
Family Relationship	Total With a Limitation	Total With a Severe Limitation	Total With a Limitation	Total With a Severe Limitation
Married, spouse present	31.0	27.0	70.7	69.1
Other family member	21.4	25.8	8.5	10.2
Not a family member[2]	47.6	47.3	20.9	20.7
Total percent	100.0	100.0	100.0	100.0

[1]Persons who have difficulty seeing, hearing, speaking, walking one-quarter mile or up one flight of stairs, lifting or carrying a full bag of groceries, getting in and out of bed, or getting around inside or outside of a house have a functional limitation. Persons with a severe limitation are unable to perform one or more of these functions.

[2]Most of these people live alone.

Source: U.S. Bureau of the Census, December 1986, Table 1.

Table 5 • MARITAL STATUS OF PERSONS AGE 15 AND OVER BY SEX, RACE, AND HISPANIC ORIGIN, MARCH 1988 (in percentages)

Marital Status	All Races		White		Black		Hispanic Origin[1]	
	Women	Men	Women	Men	Women	Men	Women	Men
Single (never married)	22.9	29.9	20.9	28.1	36.9	42.5	27.3	36.9
Married, spouse present	53.6	58.3	56.5	60.7	31.6	39.2	51.0	49.3
Married, spouse absent	3.7	2.9	2.8	2.4	9.5	6.3	7.0	6.9
Widowed	11.4	2.5	11.5	2.5	12.2	3.6	6.2	1.7
Divorced	8.4	6.4	8.2	6.2	9.8	8.5	8.5	5.2
Total percent	100.0	100.0	100.0	100.0	100.0	100.0	100.0	100.0
Total number (in thousands)	98,168	90,284	83,518	77,823	11,618	9,603	6,831	6,776

[1]Persons of Hispanic origin may be of any race.

Source: U.S. Bureau of the Census, January 1989a, Table 1.

Figure 2 • NEVER-MARRIED WOMEN AS A PERCENT OF ALL
WOMEN AGE 14 AND OVER, SELECTED YEARS,
1890–1988

Percent

[1]1980 and 1988 figures include only women age 15 and over.

Source: U. S. Bureau of the Census, September 1975, Series A160-171 and September 1988, Table 3.

Table 6 • NEVER-MARRIED WOMEN BY AGE, SELECTED
YEARS, 1940–88 (as a percent of age group)

			Year			
Age	*1940*	*1950*	*1960*[1]	*1970*	*1980*	*1988*
15-19	88.1	82.9	83.9	90.3	91.2	94.2
20-24	47.2	32.3	28.4	35.8	50.2	61.1
25-29	22.8	13.3	10.5	10.5	20.9	29.5
30-34	14.7	9.3	6.9	6.2	9.5	16.1
35-44	10.4	8.3	6.1	5.1	5.5	7.6
45-54	8.7	7.8	7.0	4.9	4.7	5.1
55-64	9.0	7.9	8.0	6.8	4.5	4.0
65 and over	9.3	8.9	8.5	7.7	5.9	5.3
All women 15 and over[2]	27.6	20.0	19.0	22.6	22.5	22.9

[1]First year that includes Alaska and Hawaii.

[2]Figures from 1940, 1950, 1960, and 1970 include 14-year-olds.

Source: U.S. Bureau of the Census, September 1975, Series A160-171 and September 1988, Table 3.

Figure 3 • BIRTH RATES[1] FOR WOMEN AGE 20-24 BY RACE,
SELECTED YEARS, 1950–85

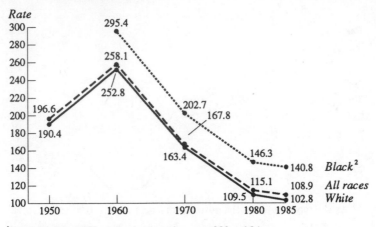

[1]Live births per 1,000 women between the ages of 20 and 24.
[2]No data available for black women in 1950.
Source: National Center for Health Statistics, March 1988, Table 2.

Table 7 • WOMEN WHO HAVE HAD A CHILD IN THE
PRECEDING YEAR BY AGE AND MARITAL
STATUS, JUNE 1987 (in percentages)

| | Age | | |
Marital Status	18-24	25-29	30-44
Married, husband present	26.2	59.2	69.8
Married, husband absent[1]	2.7	4.4	4.4
Widowed or divorced	2.6	7.7	14.9
Never married	68.4	28.7	10.9
Total percent	100.0	100.0	100.0
Total number (in thousands)	1,277	1,244	1,180

[1]Includes separated women.
Source: U.S. Bureau of the Census, May 1988, Table A and Table 4.

Table 8 • UNMARRIED-COUPLE HOUSEHOLDS BY PRESENCE
OF CHILDREN UNDER 15 YEARS OF AGE,
SELECTED YEARS, 1960–88 (in thousands)

Year	Total	Couples Without Children	Couples With Children	Percent With Children
1960	439	242	197	44.9
1970	523	327	196	37.5
1980	1,589	1,159	431	27.1
1988	2,588	1,786	802	31.0

Source: U.S. Bureau of the Census, January 1989a, Table A-7.

Table 9 • LEGAL ABORTION RATIOS BY AGE, RACE, AND
MARITAL STATUS OF WOMAN, SELECTED YEARS,
1973–83

Selected Characteristic	Abortions per 100 Live Births					
	1973	1975	1977	1979	1981	1983
Age						
Under 15	74.3	101.5	112.1	121.3	126.4	133.6
15-19	31.7	46.4	57.2	66.0	66.8	67.3
20-24	17.9	25.0	32.5	37.3	37.9	38.1
25-29	12.3	16.6	19.9	22.3	23.2	23.0
30-34	16.5	22.1	22.8	23.3	23.7	22.0
35-39	26.7	37.5	42.4	41.5	40.3	35.4
40 and over	40.2	59.9	74.2	74.7	77.6	69.1
Race						
White	17.5	22.7	26.6	30.7	31.2	29.5
All others	28.9	46.5	57.1	56.8	54.4	56.0
Marital status						
Married	6.2	8.3	9.3	10.7	9.8	9.3
Unmarried	109.8	141.1	158.5	157.8	147.5	135.2
Total	19.6	27.2	32.4	35.8	35.8	34.9

Source: National Center for Health Statistics, March 1988, Table 9.

Table 10 • HOUSEHOLD TYPE, SELECTED YEARS, 1940–88
(in percentages)

Household Type	1940	1950	1960	1970	1980	1988
Married-couple family	76.0	78.2	74.3	70.5	60.8	56.9
Other family, male householder	4.3	2.7	2.3	1.9	2.1	3.0
Other family, female householder	9.8	8.3	8.4	8.7	10.8	11.6
Nonfamily, male householder	4.6	3.8	5.1	6.4	10.9	12.4
Nonfamily, female householder	5.3	7.0	9.8	12.4	15.4	16.1
Total percent	100.0	100.0	100.0	100.0	100.0	100.0
Total number of households (in thousands)	34,949	43,554	52,799	63,401	80,776	91,066

Source: U.S. Bureau of the Census, September 1988, Table 6.

Table 11 • FAMILY TYPE BY RACE AND HISPANIC ORIGIN,
SELECTED YEARS, 1970–86 (in percentages)

Family Type	1970	1980	1985	1986
ALL RACES				
Married-couple families	86.7	81.7	80.1	79.5
Wife in paid labor force	NA	(50.2)	(54.0)	(56.2)
Wife not in paid labor force	NA	(49.8)	(46.0)	(43.8)
Female householder, no husband present	10.9	15.1	16.1	16.3
Male householder, no wife present	2.4	3.2	3.8	4.2
Total percent	100.0	100.0	100.0	100.0
Total number of families (in thousands)	51,237	60,309	63,558	65,133
WHITE				
Married-couple families	88.6	85.1	83.5	83.2
Wife in paid labor force	NA	(49.3)	(52.9)	(55.3)
Wife not in paid labor force	NA	(50.6)	(47.1)	(44.7)
Female householder, no husband present	9.1	11.9	12.9	12.9
Male householder, no wife present	2.2	3.0	3.6	3.9
Total percent	100.0	100.0	100.0	100.0
Total number of families (in thousands)	46,022	52,710	54,991	56,044
BLACK				
Married-couple families	68.0	53.7	53.2	51.3
Wife in paid labor force	NA	(59.6)	(64.1)	(65.8)
Wife not in paid labor force	NA	(40.4)	(35.9)	(34.2)
Female householder, no husband present	28.2	41.7	41.5	42.8
Male householder, no wife present	3.7	4.6	5.3	5.9
Total percent	100.0	100.0	100.0	100.0
Total number of families (in thousands)	4,774	6,317	6,921	7,177
HISPANIC ORIGIN[1]				
Married-couple families	NA	73.1	70.4	69.8
Wife in paid labor force	NA	(46.2)	(49.1)	(51.7)
Wife not in paid labor force	NA	(53.8)	(50.9)	(48.3)
Female householder, no husband present	NA	21.8	23.3	23.4
Male householder, no wife present	NA	5.1	6.3	6.8
Total percent		100.0	100.0	100.0
Total number of families (in thousands)	NA	3,235	4,206	4,588

[1]Persons of Hispanic origin may be of any race.

Source: U.S. Bureau of the Census, March 1971, Table 6; August 1981, Table 1; April 1986, Table 1; August 1988, Table 1.

Table 12 • FAMILIES BY LABOR FORCE STATUS OF
HUSBAND AND WIFE AND BY PRESENCE OF
CHILDREN, 1980, 1985, AND 1987 (in percentages)

Family Type	1980	1985	1987
Husband working, wife not in labor force	28.8	23.5	21.9
Without children	10.7	9.4	9.0
With children	18.2	14.2	12.9
Husband and wife in labor force	38.2	39.9	41.0
Without children	16.1	17.1	17.4
With children	22.1	22.8	23.6
Other family type[1]	32.9	36.6	37.0
Total percent	100.0	100.0	100.0
Total number (in thousands)	58,426	62,706	64,491

[1]Includes families headed by a single parent, married-couple families with wife only in
the labor force, and married-couple families with neither spouse in the labor force.

Source: U.S. Bureau of the Census, September 1981, Tables 1 and 18; September 1986,
Tables 1 and 17; May 1988a, Tables 1 and 18.

Table 13 • LIVING ARRANGEMENTS OF CHILDREN UNDER
AGE 18 BY RACE AND HISPANIC ORIGIN, 1980
AND 1988 (in percentages)

Children Living With	1980			1988		
	White	Black	Hispanic Origin[1]	White	Black	Hispanic Origin[1]
Two parents	82.7	42.2	75.4	78.9	38.6	66.3
One parent	15.1	45.8	21.1	18.9	54.1	30.2
Mother only	13.5	43.9	19.6	16.0	51.1	27.2
Father only	1.6	1.9	1.5	2.9	3.0	3.0
Other relatives	1.7	10.7	3.4	1.6	6.4	2.7
Nonrelatives	0.5	1.3	0.1	0.6	1.0	0.9

[1]Persons of Hispanic origin may be of any race.

Source: U.S. Bureau of the Census, January 1989a, Table A-4.

Figure 4 • FAMILIES WITH FEMALE HOUSEHOLDERS, BY
    HOUSING OWNERSHIP OR RENTERSHIP AND BY
    RACE AND HISPANIC ORIGIN OF HOUSEHOLDER,
    MARCH 1987 (in percentages)

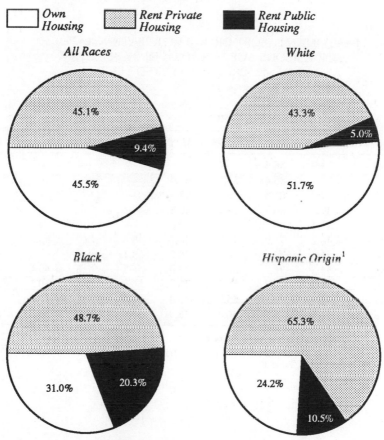

[1]Persons of Hispanic origin may be of any race.
Source: U.S. Bureau of the Census, May 1988a, Table 3.

Table 14 • CIVILIAN LABOR FORCE PARTICIPATION RATES
FOR PERSONS AGE 16 AND OVER BY SEX, RACE,
AND HISPANIC ORIGIN, SELECTED YEARS,
1950–88 (in percentages)

Year	Total Women	Total Men	White Women	White Men	Black Women	Black Men	Hispanic Origin[1] Women	Hispanic Origin[1] Men
1950	33.9	86.4	—	—	—	—	—	—
1955	35.7	85.4	34.5	85.4	—	—	—	—
1960	37.7	83.3	36.5	83.4	—	—	—	—
1965	39.3	80.7	38.1	80.8	—	—	—	—
1970	43.3	79.7	42.6	80.0	—	—	—	—
1975	46.3	77.9	45.9	78.7	48.8	70.9	43.2	80.7
1980	51.5	77.4	51.2	78.2	53.1	70.3	47.8	81.6
1985	54.5	76.3	54.1	77.0	56.5	70.8	49.4	80.4
1986	55.3	76.3	55.0	76.9	56.9	71.2	50.1	81.0
1987	56.0	76.2	55.7	76.8	58.0	71.1	52.0	81.0
1988	56.6	76.2	56.4	76.9	58.0	71.0	53.2	81.9

[1]Persons of Hispanic origin may be of any race.

Source: U.S. Bureau of Labor Statistics, June 1985, Table 5; January 1986, Table 39; January 1987, Table 39; January 1989, Table 39.

Figure 5 • CIVILIAN LABOR FORCE PARTICIPATION RATES
FOR WOMEN BY AGE, 1950, 1970, AND 1988

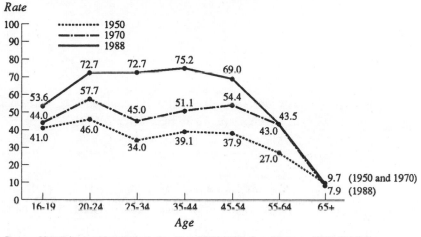

Source: U.S. Bureau of Labor Statistics, June 1985, Table 5, and January 1989, Table 3.

Table 15 • LABOR FORCE STATUS[1] BY YEARS OF SCHOOL
COMPLETED AND SEX, MARCH 1978 AND
MARCH 1988 (in percentages)

Labor Force Status	Total		Woman		Man	
	1978	1988	1978	1988	1978	1988
Labor force distribution	100.0	100.0	100.0	100.0	100.0	100.0
Less than 4 years of high school	23.8	14.7	22.0	12.4	25.0	16.5
4 years of high school	39.3	39.9	45.0	43.3	35.4	37.3
1-3 years of college	16.4	19.7	16.0	21.2	16.8	18.5
4 years of college or more	20.5	25.7	17.0	23.1	22.9	27.8
Labor force participation rate	72.5	77.5	56.5	67.1	89.8	88.6
Less than 4 years of high school	61.6	60.8	44.2	45.4	80.6	76.0
4 years of high school	72.5	76.9	58.2	66.9	92.0	89.5
1-3 years of college	77.8	82.5	61.9	74.7	93.3	91.3
4 years of college or more	85.6	88.4	70.8	80.8	95.6	94.4

[1]Includes only persons between the ages of 25 and 64.

Source: U.S. Department of Labor, August 29, 1988, Table 1.

Table 16 • FULL- AND PART-TIME WORK EXPERIENCE OF
WORKING WOMEN BY AGE, 1966 AND 1986 (in
percentages)

Work Experience	All Women Age 25-54		Age 25-34		Age 35-44		Age 45-54	
	1966	1986	1966	1986	1966	1986	1966	1986
Work at full-time job	72.9	74.8	73.8	75.3	71.3	74.3	73.5	74.7
50-52 weeks	45.5	57.1	38.6	55.1	45.2	57.8	51.7	59.8
40-49 weeks	8.3	6.5	8.8	7.2	8.2	6.0	7.8	6.0
27-39 weeks	6.5	4.2	7.6	4.6	6.2	4.2	5.8	3.3
1-26 weeks	12.6	7.0	18.8	8.4	11.7	6.3	8.2	5.6
Work at part-time job	27.2	25.3	26.1	24.7	28.7	25.8	26.2	25.2
50-52 weeks	9.8	11.4	6.8	10.3	10.9	12.0	11.2	12.7
40-49 weeks	2.9	3.3	2.5	3.3	3.0	3.1	3.0	3.3
27-39 weeks	3.1	2.8	2.7	2.7	3.4	2.9	3.0	2.6
1-26 weeks	11.4	7.8	14.1	8.4	11.4	7.8	9.0	6.6

Source: U.S. Bureau of Labor Statistics, March 1988, Table 3.

Table 17 • LABOR FORCE AND EMPLOYMENT EXPERIENCE OF WOMEN WITH YOUNG CHILDREN, 1960, 1986, AND 1988 (in percentages)

Labor Force Status	All Women			Married, Husband Present			Other, Ever Married[1]		
	1960	1985	1988[2]	1960	1985	1988[2]	1960	1985	1988[2]
Women with children age 3 and younger									
In the labor force	16.5	50.8	52.5	15.3	50.9	54.5	32.4	57.4	53.2
Employed full-time	10.4	29.7	32.5	9.5	30.7	33.7	22.2	33.1	37.0
Employed part-time	4.6	15.1	15.1	4.5	16.3	17.1	6.3	12.9	9.4
Women with children age 6 and younger									
In the labor force	20.2	54.4	56.1	18.6	53.8	57.1	39.8	64.6	60.8
Employed full-time	13.2	33.3	35.6	11.9	33.2	35.6	28.6	42.9	45.1
Employed part-time	5.3	15.1	15.7	5.2	16.5	18.0	6.3	12.3	8.6

[1]Includes widowed, divorced, and married with an absent spouse.
[2]Figures for women with children younger than age 3 or younger than age 6.

Source: U.S. Bureau of Labor Statistics (BLS), April 1961, Tables G and I; and unpublished BLS data.

Figure 6 • PERCENT OF CHILDREN WITH MOTHER IN THE
LABOR FORCE BY AGE OF CHILDREN, SELECTED
YEARS, 1970–88

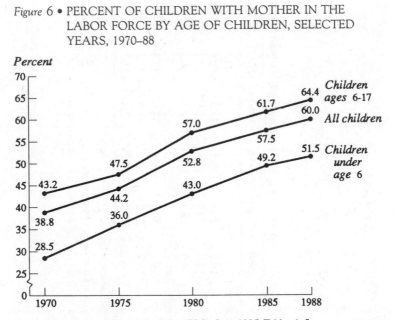

Source: U.S. Bureau of Labor Statistics (BLS), June 1985, Tables 4, 5,
and 6; September 19, 1985; and unpublished BLS data.

Table 18 • UNEMPLOYMENT RATES FOR PERSONS AGE 16
AND OVER BY SEX, RACE, AND HISPANIC
ORIGIN, SELECTED YEARS, 1950–88 (in percentages)

Year	All Races Women	Men	White Women	Men	Black Women	Men	Hispanic Origin[1] Women	Men
1950	5.7	5.1	—	—	—	—	—	—
1955	4.9	4.2	4.3	3.7	—	—	—	—
1960	5.9	5.4	5.3	4.8	—	—	—	—
1965	5.5	4.0	5.0	3.6	—	—	—	—
1970	5.9	4.4	5.4	4.0	—	—	—	—
1975	9.3	7.9	8.6	7.2	14.8	14.8	13.5	11.4
1980	7.4	6.9	6.5	6.1	14.0	14.5	10.7	9.7
1985	7.4	7.0	6.4	6.1	14.9	15.3	11.0	10.2
1987	6.2	6.2	5.2	5.4	13.2	12.7	8.9	8.7
1988	5.6	5.5	4.7	4.7	11.7	11.7	8.3	8.1

[1]Persons of Hispanic origin may be of any race.

Source: U.S. Bureau of Labor Statistics, June 1985, Table 27; January 1986, Table 39; and January 1989, Table 39.

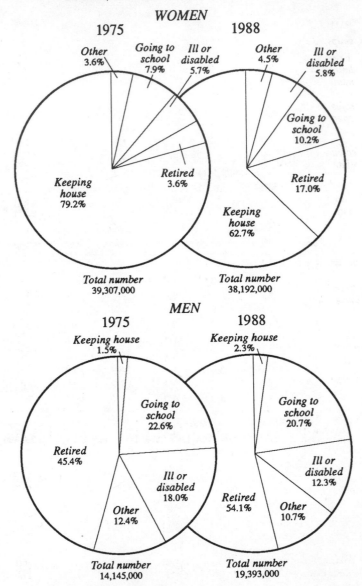

Figure 7 • REASONS FOR NOT BEING IN THE LABOR FORCE BY SEX, 1975 AND 1988[1]

WOMEN

1975

Other 3.6%
Going to school 7.9%
Ill or disabled 5.7%
Retired 3.6%
Keeping house 79.2%

Total number 39,307,000

1988

Other 4.5%
Ill or disabled 5.8%
Going to school 10.2%
Retired 17.0%
Keeping house 62.7%

Total number 38,192,000

MEN

1975

Keeping house 1.5%
Going to school 22.6%
Retired 45.4%
Ill or disabled 18.0%
Other 12.4%

Total number 14,145,000

1988

Keeping house 2.3%
Going to school 20.7%
Ill or disabled 12.3%
Retired 54.1%
Other 10.7%

Total number 19,393,000

[1]Includes only persons out of the labor force by choice.

Source: U.S. Bureau of Labor Statistics, January 1976, Table 29 and January 1989, Table A-54.

Figure 8 • OCCUPATIONAL DISTRIBUTION OF EMPLOYED
WOMEN AND MEN, 1972 AND 1988 (in percentages)

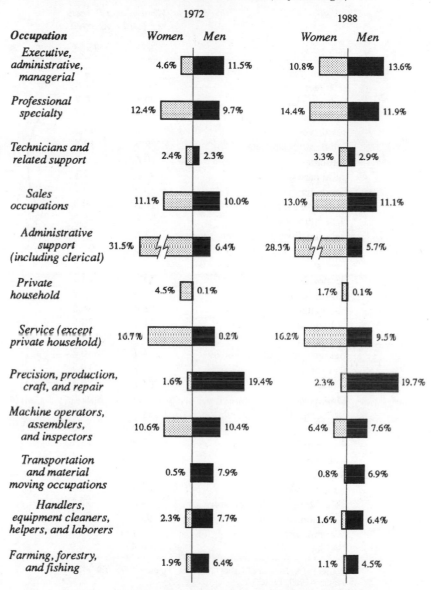

Source: U.S. Bureau of Labor Statistics, January 1984, Table 1, and January 1989, Table 21.

Table 19 • WOMEN AS A PERCENT OF ALL WORKERS IN
SELECTED OCCUPATIONS, 1975 AND 1988

Occupation	Women as a Percent of Total Employed	
	1975	1988
Airplane pilot, navigator	—	3.1
Architect	4.3	14.6
Auto mechanic	0.5	0.7
Bartender	35.2	49.6
Bus driver	37.7	48.5
Cab driver, chauffeur	8.7	12.5
Carpenter	0.6	1.5
Child care worker	93.8	97.3
Computer programmer	25.6	32.2
Computer systems analyst	14.8	29.5
Data entry keyer	92.8	88.2
Data processing equipment repairer	1.8	8.8
Dental assistant	100.0	98.7
Dentist	1.8	9.3
Economist	13.1	35.3
Editor, reporter	44.6	51.1
Elementary school teacher	85.4	84.8
College/university teacher	31.1	38.5
Firefighter	—	2.1
Garage, gas station attendant	4.7	6.2
Lawyer, judge	7.1	19.5
Librarian	81.1	85.4
Mail carrier	8.7	22.0
Office machine repairer	1.7	6.4
Physician	13.0	20.0
Police officer	2.7	13.4
Registered nurse	97.0	94.6
Secretary	99.1	99.1
Social worker	60.8	66.0
Telephone installer, repairer	4.8	12.1
Telephone operator	93.3	89.8
Waiter/waitress	91.1	82.6
Welder	4.4	4.9

Source: U.S. Bureau of Labor Statistics, January 1976, Table 2 and
January 1989, Table 22.

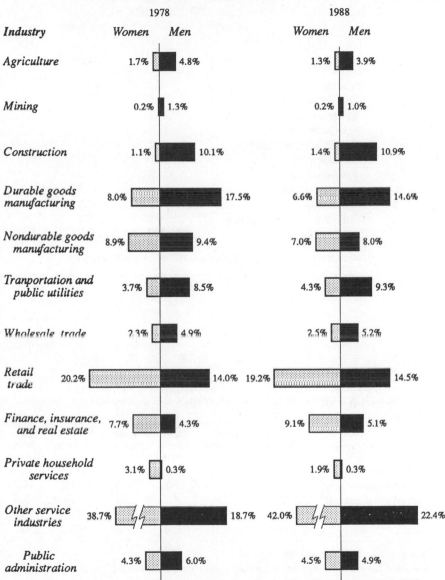

Figure 9 • INDUSTRY DISTRIBUTION OF EMPLOYED WOMEN
AND MEN, 1978 AND 1988 (in percentages)

	1978		1988	
Industry	*Women*	*Men*	*Women*	*Men*
Agriculture	1.7%	4.8%	1.3%	3.9%
Mining	0.2%	1.3%	0.2%	1.0%
Construction	1.1%	10.1%	1.4%	10.9%
Durable goods manufacturing	8.0%	17.5%	6.6%	14.6%
Nondurable goods manufacturing	8.9%	9.4%	7.0%	8.0%
Tranportation and public utilities	3.7%	8.5%	4.3%	9.3%
Wholesale trade	2.3%	4.9%	2.5%	5.2%
Retail trade	20.2%	14.0%	19.2%	14.5%
Finance, insurance, and real estate	7.7%	4.3%	9.1%	5.1%
Private household services	3.1%	0.3%	1.9%	0.3%
Other service industries	38.7%	18.7%	42.0%	22.4%
Public administration	4.3%	6.0%	4.5%	4.9%

Source: U.S. Bureau of Labor Statistics, January 1978, Table 27, and January 1989, Tables 21 and 25.

Table 20 • WOMEN AS A PERCENT OF EMPLOYED
SCIENTISTS (BY SPECIALTY) AND ENGINEERS,
1976 AND 1986

Field /Specialty	1976	1986
Scientists	18.6	27.4
Physical scientists	8.6	13.3
Mathematical scientists	23.7	25.9
Computer specialists	17.3	28.9
Environmental scientists	7.1	11.6
Life scientists	15.9	25.0
Psychologists	31.6	45.4
Social scientists	25.5	31.3
Engineers	1.6	4.1
Total scientists and engineers	8.6	15.1
Total number	199,700	698,600

Source: National Science Foundation, January 1988, Appendix Table 1.

Table 21 • EMPLOYMENT SECTOR OF FEMALE SCIENTISTS
BY RACIAL/ETHNIC GROUP AND OF ALL MALE
SCIENTISTS, 1986 (in percentages)

Sector of Employment	White Women	Black Women	Asian Women	Native American Women	Hispanic Women[1]	All Men
Business and industry	56.3	50.7	61.2	29.6	54.0	69.8
Educational institutions	21.7	17.4	16.5	25.9	19.9	12.2
Federal government	6.1	11.3	4.1	14.8	6.1	7.9
Other[2]	15.9	20.6	18.2	29.7	20.0	10.1
Total	100.0	100.0	100.0	100.0	100.0	100.0

[1]Persons of Hispanic origin may be of any race.

[2]Includes state/local/other governments, military, nonprofit organizations, hopitals/clinics, others, and no report.

Source: National Science Foundation, January 1988, Appendix Tables 15 and 16.

Table 22 • WOMEN IN ELECTIVE OFFICE, SELECTED OFFICES, 1975–89

Elected Officeholders	Percent Female										Number of Women	
	1975	1977	1979	1981	1983	1986	1987	1988	1989		1987	1989
Members of U.S. Congress	4	3	3	3	4	5	5	5	5		25	29
Statewide elective officials	10	8	11	11	13	14	14	12	14		43	45
Members of state legislatures	8	9	10	12	13	15	16	16	17		1,156	1,258

Source: Center for the American Woman and Politics, May 1986 and December 1988.

Table 23 • HISTORICAL DATA ON THE NUMBER OF WOMEN
DIRECTORS ON FORTUNE BOARDS, SELECTED
YEARS, 1969–88 (in numbers)

Year	Total Number of Women Directors	Number of Directorships Held by Women	Number of Companies with Women on Their Boards	Percentage of Companies with Women on Their Boards
1969	46	NA	NA	NA
1976	147	NA	175	13
1977	204	NA	228	18
1979	262	361	316	24
1980	317	461	378	29
1981	336	490	398	30
1982	336	499	405	31
1983	367	527	427	33
1984[1]	313	455	364	36
1985[1]	339	511	407	41
1986[1]	395	576	439	44
1987[1]	424	628	471	47
1988[1]	426	632	474	47

[1]The statistics are based on the new Fortune 1000 classification rather than the former Fortune 1350 classification and thus appear to have declined; figures actually reflect a proportionate increase.

Source: Reproduced by permission of Catalyst, 250 Park Avenue South, New York, New York 10003.

Table 24 • WOMEN IN THE ARMED SERVICES, 1973 AND
1987

Service	1973		1987	
	Number of Women	Percent of Service	Number of Women	Percent of Service
Air Force	19,750	2.9	75,308	12.5
Army	20,736	2.6	82,700	10.7
Marine Corps	2,288	1.2	9,788	4.9
Navy	12,628	2.3	53,161	9.1
Total	55,402	2.5	220,957	10.2

Source: U.S. General Accounting Office, September 1988, Table 1.1.

Table 25 • WOMEN AND MEN APPLYING TO AND BEING
ACCEPTED BY MEDICAL SCHOOLS,
1973/74–1988/89

Academic Year	No. of Applicants		No. Accepted		% Accepted	
	Men	Women	Men	Women	Men	Women
1973-74	33,304	7,202	11,488	2,847	34.5	39.5
1974-75	33,912	8,712	11,674	3,392	34.4	38.9
1975-76[1]	32,515	9,575	11,619	3,639	35.7	38.0
1976-77	31,911	10,244	11,852	3,922	37.1	38.3
1977-78	30,374	10,195	11,896	4,081	39.2	40.0
1978-79	27,075	9,561	12,352	4,175	45.6	43.7
1979-80	25,919	10,222	12,156	4,730	46.9	46.3
1980-81	25,436	10,664	12,196	4,950	47.9	46.4
1981-82	25,054	11,673	11,953	5,333	47.7	45.7
1982-83	24,045	11,685	11,843	5,451	49.3	46.7
1983-84	23,239	11,961	11,577	5,632	49.8	47.1
1984-85	23,468	12,476	11,463	5,731	48.8	45.9
1985-86	21,331	11,562	11,370	5,858	53.3	50.7
1986-87	20,056	11,267	11,159	5,933	55.6	52.7
1987-88	17,712	10,411	10,822	6,205	61.1	59.6
1988-89	16,457	10,264	10,785	6,323	65.5	61.6

[1]Excludes 213 applicants for whom gender information was not available.

Source: Association of American Medical Colleges, provided by Janet Bickel, 1989.

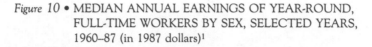

Figure 10 • MEDIAN ANNUAL EARNINGS OF YEAR-ROUND,
FULL-TIME WORKERS BY SEX, SELECTED YEARS,
1960–87 (in 1987 dollars)[1]

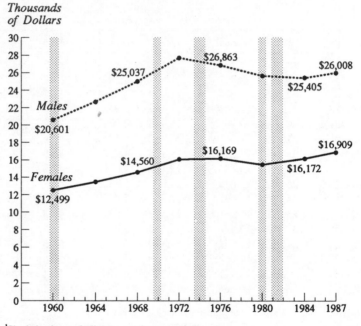

[1]Shaded columns indicate recessionary periods.

Source: U.S. Bureau of the Census, August 1988, Table A.

Figure 11 • MEDIAN USUAL WEEKLY EARNINGS OF
FULL-TIME WAGE AND SALARY WORKERS BY
SEX, RACE, AND HISPANIC ORIGIN, 1988 (in
dollars)

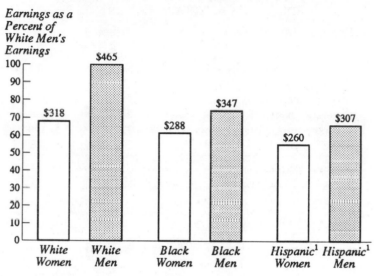

Earnings as a Percent of White Men's Earnings

[1]Persons of Hispanic origin may be of any race.

Source: U.S. Bureau of Labor Statistics, January 1989, Table 61.

Table 26 • MEDIAN WEEKLY EARNINGS OF FULL-TIME
WAGE AND SALARY WORKERS BY SEX AND AGE,
1988

Age	Median Weekly Earnings (in dollars)		
	Women	Men	Women's Earnings as a Percent of Men's Earnings
16-24	235	261	90.0
25-34	326	420	77.6
35-44	353	517	68.3
45-54	339	549	61.7
55-64	317	508	62.4
65 and over	279	394	70.8
Total, age 16 and over	315	449	70.2

Source: U.S. Bureau of Labor Statistics, January 1989, Table 61.

Table 27 • AVERAGE (MEAN) EARNINGS OF YEAR-ROUND,
FULL-TIME WORKERS[1] BY SEX AND
EDUCATIONAL ATTAINMENT, 1987 (in dollars)

Educational Attainment	Women	Men
Fewer than 8 years of school	10,940	17,789
1-3 years of high school	14,270	23,565
High school graduates	17,919	27,293
1-3 years of college	21,441	32,125
College graduates	25,544	40,962
1 or more years of post-graduate work	32,322	51,149
All education levels	20,796	32,892

[1]Workers 25 years and over.

Source: U.S. Bureau of the Census, February 1989, Table 35.

Table 28 • STATE GOVERNMENT[1] PAY EQUITY ACTIVITY,
1984, 1986, AND 1988 (number of states reporting)

Activity[2]	1984	1986	1988
Research/data collection	20	42	43
Pay equity study	11	19	23
Pay equity adjustments	4	11	20
Implementation	1	3	6
No action	27	7	7

[1]Results include the District of Columbia.

[2]Research/data collection on pay equity involves activities preliminary to a pay equity study, such as conducting general research on pay equity. Conducting a pay study involves the study of job classification and compensation systems. Pay equity adjustments are increases in salary appropriated to female-dominated or minority-dominated job categories. Implementation occurs when all elimination of sex-bias from wage-setting procedures is completed and when all appropriated salary adjustments are implemented.

Source: National Committee on Pay Equity, 1988, p. 14.

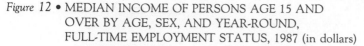

Figure 12 • MEDIAN INCOME OF PERSONS AGE 15 AND
OVER BY AGE, SEX, AND YEAR-ROUND,
FULL-TIME EMPLOYMENT STATUS, 1987 (in dollars)

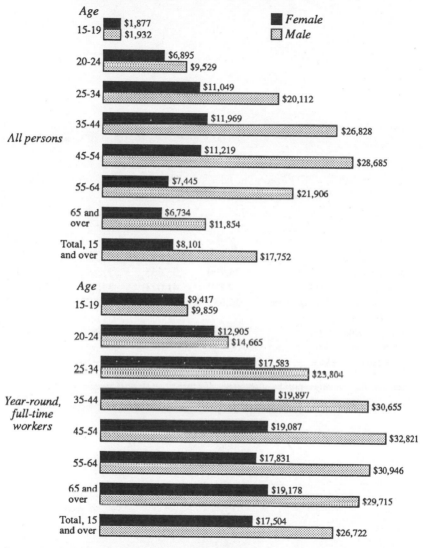

Source: U.S. Bureau of the Census, August 1988, Table 10.

Table 29 • MEDIAN ANNUAL INCOME OF FAMILIES BY
    FAMILY TYPE, RACE, AND HISPANIC ORIGIN,
    1987 (in dollars)

	Family Type		
	All Races	White	Black	Hispanic Origin[1]
Married couple	34,700	35,295	27,182	24,677
Wife in paid labor force	40,422	41,023	33,333	31,354
Wife not in paid labor force	26,652	27,394	16,822	17,967
Male householder, no wife present	24,804	26,230	17,455	19,411
Female householder, no husband present	14,620	17,018	9,710	9,805

[1]Persons of Hispanic origin may be of any race.

Source: U.S. Bureau of the Census, August 1988, Table 1.

Table 30 • SELECTED SOURCES OF INCOME FOR PERSONS AGE 15 AND OVER BY SEX, RACE, AND HISPANIC ORIGIN, 1986 (percent receiving income from source)

Source	Women				Men			
	Total	White	Black	Hispanic Origin[1]	Total	White	Black	Hispanic Origin[1]
Wage or salary	56.7	56.6	56.5	50.9	71.3	72.1	66.1	75.1
Nonfarm self-employment	3.7	4.0	1.1	2.1	8.3	8.9	3.6	5.7
Property income[2]	55.9	60.5	24.4	28.6	56.7	60.8	25.8	29.0
Interest	54.2	58.8	22.8	27.2	54.7	58.8	24.1	27.6
Social security or railroad retirement	19.9	20.9	16.1	9.9	15.7	16.2	13.9	8.1
Public assistance and supplemental security income (SSI)	6.1	4.4	18.2	12.2	2.3	1.8	5.5	3.7
Public assistance and welfare income	4.0	2.8	12.5	9.0	0.9	0.7	2.0	1.7
Supplemental security income (SSI)	2.4	1.8	6.3	3.5	1.4	1.1	3.7	2.1
Retirement and annuities	5.7	6.1	3.3	1.8	9.9	10.6	5.8	3.5

[1]Persons of Hispanic origin may be of any race.

[2]Includes dividends, interest, net rental income, income from estates or trusts, and net royalties.

Source: U.S. Bureau of the Census, June 1988, Table 37.

Table 31 • TRENDS IN POVERTY RATES OF PERSONS BY
FAMILY TYPE, RACE, AND HISPANIC ORIGIN,
SELECTED YEARS, 1960–87

Year	All Races Female-Headed	All Others	White Female-Headed	All Others	Black Female-Headed	All Others	Hispanic Origin[1] Female-Headed	All Others
1960	49.5	18.5	42.3	14.9	70.0[2]	50.7[2]	NA	NA
1965	46.0	13.2	38.5	10.3	65.1[3]	33.4[3]	NA	NA
1970	38.2	8.2	31.4	6.8	58.8	21.7	NA	NA
1976	34.4	7.1	27.3	6.0	54.7	16.9	54.3	17.9
1977	32.8	6.9	25.5	5.9	53.9	16.6	53.3	15.3
1978	32.3	6.6	24.9	5.7	53.1	15.1	53.3	14.6
1979	32.0	7.0	24.9	5.9	52.2	16.2	48.9	15.5
1980	33.8	8.0	27.1	6.9	53.1	17.9	52.5	18.5
1981	35.2	8.8	28.4	7.6	55.8	19.4	54.0	18.6
1982	36.2	9.8	28.7	8.7	57.4	20.0	57.4	22.0
1983	35.6	10.1	28.3	8.8	55.9	20.5	53.2	20.9
1984	34.0	9.3	27.3	8.2	52.9	19.1	54.3	20.9
1985	33.5	8.9	27.3	7.9	51.8	16.4	54.2	21.1
1986	34.2	8.2	27.9	7.3	52.9	15.2	51.3	19.9
1987	33.6	8.2	26.4	7.1	53.8	17.2	53.0	20.8

[1]Persons of Hispanic origin may be of any race.
[2]1959.
[3]1966.
Source: U.S. Bureau of the Census, August 1988, Table 16.

Table 32 • PERCENT OF CHILDREN[1] BELOW POVERTY LEVEL
LIVING IN FEMALE-HEADED HOUSEHOLDS BY
RACE AND HISPANIC ORIGIN, SELECTED YEARS,
1960–87

Year	All Races	White	Black	Hispanic Origin[2]
1960	23.7	21.0	29.4[3]	NA
1965	31.7	27.1	44.1[4]	NA
1970	45.8	36.6	60.7	NA
1976	55.4	45.0	73.9	44.6
1977	56.4	45.3	74.9	48.9
1978	58.5	46.3	78.0	48.9
1979	56.4	44.5	77.1	44.4
1980	52.8	41.3	75.4	47.1
1981	52.2	42.0	73.2	48.5
1982	51.0	39.2	71.5	46.8
1983	50.2	39.7	74.6	45.2
1984	52.4	41.8	74.9	47.2
1985	53.8	43.0	78.4	49.6
1986	56.7	45.7	80.5	49.5
1987	56.9	46.0	79.0	47.2

[1]Refers to related children under age 18 in families.
[2]Persons of Hispanic origin may be of any race.
[3]1959.
[4]1966.
Source: U.S. Bureau of the Census, August 1985, Table 16 and August 1988, Table 16.

Chapter Notes

O N E **A Portrait of African American Families in the United States**

1. Unless otherwise indicated, the statistics in this chapter can be found in the Census Bureau publications listed in the references.
2. African Americans are now moving back to the South to take advantage of new employment opportunities and the more desirable quality of life outside of large northern cities. They are also expressing a desire to be closer to their extended families. This reverse migration will show up even more sharply in the 1990 census than it has to date (Weiss, 1989).

T W O **Women and Affordable Housing**

1. Unless otherwise indicated, all data used in this chapter are derived from the American Housing Survey (AHS) for 1985, the most recent year for which there are published AHS data. The AHS reported a total of 99.9 million housing units, including mobile homes, in the United States in that year. Of this total, 3.2 million units were seasonal (U.S. Department of Housing and Urban Development and U.S. Bureau of the Census, December 1988, Table 1-6). Of the remaining 96.7 million "year-round" units, 8.3 million were vacant for various reasons (2.5 million of these were for rent). The housing survey data in this chapter regarding households pertain to households in the 88.4 million housing units that were *occupied* in 1985.
2. For convenience, the terms used by the Census Bureau in the Housing Survey have been shortened for this chapter. The term "married couples" is used instead of "married couples, no nonrelatives present"; the term "families" is used instead of "two-or-more person households"; and "single" men or women, as the case may be, instead of "male" or "female one-person households."

   It should also be noted here that the Housing Survey category of "married couple, no nonrelatives present" is not strictly comparable to the "married couple" category used in the Current Population Survey (CPS). However, since CPS figures for March 1985 show that 99 percent

of married-couple households had no nonrelatives present, this distinction is ignored here.

3. The Bureau of Labor Statistics (BLS) used to publish a series of "urban
family budgets" for a family of four, with adjustments for other household types. A rough measure of the cost of nonhousing needs for various
household types in 1985 can be estimated by using the 1981 Bureau of
Labor Statistics "lower budget" adjusted by the change in the Consumer Price Index since 1981. This is a higher standard than the poverty
level (which is calculated by multiplying the estimated cost of a bare
subsistence-level food budget by three). BLS in the past has described its
"lower budget" as providing a modest but adequate standard of living.

4. This analysis is based on the federal government's "housing assistance"
budget subfunction, which comprises federal programs and activities
that directly relate to housing. It therefore excludes the amount of federal cash payments (such as social security, Supplemental Security Income [SSI], or Aid to Families with Dependent Children [AFDC]) spent
on housing by recipients of those payments.

5. The term "incremental reservations" is used to denote either additional
households to be assisted through vouchers and Section 8 Existing, or
additional subsidized *units* to be provided through such programs as
Section 202 housing for elderly and handicapped persons and/or public
housing. Each year, in addition to incremental reservations, HUD budget authority is provided for some units or households that are currently
subsidized (for example, to replace units that are demolished or otherwise lost to the inventory).

T H R E E **Child Care in the United States**

1. More recently, some states have attempted to integrate—at least partially—education and child care needs. In at least four states (Massachusetts, Vermont, Florida, and New Jersey), recent prekindergarten legislation permits school districts to fund full working-day child care, and,
indeed, a number of these programs are being funded.

2. Congressional interest in child care legislation did not die with the
100th Congress. As this chapter is written, the full Senate has already
acted on S. 5, a compromise bill that seeks to satisfy some of the major
concerns about ABC.

   The key provisions of S. 5 include $1.75 billion in spending for
direct services, making the dependent care tax credit refundable for
low-income families, allowing states to set their own minimum health
and safety standards with the help of federal incentive grants and model
federal standards, and permitting child care vouchers to be used for care
in sectarian programs, while prohibiting such programs to discriminate
on the basis of religion in hiring staff or admitting children. S. 5 would

also provide a health tax credit to families with incomes under $18,000. The Senate defeated an administration-backed amendment that would have relied mainly on tax credits to help low-income families purchase child care services, rather than on spending for direct services.

The House Education and Labor Committee, meanwhile, completed work on H.R. 3. As finally approved by the committee, H.R. 3 would authorize $1.75 billion in direct spending. Funds would be allocated to expand Head Start to provide full-day care for children of working parents; develop school-based before- and after-school care; help states improve day care programs for infants, toddlers, and children under 13; and help states coordinate child care services. The bill does not set minimum federal health and safety standards, and states would have considerable leeway in meeting the bill's requirement to upgrade health and safety, licensing, and training standards.

F O U R **Gender Equality and Employment Policy**

1. A more extended discussion of these issues appears in Rhode, 1989a and 1989b.
2. For example, recent data suggest that males and females with comparable qualifications holding comparable jobs do not have different turnover rates in most job contexts (Waite and Berryman, 1985; Reskin and Hartmann, 1986).
3. The most important have been the Equal Pay Act of 1963, 29 U.S.C. Section 206 (banning sex discrimination in wages); Title VII of the Civil Rights Act of 1964 (prohibiting sex discrimination in hiring, advancement, termination, and related terms of employment), and Executive Order 11375 (requiring federal contractors to establish affirmative action programs for women).
4. For example, disputes often arise about how to define the relevant applicant pool, which individuals best satisfy given job requirements, and what counts as sufficient good-faith efforts to meet goals and timetables (see Bartholet, 1982).

Women in Business

1. Because partnerships and subchapter S corporations typically have more than one owner, the analyses discussed in this chapter are restricted to sole proprietorships. Researchers and policymakers do not agree on how to identify "the" owner in a multiple owner firm. The reader interested in comparing all women-owned sole proprietorships with all women-owned partnerships or corporations may wish to consult U.S. Bureau of the Census, August 1987. In addition, the 1982 Charac-

teristics of Business Owners contains much more information than can
be discussed in this brief chapter. The reader is encouraged to contact
the original source for other information that might be of interest.

2. Other factors than those discussed in this chapter also determine performance; these include choice of goods or services to produce or provide, geographic location of the business, the owner's or firm's "social"
capital, the firm's financial capital, and product markets.

3. The CBO survey also obtained information on profits, which may also
be used to measure performance. However, there are two reasons why
receipts may be a better measure of performance than profits. First,
profits are viewed as somewhat discretionary in small owner-managed
firms (for example, an owner can elect to take his or her compensation
as salary rather than as profits). Second, there is some question about
the reliability of CBO profit data (Ando, 1988b).

The Emergence and Growth of Women's Studies Programs

1. An earlier version of this paper appeared in *Thought and Action*, the
National Education Association Higher Education Journal, Volume IV,
Fall 1988.

References

Editor's Note

Bergmann, Barbara R. *The Economic Emergence of Women*. New York: Basic Books, 1986.

Older Women's League (OWL). *Failing America's Caregivers: A Status Report on Women Who Care*. Washington, D.C.: OWL, 1989.

Whited, Charles. "It's Still Tough to Be a Woman in Work World." *Miami Herald*, February 9, 1989.

O N E A Portrait of African American Families in the United States

Ahmed, Feroz. *Infant Mortality in Washington, D.C.: A Study of Risk Factors Among Black Residents*. Washington, D.C.: Institute for Urban Affairs and Research, 1987.

Billingsly, Andrew. *Black Families in White America*. Englewood Cliffs, New Jersey: Prentice Hall, 1968.

Califano, Joseph. "Tough Talk for Democrats." *New York Times Magazine*, January 8, 1989.

Cross, William. "Black Family and Black Identity: A Literature Review." *Western Journal of Black Studies* 2 (Summer, 1978): 111-124.

Dash, Leon. *When Children Want Children, The Urban Crisis of Teenage Childbearing*. New York: William Morrow and Company, 1989.

Edelman, Marian W. *Families in Peril, An Agenda for Social Change*. Cambridge, Massachusetts: Harvard University Press, 1987.

Farley, Reynolds and Walter Allen. *The Color Line and the Quality of Life in America*. New York: Russell Sage Foundation, 1987.

Frazier, E. Franklin. *The Negro Family in the United States*. Chicago: University of Chicago Press, 1939.

Furstenberg, Frank. "The Social Consequences of Teen Parenthood." In *Teen Sexuality, Pregnancy, and Childbearing*, edited by F. Furstenberg, R. Lincoln, and J. Menken. Philadelphia: University of Pennsylvania Press, 1981.

Glick, Paul. "Demographic Pictures of Black Families." In *Black Families*,

2nd edition, edited by Harriette McAdoo. Newbury Park, California: Sage Publications, 1988.

Hall, Robert and Carol Stack. *Holding on to the Land and the Lord: Kinship, Ritual, Land Tenure, and Social Policy in the Rural South*. Athens, Georgia: University of Georgia Press, 1982.

Harrison, Algea. "The Black Family's Socializing Environment: Self-Esteem and Ethnic Attitudes Among Black Children." In *Black Children: Social, Educational, and Parental Environments*, edited by Harriette McAdoo. Beverly Hills, California: Sage Publications, 1985.

Hill, Robert. *The Strengths of Black Families*. New York: Emerson-Hall, 1971.

Johnson, Julie. "Blacks and Whites are Found [World Apart]." *New York Times*, January 12, 1989a.

———. "Schools Faulted on Educating Blacks." *New York Times*, May 24, 1989b.

Kunjufu, Jawanza. *Countering the Conspiracy to Destroy Black Boys*. Vol. II. Chicago: African-American Images, 1986.

McAdoo, Harriette. "The Development of Self Concept and Race Attitudes of Young Black Children Over Time." In *Third Conference on Empirical Research in Black Psychology*, edited by W.E. Cross. Washington, D.C.: National Institute of Education, 1977.

———. "Factors Related to the Stability of Upwardly Mobile Black Families." *Journal of Marriage and the Family* 40 (November 1978): 761-776.

———. "Family Changes Within African-American Families." *Smith College School for Social Work Journal* 5 (Spring 1987): 19-22.

———. "Transgenerational Patterns of Upward Mobility in African American Families." In *Black Families*, 2nd edition, edited by Harriette McAdoo. Newbury Park, California: Sage Publications, 1988.

Nash, Margaret and Margaret Dunkle. *The Need for a Warming Trend: A Survey of the School Climate for Pregnant and Parenting Teens*. Washington, D.C.: Equality Center, 1989.

Schmidt, William. "Study Links Male Employment and Single Mothers in Chicago." *New York Times*, January 16, 1989.

U.S. Bureau of the Census. *Current Population Reports*. Series P-20, No. 410. *Marital Status and Living Arrangements: March 1985*. Washington, D.C.: U.S. Government Printing Office, November 1986.

———. *Current Population Reports*. Series P-20, No. 423. *Marital Status and Living Arrangements: March 1987*. Washington, D.C.: U.S. Government Printing Office, April 1988.

———. *Current Population Reports*. Series P-20, No. 424. *Household and Family Characteristics: March 1987*. Washington, D.C.: U.S. Government Printing Office, May 1988.

———. *Current Population Reports*. Series P-20, No. 429. *School Enrollment—Social and Economic Characteristics of Students: October 1986*.

Washington, D.C.: U.S. Government Printing Office, August 1988a.

————. Current Population Reports. Series P-60, No. 161. *Money Income and Poverty Status in the United States: 1987*. Washington, D.C.: U.S. Government Printing Office, August 1988b.

————. Current Population Reports. Series P-20, No. 433. *Marital Status and Living Arrangements: March 1988*. Washington, D.C.: U.S. Government Printing Office, January 1989a.

————. Current Population Reports. Series P-25, No. 1018. *Projections of the Population of the United States by Age, Sex, and Race: 1988 to 2080*. Washington, D.C.: U.S. Government Printing Office, January 1989b.

————. Current Population Reports. Series P-60, No. 162. *Money Income of Households, Families, and Persons in the United States: 1987*. Washington, D.C.: U.S. Government Printing Office, February 1989.

————. Current Population Reports. Series P-23, No. 154. *Child Support and Alimony: 1985*. Washington, D.C.: U.S. Government Printing Office, March 1989.

————. Current Population Reports. Series P-20, No. 436. *Fertility of American Women*. Washington, D.C.: U.S. Government Printing Office, May 1989.

U.S. Bureau of Labor Statistics. *Employment and Earnings*. Washington, D.C.: U.S. Government Printing Office, January 1989.

Vobejda, Barbara. "Black Males Increasingly Rare in College." *Washington Post*, January 16, 1989.

Weiss, Kenneth. "Migration By Blacks From the South Turns Around." *New York Times*, June 11, 1989.

Willie, Charles. "The Black Family: Striving Toward Freedom." In *The State of Black America 1988*, edited by Janet Deward. New York: National Urban League, Inc., 1988a.

————. *A New Look at Black Families*, 3rd edition. Dix Hills, New York: General Hall, 1988b.

Wilson, William. "Social Policy and Minority Groups: What Might Have Been and What Might We See in the Future?" In *Divided Opportunities: Minorities, Poverty, and Social Policy*, edited by Gary Sandefur and Marta Tienda. New York: Plenum Press, 1988.

T W O **Women and Affordable Housing**

Leonard, Paul A., Cushing N. Dolbeare, and Edward B. Lazere. *A Place to Call Home: The Crisis in Housing for the Poor*. Washington, D.C.: Center on Budget and Policy Priorities and Low Income Housing Information Service, 1989.

National Low Income Housing Coalition, Women and Housing Task

Force. "Memorandum to the Transition and the Incoming Administration." Washington, D.C.: National Low Income Housing Coalition, 1988.

National Low Income Housing Preservation Commission. *Preventing the Disappearance of Low Income Housing*. Washington, D.C.: National Low Income Housing Preservation Commission, 1988.

U.S. Bureau of the Census. Current Population Reports. Series P-60, No. 155. *Receipt of Selected Noncash Benefits: 1985*. Washington, D.C.: U.S. Government Printing Office, January 1987.

————. Current Population Reports. Series P-60, No. 158. *Poverty in the United States 1985*. Washington, D.C.: U.S. Government Printing Office, October 1987.

U.S. Bureau of Labor Statistics (BLS). "Autumn 1981 Urban Family Budgets and Comparative Indexes for Selected Urban Areas." Press release USDL 82-129. Washington, D.C.: BLS, 1982.

U.S. Congress. Joint Committee on Taxation. *Estimates of Federal Tax Expenditures for Fiscal Years 1986-1990*. Washington, D.C.: U.S. Government Printing Office, 1985.

U.S. Department of Housing and Urban Development and U.S. Bureau of the Census. Current Housing Reports, H-150-85. *American Housing Survey for the United States in 1985*. Washington, D.C.: U.S. Government Printing Office, December 1988.

U.S. General Accounting Office (GAO). *Rental Housing: Potential Reduction in the Privately Owned and Federally Assisted Inventory*. GAO/RCED-86-176FS. Washington, D.C.: GAO, 1986.

————. *Rental Housing: Potential Reduction in the Section 8 Existing and Voucher Inventory*. GAO/RCED-87-20FS. Washington, D.C.: GAO, 1987.

————. *Rural Rental Housing: Impact of Section 515 Loan Prepayments on Tenants and Housing Availability*. GAO/RCED-88-15BR. Washington, D.C.: GAO, 1988.

THREE **Child Care in the United States**

Berrueta-Clement, John R., Laurence J. Schweinhart, W. Steven Barnett, Ann S. Epstein, and David P. Weikart. *Changed Lives: The Effects of the Perry Preschool Program on Youth Through Age 19*. Ypsilante, Michigan: High/Scope Press, 1984.

Besharov, Douglas J. and Paul N. Tramontozzi. "Child Care Subsidies: Mostly for the Middle Class." *Washington Post*, May 2, 1988.

Blank, Helen, Amy Wilkins, and Margaret Crawley. *State Child Care Fact Book 1987*. Washington, D.C.: Children's Defense Fund, 1987.

Blau, D.M. and P.K. Robins. "Child Care and Family Labor Supply." *The Review of Economics and Statistics* 70 (1988): 374-381.

Bureau of National Affairs (BNA). *Latchkey Children: A Guide for Employers*. Washington, D.C.: BNA, 1984.

Burud, Sandra L., Pamela R. Aschbacher, and Jacqueline McCroskly. *Employer-Supported Child Care: Investing in Human Resources*. Boston: Auburn House, 1984.

Children's Defense Fund. *Child Care: The Time Is Now*. Washington, D.C.: Children's Defense Fund, 1987.

Committee on Economic Development. *Children in Need: Investment and Strategies for the Educationally Disadvantaged*. New York: Committee for Economic Development, 1987.

Commonwealth of Massachusetts. *Caring for Our Common Wealth: The Economics of Child Care in Massachusetts*. Boston: Commonwealth of Massachusetts Office for Children, 1988.

Family Impact Seminar. *The Child Care Market: Supply, Demand, Price, and Expenditures*. Washington, D.C.: Family Impact Seminar, January 1989.

Friedman, Dana. "Estimates From the Conference Board and Other National Monitors of Employer-Supported Child Care." Unpublished memo. New York: The Conference Board, 1988.

Galinsky, Ellen. *Business Competitive Policies and Family Life: The Promise and Potential Pitfalls of Emerging Trends*, in press.

Galinsky, Ellen and Dana Friedman. *Investing in Quality Child Care: A Report for AT&T*. New York: Bank Street College of Education, November 1986.

Goodman, Irene and Joan Brady. *The Challenge of Coordination: Head Start's Relationship to State Funded Preschool Initiatives*. Newton, Massachusetts: Education Development Center, Inc., May 1988.

Gray, W., L. Kafalas, and D. Knight. *An Evaluation of the Massachusetts Voucher Day Care*. Boston: Commonwealth of Massachusetts Department of Social Services, 1984.

Harris, Louis and Associates, Inc. *The Metropolitan Life Survey of the American Teacher 1987: Strengthening Links Between Home and School*. New York: Metropolitan Life Insurance Company, 1987.

Hartmann, Heidi and Diana M. Pearce. *High Skill and Low Pay: The Economics of Child Care Work*. Executive summary. Washington, D.C.: Institute for Women's Policy Research, February 1989.

Hofferth, Sandra L. and Deborah A. Phillips. "Child Care in the United States, 1970 to 1995." *Journal of Marriage and the Family* 49 (August 1987): 559-571.

Honig, L., D. Wittmer, R. Lally, and P. Magione. *An Early Intervention Program 10 Years Later: What Happened to High Risk Infants Who Received Quality Early Childhood Education—The Syracuse University Study*. Paper presented at the National Association for the Education of Young Children Conference, Washington, D.C., November 1986.

Kahn, Alfred J. and Sheila B. Kamerman. *Child Care: Facing the Hard Choices*. Dover, Massachusetts: Auburn House, 1987.

Lazar, Irving and the Consortium on Developmental Continuity. *The Persistence of Preschool Effects*. Denver, Colorado: Education Commission of the States, 1977.

Lindsey, Laurence B. "Better Child Care, Cheaper." *Wall Street Journal*, July 5, 1988.

Marx, Fern. "Child Care." In *Services to Young Families: Program Review and Policy Recommendations*, edited by H. McAdoo and T.M.J. Parkam. Washington, D.C.: American Public Welfare Association, 1985.

Marx, Fern and Michelle Seligson. *The Public School Early Childhood Study: The State Survey*. New York: Bank Street College of Education, 1988.

Mitchell, Anne. *The Public School Early Childhood Study: The District Survey*. New York: Bank Street College of Education, 1988.

National Association of Elementary School Principals. "Child Care Survey." Press release. Alexandria, Virginia: National Association of Elementary School Principals, January 28, 1988.

National Governor's Association. *Focus on the First 60 Months: Proceedings of the National Early Childhood Conference*. Washington, D.C.: National Governor's Association, 1986.

O'Connor, Alice. "The Family Support Bill: Living Up to Its Name?" *Child Care Action News* 5 (November-December 1988).

Pekow, Charles. "Legislative Failure: Why ABC Didn't Pass in 1988." *Special Report* 17. Washington, D.C.: Day Care Information Service, December 1988.

Phillips, Deborah A. and Carollee Howes. "Indicators of Quality Child Care: Review of the Research" in *Quality in Child Care: What Does the Research Tell Us?* edited by Deborah A. Phillips. Washington, D.C.: National Association for the Education of Young Children, 1987.

Porter, Toni B. *Lives on Hold*. New York: Child Care, Inc., 1988.

Presser, Harriet. "Shift Work and Child Care Among Young Dual Earner American Parents." *Journal of Marriage and the Family* 50 (February 1988): 133-149.

Rector, Robert. "The American Family and Day Care." *Issue Bulletin* 138. Washington, D.C.: The Heritage Foundation, April 6, 1988.

Samuelson, Robert J. "The Debate Over Day Care." *Newsweek*, June 27, 1988, 45.

Seligson, Michelle. "Child Care for the School-Age Child." *Phi Delta Kappan* 67 (May 1986): 20-23.

U.S. Bureau of the Census. Current Population Reports. Series P-23, No. 129. *Child Care Arrangements of Working Mothers: June 1982*. Washington, D.C.: U.S. Government Printing Office, 1983.
————. Current Population Reports. Series P-70, No. 9. *Who's Minding the Kids? Child Care Arrangements: Winter 1984-85*. Washington, D.C.: U.S. Government Printing Office, May 1987.

F O U R **Gender Equality and Employment Policy**

Abramson, Jill and Barbara Franklin. *Where Are They Now: The Women of Harvard Law*. Garden City, New York: Doubleday, 1986.
Aisenberg, Nadya and Mona Harrington. *Women of Academe*. Amherst, Massachusetts: University of Massachusetts Press, 1988.
American Bar Association (ABA). Commission on Women in the Professions. *Report to the House of Delegates*. Chicago: ABA, 1988.
Bartholet, Elizabeth. "Application of Title VII to Jobs in High Places." *Harvard Law Review* 95 (March 1982): 947-1027.
Becker, Gary. *The Economics of Discrimination*, 2nd edition. Chicago: University of Chicago Press, 1971.
————. *Human Capital*. New York: Columbia University Press, 1975.
Becker, Mary E. "Prince Charming: Abstract Equality." *Supreme Court Review*. Chicago: University of Chicago Press, 1987, 201-247.
Beller, Andrea H. "Occupational Segregation and the Earnings Gap." In *Comparable Worth: Issue for the 80's*. Vol. 1. Washington, D.C.: U.S. Commission on Civil Rights, 1984.
Bernard, Jessie. "Sex Difference: An Overview." In *Beyond Sex-Role Stereotypes*, edited by Alexandra Kaplan and Joan Bean. Boston: Little, Brown, 1976.
Bielby, William T. and James N. Baron. "A Woman's Place is With Other Women: Sex Segregation Within Organizations." In *Sex Segregation in the Workplace: Trends, Explanations, Remedies*, edited by Barbara F. Reskin. Washington, D.C.: National Academy Press, 1984.
Blau, Francine D. "Occupational Segregation and Labor Market Discrimination." In *Sex Segregation in the Workplace: Trends. Explanations, Remedies*, edited by Barbara F. Reskin. Washington, D.C.: National Academy Press, 1984.
Block, Walter E. and Michael A. Walker. *Discrimination, Affirmative Action, and Equal Opportunity: An Economic and Social Perspective*. Vancouver: The Fraser Institute, 1982.
Caribbean Marine Services v. Baldridge, 844 F2d 668 (9th Cir. 1988).
Citizens' Commission on Civil Rights. *Affirmative Action: To Open the Doors of Job Opportunity, A Policy of Fairness and Compassion That Has Worked*. Washington, D.C.: Citizens' Commission on Civil Rights, 1984.

Clauss, Carin Anne. "Comparable Worth: The Theory, Its Legal Foundation, and the Feasibility of Implementation." *Journal of Law Reform* 20 (Fall 1986): 7-97.

Duncan, Gregory. *Years of Poverty, Years of Plenty.* Ann Arbor: University of Michigan, Survey Research Center, Institute for Social Research, 1984.

Employee Benefit Research Institute (EBRI). *Issue Brief* 85 (December 1988): 15.

Epstein, Cynthia Fuchs. *Deceptive Distinction: Sex, Gender, and the Social Order.* New Haven, Connecticut: Yale University Press, 1988.

Fallon, Richard H. "To Each According to His Ability; From None According to His Race: The Concept of Merit in the Law of Antidiscrimination." *Boston Law Review* 60 (November 1980): 815-877.

Fernandez, John. *Racism and Sexism in Corporate Life.* Lexington, Massachusetts: Lexington Books, 1981.

Fishel, Daniel and Edward P. Lazear. "Comparable Worth and Discrimination in Labor Markets." *University of Chicago Law Review* 53 (Summer 1986): 891-952.

Gold, Michael Evan. *A Dialogue on Comparable Worth.* Ithaca, New York: ILR Press, 1983.

Goldman, Alan H. *Justice and Reverse Discrimination.* Princeton, New Jersey: Princeton University Press, 1979.

Gutek, Barbara (editor). *Sex Role Stereotyping and Affirmative Action Policy.* Los Angeles: Institute of Industrial Relations, 1982.

Hartmann, Heidi I. "Comparable Worth and Women's Economic Independence." In *Ingredients for Women's Employment Policy,* edited by Christine Bose and Glenna Spitze. Albany, New York: State University of New York Press, 1987.

Hartmann, Heidi I., Patricia A. Roos, and Donald J. Treiman. "An Agenda for Basic Research on Comparable Worth." In *Comparable Worth: New Directions for Research,* edited by Heidi I. Hartmann. Washington, D.C.: National Academy Press, 1985.

Howe, Louise Kapp. *Pink Collar Workers.* New York: G.P. Putnam's Sons, 1977.

Kamerman, Sheila B. and Alfred J. Kahn. *The Responsive Workplace.* New York: Columbia University Press, 1987.

Kanter, Rosabeth Moss. *Men and Women of the Corporation.* New York: Basic Books, 1977.

Kaufman, Debra R. and Barbara L. Richardson. *Achievement and Women: Challenging the Assumptions.* New York: The Free Press, 1982.

Killingsworth, Mark R. "The Economics of Comparable Worth: Analytic, Empirical, and Policy Questions." In *Comparable Worth: New Directions for Research,* edited by Heidi I. Hartmann. Washington, D.C.: National Academy Press, 1985.

Kirp, David L., Marlene Strong, and Mark G. Yudof. *Gender Justice*. Chicago: University of Chicago Press, 1985.

Larwood, Laurie and Marion Wood. *Women in Management*. Lexington, Massachusetts: Lexington Books, 1977.

Lauter, David. "How to Factor the Value of Workers' Skills." *National Law Journal* January 2, 1984: 24.

Lawrence, Charles R. "The Id, the Ego, and Equal Protection: Reckoning with Unconscious Racism." *Stanford Law Review* 39 (1987): 317-388.

Lott, Bernice. "The Devaluation of Women's Competence." *Journal of Social Issues* 41 (Winter 1985): 43-60.

McBroom, Patricia. *The Third Sex*. New York: William Morrow, 1986.

MacKinnon, Catharine. *Sexual Harassment of Working Women: A Case of Sex Discrimination*. New Haven, Connecticut: Yale University Press, 1979.

Marano, Cynthia. Prepared statement for the Subcommittee on Employment Opportunities of the Committee on Education and Labor, U.S. House of Representatives, 2d Session. *Hearing on Women in the Workforce: Supreme Court Issues*. Washington, D.C.: U.S. Government Printing Office, 1986.

Marini, Margaret Mooney and Mary C. Brinton. "Sex Typing in Occupational Socialization." In *Sex Segregation in the Workplace: Trends, Explanations, Remedies*, edited by Barbara F. Reskin. Washington, D.C.: National Academy Press, 1984.

Matthaei, Julie A. *An Economic History of Women in America*. New York: Shocken, 1982.

Mead, Margaret. *Male and Female: A Study of the Sexes in a Changing World*. New York: William Morrow, 1968.

Mednick, Martha T. "Women and the Psychology of Achievement: Implications for Personal and Social Change." In *Women in the Work Force*, edited by H. John Bernadin. New York: Praeger, 1982.

Menges, Robert J. and William H. Exum. "Barriers to the Progress of Women and Minority Faculty." *Journal of Higher Education* 54 (March/April 1983): 123-144.

Meritor Savings Bank FSB v. Vinson, 477 U.S. 57 (1986).

Mirande, Alfredo and Evangelina Enriquez. *La Chicana*. Chicago: University of Chicago Press, 1979.

Muller v. Oregon, 208 U.S. 412, 421 (1908).

National Committee on Pay Equity. *Pay Equity: An Issues of Race, Ethnicity, and Sex*. Washington, D.C.: National Committee on Pay Equity, 1987.

———. *Briefing on the Wage Gap*. Washington, D.C.: National Committee on Pay Equity, 1989.

New York State Club Association v. City of New York, 108 S. Ct. 2225 (1988).

Remick, Helen and Ronnie Steinberg. "Technical Possibilities and Political Realities: Concluding Remarks." In *Comparable Worth and Wage Discrimination*, edited by Helen Remick. Philadelphia: Temple University Press, 1984.

Reskin, Barbara F. and Heidi I. Hartmann. *Women's Work, Men's Work: Sex Segregation on the Job*. Washington, D.C.: National Academy Press, 1986.

Rhode, Deborah L. "Association and Assimilation." *Northwestern Law Review* 1 (Fall 1986): 106-145.

———. "Perspectives on Professional Women." *Stanford Law Review* 40 (May 1988): 1163-1207.

———. *Justice and Gender*. Cambridge, Massachusetts: Harvard University Press, 1989a.

———. "Occupational Inequality." *Duke University Law Journal* (forthcoming, 1989b).

Roberts v. United States Jaycees, 468 U.S. 628 (1984).

Roos, Patricia A. *Gender and Work: A Comparative Analysis of Industrial Societies*. Albany, New York: State University of New York Press, 1985.

Roos, Patricia A. and Barbara Reskin. "Institutional Factors Contributing to Sex Segregation in the Workplace." In *Sex Segregation in the Workplace: Trends, Explanations, Remedies*, edited by Barbara F. Reskin. Washington, D.C.: National Academy Press, 1984.

Savage, David. "San Jose's Equal Pay Plan Survives." *Los Angeles Times*, September 12, 1983.

Scales-Trent, Judy. "Comparable Worth: Is This a Theory for Black Workers?" *Women's Rights Law Reporter* 8 (Winter 1984): 51-58.

Shepela, Sharon Toffey and Ann T. Viviano. "Some Psychological Factors Affecting Sex Discrimination and Wages." In *Comparable Worth and Wage Discrimination*, edited by Helen Remick. Philadelphia: Temple University Press, 1984.

Steinberg, Ronnie J. "Identifying Wage Discrimination and Implementing Pay Equity Adjustments." In *Comparable Worth: Issue for the 80's*. Vol. 1. Washington, D.C.: U.S. Commission on Civil Rights, 1984.

Steinberg, Ronnie J. and Lois Haignere. "Equitable Compensation: Methodological Criteria for Comparable Worth." In *Ingredients for Women's Employment Policy*, edited by Christine Bose and Glenna Spitze. Albany, New York: State University of New York Press, 1987.

Strober, Myra H. and Sanford N. Dornbush. "Public Policy Alternatives." In *Feminism, Children, and the New Families*, edited by Sanford N. Dornbush and Myra H. Strober. New York: Guilford Press, 1988.

Treiman, Donald J. and Heidi I. Hartmann. *Women, Work and Wages: Equal Pay for Jobs of Equal Value*. Washington, D.C.: National Academy Press, 1981.

U.S. Bureau of the Census. *Census of Population, 1960, Volume One, Characteristics of the Population: U.S. Summary*. Washington, D.C.: U.S. Government Printing Office, 1964.

U.S. Bureau of Labor Statistics. *Employment and Earnings*. Washington, D.C.: U.S. Government Printing Office, 1968.

Waite, Linda J. and Sue E. Berryman. *Women in Non-Traditional Occupations: Choice and Turnover*. Santa Monica, California: Rand, 1985.

Walshok, Mary L. *Blue Collar Women: Pioneers on the Male Frontier*. Garden City, New York: Anchor, 1981.

Weiler, Paul. "The Wages of Sex: Limits of Comparable Worth." *Harvard Law Review* 99 (June 1986): 1728-1807.

Zigler, Edward and Meryl Frank. *The Parental Leave Crisis: Toward a National Policy*. New Haven, Connecticut: Yale University Press, 1988.

Women in Brief

Alloway, Lawrence. "Women's Art in the '70s." *Art in America*. (May/June 1976): 64-72.

American Medical Association (AMA). *In the Marketplace: Work Patterns, Practice Characteristics and Incomes of Women Physicians*. Chicago: AMA, 1987.

Ando, Faith H. "Capital Issues and the Minority-Owned Business." *The Review of Black Political Economy* 16 (Spring 1988a): 77-109.

———. *Minorities, Women, Veterans and the 1982 Characteristics of Business Owners Survey: A Preliminary Analysis*. Report to the U.S. Small Business Administration and the U.S. Minority Business Development Agency, SBA 3026-OA-88. Haverford, Pennsylvania: Faith Ando & Associates, 1988b.

Arnold, Robert, Steven C. Martin, and Ruth M. Parker. "Taking Care of Patients: Does It Matter When the Doctor Is a Woman?" *Western Journal of Medicine* 149 (1988): 729-733.

Association of American Medical Colleges (AAMC). *Medical School Admission Requirements, 1990-91*. Washington, D.C.: AAMC, 1989.

Barrett, Nancy S. "Women and the Economy." In *The American Woman 1987-88: A Report in Depth*, edited by Sara E. Rix. New York: W. W. Norton and Company, 1987.

Behr, Shulamith. *Women Expressionists*. New York: Rizzoli, 1988.

Bell, Susan G. and Karen M. Offen (editors). *Women, the Family, and Freedom: The Debate in Documents*. Stanford, California: Stanford University Press, 1983.

Belous, Richard S. "How Firms Adjust to the Shift Toward Contingent Workers." *Monthly Labor Review* 112 (March 1989): 7-12.

Benham, Lee. "Benefits of Women's Education Within Marriage." *Journal of Political Economy* 82, 2, part II (March/April 1974): S57-S71.

Bianchi, Suzanne M. and Daphne Spain. *American Women in Transition*. New York: Russell Sage Foundation, 1986.

Bickel, Janet. "Women in Medical Education: A Status Report." *The New England Journal of Medicine* 319 (December 15, 1988): 1579-1584.

Bielby, William T. and Denise D. Bielby. *The 1989 Hollywood Writers' Report: Unequal Access, Unequal Pay*. West Hollywood, California: Writers Guild of America, West, 1989.

Bonilla-Santiago, Gloria. *Hispanic Women in New Jersey: A Survey of Women Raising Families Alone*. Camden, New Jersey: Hispanic Women's Task Force of New Jersey, Rutgers University, 1988.

Bowman, Marjorie A. and Marcie Lynn Gross. "Overview of Research on Women in Medicine—Issues for Public Policymakers." *Public Health Reports* 101 (May/June 1986): 513-521.

Broude, Norma. "Degas's Misogyny." *Art Bulletin* 59 (March 1977): 95-107.

Bureau of National Affairs (BNA). *The Changing Workplace: New Directions in Staffing and Scheduling*. Washington, D.C.: BNA, 1986.

Calkins, E., Louise M. Arnold, and T. Lee Willoughby. "Gender Differences in Predictors of Performance in Medical Training." *Journal of Medical Education* 62 (August 1987): 682-685.

Camp, Sharon L. (editor). *Country Rankings of the Status of Women: Poor, Powerless, and Pregnant*. Washington, D.C.: Population Crisis Committee, 1988.

Castro, Janice. "Women Entrepreneurs: She Calls All the Shots." *Time*, July 4, 1988, 54-57.

Chadwick, Whitney. *Women Artists in the Surrealist Movement*. Boston: Little, Brown, 1985.

Chen, Gavin, Norman Hurwitz, Bruce Kirchhoff, and Richard Stevens. *Minority Business Enterprise Today: Problems and Their Causes*. NTIS Report Number PB-82-194986. Washington, D.C.: U. S. Department of Commerce, Minority Business Development Agency, January 1982.

Chiti, Judith. "Review of *Reflections: Women in Their Own Image*." *Woman's Art Journal* 7 (Spring/Summer 1986): 46-47.

Christensen, Kathleen. Testimony Before the Employment and Housing Subcommittee, Committee on Government Operations, U.S. House of Representatives, May 19, 1988.

Clark, J. and P. P. Rieker. "Gender Differences in Relationships and Stress of Medical and Law Students." *Journal of Medical Education* 61 (January 1986): 32-40.

Curti, Merle. *The American Peace Crusade 1815-1860*. Durham, North Carolina: Duke University Press, 1929.
———. *Peace or War: The American Struggle 1636-1936*. New York: W. W. Norton and Company, 1936.
Davidson, Nicholas. *The Failure of Feminism*. Buffalo, New York: Prometheus Books, 1988.
DeBenedetti, Charles. *The Peace Reform in American History*. Bloomington, Indiana: Indiana University Press, 1980.
Degen, Marie Louise. *The History of the Woman's Peace Party*. Baltimore: The Johns Hopkins University Press, 1939.
Dieppa, Ismael and Miguel Montiel. "Hispanic Families: An Exploration." In *Hispanic Families*, edited by Jan Curren. Washington, D.C.: National Coalition of Hispanic Mental Health and Humans Services Organizations, 1978.
Downie, Susanna (editor). *Decade of Achievement: 1977-1987—A Report of a Survey Based on the National Plan of Action for Women*. Beaver Dam, Wisconsin: National Women's Conference Committee, 1988.
Duncan, Carol. "Happy Mothers and Other New Ideas in French Art." *Art Bulletin* 55 (December 1973): 570-583.
Elshtain, Jean Bethke. "Women, War and Feminism." *Nation* 230 (June 14, 1980): 705-722.
Emmons, David W. "Changing Dimensions of Practice Arrangements." *Medical Care Review* 45 (Spring 1988): 101-128.
Fahlman, Betsy. "Reviews." *Woman's Art Journal* 8 (Fall 1987/Winter 1988): 55-59.
Fine, Elsa Honig. *Women and Art: A History of Women Painters and Sculptors from the Renaissance to the 20th Century*. Montclair/London: Allenheld and Schram/Prior, 1978.
Fraser, Arvonne. *U.N. Decade for Women: Documents and Dialogue*. Boulder, Colorado: Westview Press, 1987.
Galey, Margaret E. "Promoting Nondiscrimination Against Women: The U.N. Commission on the Status of Women." *International Studies Quarterly* 23 (June 1979): 273-302.
Glenn, Evelyn Nakano. *Issei, Nisei, War Bride: Three Generations of Japanese American Women in Domestic Service*. Philadelphia: Temple University Press, 1986.
Gouma-Peterson, Thalia and Patricia Mathews. "The Feminist Critique of Art History." *Art Bulletin* 69 (September 1987): 326-357.
Grant, Linda. "The Gender Climate of Medical School: Perspectives of Women and Men Students." *Journal of the American Medical Women's Association* 43 (July/August 1988): 109-119.
Grefe, Mary. Testimony Before the 32nd Session of the U.N. Commission on the Status of Women, Vienna, March 18, 1988.

Heller, Nancy. *Women Artists: An Illustrated History*. New York: Abberville Press, 1987.

Hobbs, Robert. "Sally Michel: The Other Avery." *Woman's Art Journal* 8 (Fall 1987/Winter 1988): 3-14.

Institute for Defense and Disarmament Studies. *American Peace Directory*, edited by Melinda Fine and Peter Stevens. Cambridge, Massachusetts: Ballinger Publishing, 1984.

―――. *Peace Resource Book*, edited by Carl Conetta. Cambridge, Massachusetts: Ballinger Publishing, 1988.

International Congress of Women. *International Congress of Women, The Hague Report*. Amsterdam: N.V. Concordia, 1915.

―――. *Report of the International Congress of Women, Zurich, 1918*. Geneva: International Congress of Women, 1918.

Katz, Barry. "The Women of Futurism." *Woman's Art Journal* 7 (Fall 1986/ Winter 1987): 3-13.

Kim, Bok-Lim C., Amy I. Okamura, Naomi Ozawa, and Virginia Forrest. *Women in Shadows. A Handbook for Service Providers Working with Asian Wives of U.S. Military Personnel*. LaJolla, California: National Committee Concerned with Asian Wives of U.S. Servicemen, 1981.

Kim, Elaine with Janice Otani. *With Silk Wings: Asian American Women at Work*. Oakland, California: Asian Women United of California, 1983.

Lauter, Paul. *Reconstructing American Literature*. Old Westbury, New York: The Feminist Press, 1983.

Lerner, Gerda *Teaching Women's History*. Washington, D.C.: American Historical Association, 1981.

Levitan, Sar A. and Elizabeth A. Conway. "Part-Timers: Living on Half-Rations." *Challenge* 31 (May/June 1988): 8-16.

Lippard, Lucy. "Sweeping Changes: The Contributions of Feminism to the Art of the 1970s." *College Art Journal* 40 (Fall/Winter 1980): 362-365.

Lloyd, C. and N. Gartrell. "Sex Differences in Medical Student Mental Health." *American Journal of Psychiatry* 138 (October 1981): 1346-1351.

Lorber, Judith. *Women Physicians: Career, Status and Power*. New York: Tavistock, 1984.

Lott, Juanita (editor). *Pan Asian Women: A Vital Force*. Washington, D.C.: Organization of Pan Asian American Women, 1985.

Lott, Juanita and Canta Pian. *Beyond Stereotypes and Statistics: Emergence of Asian and Pacific American Women*. Hyattsville, Maryland: Council Press, 1979.

Loughery, John. "Mrs. Holladay and the Guerrilla Girls." *Arts Magazine* 62 (October 1987): 61-65.

Mark, Diane Mei Lin and Ginger Chih. *A Place Called Chinese America*. Dubuque, Iowa: Kendall/Hunt Publishing Company, 1982.

Miller, Jean Baker. *Toward a New Psychology of Women*. Boston: Beacon Press, 1976.

Mincer, Jacob and Solomon Polachek. "Family Investments in Human Capital: Earnings of Women." *Journal of Political Economy* 82, 2, part II (March/April 1974): S76-S108.

Munsterberg, Hugo. *A History of Women Artists*. New York: C.N. Potter Crown, 1975.

Natera, Maria. *Hispana Perspective*. Los Angeles: California State Department of Education, Career-Vocational Preparation Division, 1988.

National Council of La Raza. *Hispanics in the Work Force: Hispanic Women Part II*. Washington, D.C.: Policy Analysis Center, 1988.

Nemser, Cindy. *Art Talk: Conversations With 12 Artists*. New York: Scribner, 1975.

Nochlin, Linda. "Why Have There Been No Great Women Artists?" *Art News* 69 (January 1971): 22-39.

Owen, John D. "Why Part-Time Workers Tend to be in Low-Wage Jobs." *Monthly Labor Review* 101 (June 1978): 11-14.

Petersen, Karen and J.J. Wilson. *Women Artists: Recognition and Reappraisal*. New York: Harper Colophon, 1976.

Plauche, Warren C. and Joseph M. Miller, Jr. "Performances of Female Medical Students in an Obstetrics and Gynecology Clerkship." *Journal of Medical Education* 61 (April 1986): 323-325.

Preven, David W., Elizabeth Krajic Kachur, Robin B. Kupfer, and Jane A. Waters. "Interviewing Skills of First-Year Medical Students." *Journal of Medical Education* 61 (October 1986): 842-844.

Riley, John G. "Testing the Educational Screening Hypothesis." *Journal of Political Economy* 87, 5, part II (October 1979): S227-S252.

Rizzo-Harvi, Renata. "Women's Work." *Nuclear Times* (July/August 1987): 19-23.

Rom, Christine C. "One View: The Feminist Art Journal." *Woman's Art Journal* 2 (Fall 1981/Winter 1982): 19-24.

Sandefur, Gary D. and Arthur Sakamoto. "American Indian Household Structure and Income." *Demography* 25 (February 1988): 71-80.

Seifert, Carolyn. "Images of Domestic Madness in the Art and Poetry of American Women." *Woman's Art Journal* 1 (Fall 1980/Winter 1981): 1-6.

Shefer, Elaine. "Woman's Mission." *Woman's Art Journal* 7 (Spring/Summer 1986): 8-12.

Sherman, Julia and Evelyn Torton Beck (editors). *The Prism of Sex*. Madison, Wisconsin: The University of Wisconsin Press, 1981.

Sparrow, W.S. *Women Painters of the World*. London: Hodder and Stoughton, 1905.

Spence, Michael A. *Market Signalling: Information Transfer in Hiring and Related Screening Processes*. Cambridge, Massachusetts: Harvard University Press, 1974.

Spender, Dale (editor). *Men's Studies Modified*. Oxford, England: Pergamon Press, 1981.

Steinson, Barbara J. *American Women's Activism During World War I*. New York: Garland Publishing, 1982.

Stiglitz, Joseph E. "The Theory of 'Screening,' Education, and the Distribution of Income." *American Economic Review* 65 (June 1975): 283-300.

Stinson, John F., Jr. "Moonlighting by Women Jumped to Record High." *Monthly Labor Review* 109 (November 1986): 22-25.

Swerdlow, Amy. "Women's Peace Festival." *Women's Studies Quarterly* 12 (Summer 1984): 29.

Tinker, Irene (editor). *Women in Washington: Advocates for Public Policy*. Beverly Hills, California: Sage Publications, 1983.

Tinker, Irene and Michele Bo Bramsen. *Women and World Development*. Washington, D.C.: Overseas Development Council, 1976.

Tudor, Cynthia and Diane Lindley. *Trends in Medical School Applicants and Matriculants, 1978-1987*. Washington, D.C.: Association of American Medical Colleges, 1988.

Tufts, Eleanor. *Our Hidden Heritage: Five Centuries of Women Artists*. New York: Paddington Press, 1974.

United Nations. *The Forward-Looking Strategies for the Advancement of Women*. New York: United Nations, 1985.

U.S. Bureau of the Census. PC80-1-C1. *General Social and Economic Characteristics: United States Summary*. Washington, D.C.: U.S. Government Printing Office, December 1983a.

————. *Statistical Abstract of the United States 1984*. Washington, D.C.: U.S. Government Printing Office, December 1983b.

————. *Current Population Reports*. Series P-20, No. 390. *Educational Attainment in the United States: March 1981 and 1980*. Washington, D.C.: U.S. Government Printing Office, August 1984.

————. WB82-1. *1982 Economic Censuses: Women Owned Businesses*. Washington, D.C.: U.S. Government Printing Office, April 1986.

————. 82CBO-1. *1982 Characteristics of Business Owners*. Washington, D.C.: U.S. Government Printing Office, August 1987.

————. PC80-2-1E. *Asian and Pacific Islander Population in the United States: 1980*. Washington, D.C.: U.S. Government Printing Office, January 1988.

————. *Current Population Reports*. Series P-20, No. 427. *Fertility of American Women: June 1987*. Washington, D.C.: U.S. Government Printing Office, May 1988.

————. *Current Population Reports*. Series P-20, No. 428. *Educational*

Attainment in the United States: March 1987 and 1986. Washington, D.C.: U.S. Government Printing Office, August 1988a.

————. Current Population Reports. Series P-20, No. 431. *The Hispanic Population in the United States: March 1988*. Washington, D.C.: U.S. Government Printing Office, August 1988b.

————. Current Population Reports. Series P-60, No. 161. *Money Income and Poverty Status in the United States: 1987*. Washington, D.C.: U.S. Government Printing Office, August 1988c.

U.S. Bureau of Labor Statistics. *Employment and Earnings*. Washington, D.C.: U.S. Government Printing Office, January 1988 and January 1989.

U.S. Congress. House. Committee on Small Business. 100th Congress, 2d Session. *New Economic Realities: The Rise of the Woman Entrepreneur*. Washington, D.C.: U.S. Government Printing Office, 1988.

Valdivieso, Rafael and Cary Davis. *U.S. Hispanics: Challenging Issues for the 1990s*. Washington, D.C.: Population Reference Bureau, 1988.

Wallis, Lila A., H. Gilder, and H. Thaler. "Advancement of Men and Women in Medical Academia." *Journal of the American Medical Association* 246 (November 20, 1981): 2350-2353.

Weinberg, Ethel and James F. Rooney. "The Academic Performance of Women Students in Medical School." *Journal of Medical Education* 48 (March 1973): 240-247.

Whittick, Arnold. *Woman Into Citizen*. Santa Barbara, California: ABC-Clio, 1979.

Williams, Harry B. "What Temporary Workers Earn: Findings From a New BLS Survey." *Monthly Labor Review* 112 (March 1989): 3-6.

Young, Nancy Foon and Judy R. Parish (editors). *Montage: An Ethnic History of Women in Hawaii*. Honolulu: State Commission on the Status of Women, 1977.

American Women Today: A Statistical Portrait

Catalyst. "Historical Data on the Number of Women Directors on Fortune Boards During the Last 17 Years" (fact sheet). New York: Catalyst, 1986.

Center for the American Woman and Politics (CAWP). *Women Candidates for Congress and Statewide Offices: 1988 Election Results*. New Brunswick, New Jersey: CAWP, 1988.

Hubbard, Lisa, with the assistance of Cynthia Coleman. *National Committee on Pay Equity Survey of State-Government Level Pay Equity Activity 1988*. Washington, D.C.: National Committee on Pay Equity, 1988.

National Center for Health Statistics. *Health, United States, 1987*, No. (PHS) 88-1232. Washington, D.C.: U.S. Government Printing Office, March 1988.

————. "Annual Summary of Births, Marriages, Divorces, and Deaths: United States, 1987." *Monthly Vital Statistics Report* 36, 13, No. (PHS) 88-1120. Hyattsville, Maryland: U.S. Public Health Service, July 1988.

National Science Foundation (NSF). *Women and Minorities in Science and Engineering*. Washington, D.C.: NSF, 1988.

U.S. Bureau of the Census. Current Population Reports, Series P-20, No. 218. *Household and Family Characteristics: March 1970*. Washington, D.C.: U.S. Government Printing Office, March 1971.

————. *Historical Statistics of the United States, Colonial Times to 1970, Part 1*. Washington, D.C.: U.S. Government Printing Office, September 1975.

————. Current Population Reports. Series P-60, No. 127. *Money Income and Poverty Status of Families in the United States: 1980*. Washington, D.C.: U.S. Government Printing Office, August 1981.

————. Current Population Reports. Series P-20, No. 366. *Household and Family Characteristics: March 1980*. Washington, D.C.: U.S. Government Printing Office, September 1981.

————. Current Population Reports. Series P-60, No. 151. *Money Income of Households, Families, and Persons in the United States: 1984*. Washington, D.C.: U.S. Government Printing Office, April 1986.

————. Current Population Reports. Series P-60, No. 154. *Money Income and Poverty Status of Families and Persons in the United States: 1985*. Washington, D.C.: U.S. Government Printing Office, August 1986.

————. Current Population Reports. Series P-20, No. 411. *Household and Family Characteristics: March 1985*. Washington, D.C.: U.S. Government Printing Office, September 1986.

————. Current Population Reports. Series P-70, No. 8. *Disability, Functional Limitation, and Health Insurance Coverage: 1984/1985*. Washington, D.C.: U.S. Government Printing Office, December 1986.

————. Current Population Reports. Series P-20, No. 424. *Household and Family Characteristics: March 1987*. Washington, D.C.: U.S. Government Printing Office, May 1988a.

————. Current Population Reports. Series P-20, No. 427. *Fertility of American Women: June 1987*. Washington, D.C.: U.S. Government Printing Office, May 1988b.

————. Current Population Reports. Series P-60, No. 159. *Money Income of Households, Families, and Persons in the United States: 1986*. Washington, D.C.: U.S. Government Printing Office, June 1988.

————. Current Population Reports. Series P-60, No. 161. *Money Income and Poverty Status in the United States: 1987*. Washington, D.C.: U.S. Government Printing Office, August 1988.

————. Current Population Reports. Series P-20, No. 432. *Households, Families, Marital Status and Living Arrangements: March 1988 (Ad-*

vance Report). Washington, D.C.: U.S. Government Printing Office, September 1988.
————. Current Population Reports. Series P-20, No. 433. *Marital Status and Living Arrangements: March 1988.* Washington, D.C.: U.S. Government Printing Office, January 1989a.
————. Current Population Reports. Series P-25, No. 1018. *Projections of the Population to the Year 2000.* Washington, D.C.: U.S. Government Printing Office, January 1989b.
————. Current Population Reports. Series P-60, No. 162. *Money Income of Households, Families, and Persons in the United States: 1987.* Washington, D.C.: U.S. Government Printing Office, February 1989.
U.S. Bureau of Labor Statistics. *Marital and Family Characteristics of Workers: March 1960.* Washington, D.C.: U.S. Bureau of Labor Statistics, April 1961.
————. *Employment and Earnings.* Washington, D.C.: U.S. Government Printing Office, January 1976.
————. *Employment and Earnings.* Washington, D.C.: U.S. Government Printing Office, January 1979.
————. *Employment and Earnings.* Washington, D.C.: U.S. Government Printing Office, January 1984.
————. *Handbook of Labor Statistics.* Washington, D.C.: U.S. Government Printing Office, June 1985.
————. "Labor Force Activity of Mothers of Young Children Continues at Record Pace." *News,* USDL 85-381, September 19, 1985.
————. *Employment and Earnings.* Washington, D.C.: U.S. Government Printing Office, January 1986.
————. *Employment and Earnings.* Washington, D.C.: U.S. Government Printing Office, January 1987.
————. *Monthly Labor Review* 111 (March 1988): 7.
————. "Educational Level of U.S. Labor Force Continues to Rise." *News,* USDL 88-423, August 29, 1988.
————. *Employment and Earnings.* Washington, D.C.: U.S. Government Printing Office, January 1989.
U.S. General Accounting Office (GAO). *Women in the Military: More Military Jobs Can Be Opened Under Current Status.* GAO/NSIAD-88-222. Washington, D.C.: GAO, September 1988.

Notes on the Contributors

Faith H. Ando is president of Faith Ando & Associates, Inc., a suburban Philadelphia economics and statistics consulting firm. A Harvard Ph.D., Dr. Ando began her formal research into issues of minority entrepreneurship in 1982 with support from the Minority Business Development Agency (MBDA). Since then, she has directed many empirical minority entrepreneurship studies and contributed her findings to numerous professional journals.

Janet Bickel is director for women's programs and senior staff associate in the Division of Institutional Planning and Development at the Association of American Medical Colleges (AAMC). She previously worked as the project director of an AAMC study on the integration of human values curricula into medical students' clinical education, and as staff director for the Organization of Student Representatives. Before joining AAMC, she was admissions and financial aid coordinator at Brown University's Program in Medicine.

Gloria Bonilla-Santiago is an assistant professor at the Graduate School of Social Work at Rutgers University and chairperson of the Hispanic Women's Task Force of New Jersey. Dr. Bonilla-Santiago has been instrumental in passing legislation for Hispanic women in New Jersey; this includes landmark legislation that appropriates funding for Hispanic women's centers. Among her publications are *Puerto Rican Migrant Farmworkers: The New Jersey Experience* and numerous articles on the conditions of Hispanic women in the United States.

Mariam Chamberlain is president of the National Council for Research on Women. She has served as a program officer in education and research at the Ford Foundation, and as a resident scholar and chair of the Task Force on Women in Higher Education at the Russell Sage Foundation. An economist by training, she is the author of several articles on women's studies and editor of *Women in Academe: Progress and Prospects* (1988).

Elizabeth Conway is a research associate at the Center for Social Policy Studies at The George Washington University. A former fellow with the Congressional Fellowships on Women and Public Policy Program of the Women's Research and Education Institute, Ms. Conway writes about labor economics, health care, and family policy issues.

Cushing N. Dolbeare has been a housing and public policy consultant since 1971, except for an interval when she served as president of the National Low Income Housing Coalition, which she founded. She is chair of the National Low Income Housing Coalition, as well as chair of its Women and Housing Task Force.

Betty Parsons Dooley has been director of the Women's Research and Education Institute since 1977. An early Texas feminist, she was active in state politics before moving to Washington, D.C. In 1964, she was a candidate for the U.S. House of Representatives from the 16th congressional district of Texas. She served for several years as director of the Health Security Action Council, an advocacy organization that worked for comprehensive national health insurance.

Elsa Honig Fine is editor and publisher of *Woman's Art Journal*, which she established in 1980. She is also the author of *Women and Art: A History of Women Painters and Sculptors from the Renaissance to the 20th Century* (1978) and *The Afro-American Artist: A Search for Identity* (1973), and coeditor of *Women's Studies and the Arts* (1978).

Arvonne S. Fraser is a senior fellow at the Hubert H. Humphrey Institute of Public Affairs at the University of Minnesota, where she directs the Women, Public Policy and Development Project and codirects the International Women's Rights Action Watch. During the Carter administration, she served as coordinator of the Office of Women in Development at the U.S. Agency for International Development. Dr. Fraser attended all three world women's conferences (two as a U.S. delegate) and acted as a U.S. advisor to the United Nations Commission on the Status of Women.

Sarah Harder is women's studies coordinator and a tenured faculty member at the University of Wisconsin-Eau Claire. Cochair of the National Women's Conference Committee, she is also a leader of the Wisconsin Women's Network, Council of Presidents, and Women for a Meaningful Summit. Dr. Harder is a former president of the American Association of University Women and chair of the Wisconsin Women's Council.

Juanita Tamayo Lott is president of Tamayo Lott Associates of Silver Spring, Maryland. She chaired the Census Bureau Advisory Committee on Asian and Pacific Islander Populations for the 1990 census, served on the U.S. Commission on Civil Rights as deputy director of the Women's Rights Program and as director of the Program Analysis Division, and headed the Department of Health, Education and Welfare's Asian American Affairs Division. Her publications include *Pan Asian Women: A Vital Force* (1985) and *Beyond Stereotypes and Statistics* with Canta Pian (1979).

Harriette Pipes McAdoo is a professor at Howard University in the School of Social Work. A University of Michigan Ph.D., she has done post-doctoral work at Harvard University. Dr. McAdoo was the first recipient of the National Council on Family Relations' Marie Peters Award for Outstanding Scholarship, Leadership, and Service in the Area of Ethnic Minority Families. She has edited and written numerous works concerning black families. Most recently, she coedited *Services to Young Families, Program Review and Policy Recommendations*, and *Black Children: Social, Educational, and Parental Environments*.

Kate McGuinness is a 1983 graduate of Barnard College. She currently is working on her Master's degree in peace studies at the University of Lancaster in England. She is coauthor of "Women in Law Enforcement," *The American Woman, 1988-89*.

Fern Marx is a mid-career fellow at the Bush Center in Child Development and Social Policy at Yale University. A doctoral candidate at the Florence Heller School for Advanced Studies in Social Welfare at Brandeis University, Ms. Marx has participated in many studies of child care at the Wellesley College Center for Research on Women. Her recent publications include *The Public School Early Childhood Study: The State Survey* (1988) and *The Child Day Care Affordability Study: Technical Report* (1988).

Deborah L. Rhode is a professor of law and director of the

Institute for Research on Women and Gender at Stanford University. She graduated from Yale College and Yale Law School. The author of *Justice and Gender* (1989) and editor of *Theoretical Perspectives on Sexual Difference* (1990), she has written extensively on gender discrimination.

Michelle Seligson is the associate director/project director of the Center for Research on Women at Wellesley College. A graduate of the Harvard Graduate School of Education, Ms. Seligson has developed and directed national long-term studies on child care and early education. She is the coauthor of *Between Promise and Practice: Early Childhood Programs and the Public Schools* (1988) and *When School's Out and Nobody's Home* (1985).

C. Matthew Snipp is a fellow of the Center for Advanced Studies in the Behavioral Sciences in Palo Alto, California. Before joining the center, he was an associate professor of rural sociology at the University of Wisconsin-Madison. His most recent publication is *American Indians: The First of This Land* (1989).

Jean Stapleton is president of the board of directors of the Women's Research and Education Institute. A three-time Emmy award winner, Ms. Stapleton is an actor and singer in the theater, television, and film. She is a member of the national advisory board of the World Federalist Association and was a commissioner at the National Women's Conference in Houston in 1977. She is a leading proponent of the Equal Rights Amendment.

Sally Steenland is deputy director of the National Commission on Working Women, where she directs the organization's media projects. She has also worked for Ralph Nader and for the National Citizens Committee for Broadcasting. She is author of "Women in Broadcasting," *The American Woman, 1987-88*.

Anne J. Stone has been a research associate at WREI since 1981, having previously served on the Washington staff of then-U.S. Representative Elizabeth Holtzman. Ms. Stone has authored and coauthored policy analyses on various subjects, including the federal budget, employment issues for women, and tax reform legislation.

About the Women's Research and Education Institute

BETTY PARSONS DOOLEY, *Executive Director*
SARA E. RIX, *Director of Research*
ANNE J. STONE, *Research Associate*
ALISON DINEEN, *Fellowship Program Director*
TERRY A. WALKER, *Office Manager*

THE WOMEN'S RESEARCH AND EDUCATION INSTITUTE (WREI) is a nonprofit (501[c][3]) organization located in Washington, D.C. Established in 1977, WREI provides information, research, and policy analysis to the bipartisan Congressional Caucus for Women's Issues, as well as to other members of Congress.

From its inception, WREI has sought to facilitate and strengthen links between researchers and policymakers concerned with issues of particular importance to women. WREI gives high priority to:

- Encouraging researchers to consider the broader implications of their work, especially as it relates to public policy;

- Fostering the exchange of ideas and expertise between researchers with technical knowledge and policymakers familiar with the realities of the legislative process and political constraints; and

- Promoting both the informed examination of policies from the perspective of their effect on women and the formulation of policy options that recognize the needs of today's women and men and their families.

WREI's activities include publishing research reports and preparing briefing papers, holding conferences and symposia, and undertaking individual research projects. WREI sponsors the Congressional Fellowships on Women and Public Policy, a program open to graduate students with strong academic skills and a proven commitment to equity for women. The fellowship program has a dual purpose: to enhance the research capacity of congressional offices, especially with respect to the implications for women of existing and proposed legislation, and to provide promising women with hands-on experience in the federal legislative process.

WREI's research coordination and dissemination efforts are by no means restricted to federal policymakers, however, and WREI receives an increasing number of requests for information from the press, state and local officials, other organizations, and the public.

Board of Directors

JEAN STAPLETON, *President*

DOROTHY GREGG, *Vice President*

DOROTHY HEIGHT, *Secretary*

ESTHER COOPERSMITH, *Treasurer*

J. MICHAEL BROWN

SHARON PRATT DIXON

EVELYN DUBROW

MARGARET M. HECKLER

MATINA HORNER

JUANITA KREPS

HELEN S. MEYNER

HELEN MILLIKEN

ALMA RANGEL

ANNETTE STRAUSS

CELIA G. TORRES

PAQUITA VIVÓ

DIANE E. WATSON

Index

About the Editor

SARA E. RIX is director of research at the Women's Research and Education Institute (WREI), where she specializes in policy research and analysis. Her primary research interests are employment policy, retirement policy, and the economics of aging. She holds a Ph.D. from the University of Virginia.

Dr. Rix is chair of the research, education, and practice committee of the Gerontological Society of America, a member of the board of directors of the National Center on Women and Retirement Research, and a member of the American Sociological Association's ad hoc committee on federal standards for the employment of sociologists. She is, or has been, an adviser on or consultant to projects of the General Accounting Office, Working Women, the Office of Technology Assessment, the National Senior Citizens Education and Research Center, the National Council for Alternative Work Patterns, and the 1981 White House Conference on Aging.

Dr. Rix has studied, written on, and spoken about the work and retirement income needs of middle-aged and older women and men for over 10 years. She is the coauthor of *The Graying of Working America* (with Harold L. Sheppard) and of *Retirement-Age Policy: An International Perspective* (with Paul Fisher). Before she came to WREI, she was a research scientist at the American Institutes for Research.